AF838820

EU Copyright Law

EU Copyright Law

Subsistence, Exploitation and Protection of Rights

Morten Rosenmeier
Kacper Szkalej
Sanna Wolk

Wolters Kluwer

Published by:
Kluwer Law International B.V.
PO Box 316
2400 AH Alphen aan den Rijn
The Netherlands
E-mail: international-sales@wolterskluwer.com
Website: lrus.wolterskluwer.com

Sold and distributed in North, Central and South America by:
Wolters Kluwer Legal & Regulatory U.S.
7201 McKinney Circle
Frederick, MD 21704
United States of America
Email: customer.service@wolterskluwer.com

Sold and distributed in all other countries by:
Air Business Subscriptions
Rockwood House
Haywards Heath
West Sussex
RH16 3DH
United Kingdom
Email: international-customerservice@wolterskluwer.com

ISBN 978-90-411-8369-9

e-Book: ISBN 978-90-411-8370-5
web-PDF: ISBN 978-90-411-8371-2

© 2019 Kluwer Law International BV, The Netherlands

All rights reserved. No part of this publication may be reproduced, stored in a retrieval system, or transmitted in any form or by any means, electronic, mechanical, photocopying, recording, or otherwise, without written permission from the publisher.

Permission to use this content must be obtained from the copyright owner. More information can be found at: lrus.wolterskluwer.com/policies/permissions-reprints-and-licensing

About the Authors

Morten Rosenmeier, Professor, LLD, is a researcher within the field of copyright law at the Faculty of Law, University of Copenhagen. He has written a number of academic publications in his research field.

Kacper F. Szkalej, LLB (Hons), LLM (IT Law), LLM (IP Law), PhD Researcher in copyright law at the Institute of Intellectual Property, Marketing and Competition Law (IMC), Uppsala University. Lecturer at Uppsala University and KTH – Royal Institute of Technology.

Sanna Wolk, Professor, LLD, is a researcher within the field of Intellectual Property at the Faculty of Law, Uppsala University and also Head of IP at Cirio Law Firm. She has published many academic articles and books in her research field. In addition, she is the founder and also chair of the Institute of Intellectual Property, Marketing and Competition Law (IMC) at Uppsala University, which is the leading research and education institute in Sweden.

Table of Contents

Preface

Today many authors, performers, producers and companies are well aware of the value of copyright. Societal and economic changes and the further growth of electronic commerce are making copyright and related rights protection an increasingly important field of law.

General economic and technological development is closely linked to the development of copyright law. New information technology, in particular digital technology, has in recent years had a considerable influence on copyright. Legislators in many countries, including the European Union (EU) Member States, have attempted to adapt their laws to the demands of new technology. In the EU no less than ten copyright-specific directives and two regulations have been adopted to regulate different aspects of the copyright system in a new technological and economic order. These instruments cover and harmonise the protection of computer programs, rental and lending rights, the term of protection, satellite and cable transmissions, databases, copyright in the information society (including the exclusive rights, limitations and exceptions and technological protection measures (TPMs)), certain aspects of enforcement, resale rights, orphan works, aspects of collective rights management, accessibility to works by visually-impaired persons, and the cross-border access to content. Additionally, instruments generally regulating e-commerce are also relevant in the copyright context. As this book goes into production the EU legislator is working on yet another directive, the Digital Single Market (DSM) Directive, introducing new rights and exceptions and regulating the obligations of Internet content sharing platforms.

The Court of Justice of the European Union (CJEU) has also played a significant role in shaping the EU copyright framework. With a growing amount of judgements on the interpretation of, thus far, the directives, the Court's case law plays no lesser role in harmonising the EU copyright framework. The Court's contributions to forming the EU copyright framework is best seen in its many judgements concerning the communication to the public right (Article 3 InfoSoc Directive) which is, arguably, becoming technology specific. The Court has, for example, been called upon to rule on the legality of linking to protected subject matter, which has been legally uploaded to the Internet, by the provision of an ordinary hyperlink (C-466/12 *Svensson*, C-279/13 *C More Entertainment*) on the one hand, and the embedding of content on a website by using a frame/inline link (C-348/13 *BestWater*) on the other hand, linking to protected subject matter which has been uploaded to the Internet unlawfully (C-160/15 *GS Media*), the sale of a multimedia streaming device pre-loaded with add-ons linking to various websites (C-527/15 *Stichting Brein*), management of a platform indexing metadata relating to protected subject matter and the provision of a search engine relating to that metadata (C-610/15 *Stichting Brein II*).

The continued expansion of copyright law with all-new laws and the growing body of case law from the CJEU make this dynamic legal area, especially in the digital environment, increasingly more complex and difficult to comprehend. With this book we hope to provide a current presentation of the EU copyright law framework and trends to a wider audience.

September 2018
Morten Rosenmeier Kacper Szkalej Sanna Wolk

CHAPTER 1

Copyright in the International Context

§1.01 INTRODUCTION

Copyright protection provides incentives for creators to create works of art or architecture or other creations of cultural and societal interest. Protection is granted regardless of the usefulness or commercial value of the information embedded in the work. Without such protection creators would likely not invest the same amount of time and effort to create, and many business models or ways of accessing copyright-protected works would likely not be created. Copyright serves therefore a very important function for the economy and society. Protection is however not absolute, neither in time nor in scope, and this serves to facilitate, *inter alia*, access to knowledge and culture.

Copyright protection is said to be limited territorially. This means that instead of being protected across borders, it is protected by every country separately. However, because there are many international conventions and treaties that regulate copyright, exploitation rights, so-called economic rights, and moral rights can be said to be aligned to a large extent. Differences relate primarily to the scope of limitations and exceptions, so certain uses that may be permitted in one country might not be permitted in another country.

§1.02 THE NATURE OF COPYRIGHT

Copyright law is part of the legal body of rules known as intellectual property rights (IPRs). The term *intellectual property rights* is a collective designation for *inter alia* copyright law, patent law, design law and trademark law. Intellectual property rights give authors, inventors, designers and firms an exclusive right to the economic exploitation of works and other copyright-protected material, inventions, design and trademarks respectively. Intellectual property rights are said to be 'intellectual' since the protected objects are not physical things. For example, if a person writes a book the author has copyright in the manuscript. This allows the author to forbid others to:

- make a copy of the manuscript, i.e., to make other identical manuscripts;
- produce (print) and distribute manuscripts which resemble the original manuscript without being identical to it;
- translate the manuscript into a foreign language;
- print books based on the manuscript;
- make comic strip books which build on the plot of the manuscript;
- make movies or animated cartoons based on the manuscript.

Thus, copyright does not concern a certain physical object such as the property in e.g., a house. Instead, copyright protects the work as an incorporeal object. The situation is similar within the other intellectual property rights. If, for instance, a firm's logo is protected by trademark law, the firm can prohibit the use of similar logos on shop fronts, in television commercials, in printed advertisements etc.

§1.03 THE VARIOUS TYPES OF COPYRIGHT AND RELATED RIGHTS

Essentially, copyright law protects two things. First, copyright law confers protection on *original literary and artistic works*. They are subject to *copyright protection*. The protection lasts for seventy years after the death of the author. Copyright protection means that one has to obtain permission from the author (or whomever the author may have transferred their rights to) to be able to reproduce the work or exploit it economically. Moreover, copyright also protects certain intellectual efforts which are not (or are not necessarily) protected *works*, but which nevertheless have been considered to require protection, such as performances of performing artists, sound recordings, broadcasts etc. Rights associated with such intellectual efforts are called *neighbouring rights* or *related rights*. Protection conferred by related rights is typically shorter than true copyright protection of literary and artistic works. Additionally, related rights are not as extensive as copyright protection of literary and artistic works. However, European Union (EU) law has harmonised copyright protection and the related rights to a large extent, albeit not exhaustively.

§1.04 MAJOR COPYRIGHT CONVENTIONS AND AGREEMENTS

While the legal framework is yet to see the introduction of a truly international, unitary copyright system, the scope of substantive copyright can be said to be aligned to a significant extent as a result of a number of legal instruments, in particular, dealing specifically with copyright are:

- *Berne Convention for the Protection of Literary and Artistic Works of 1886 (as amended).*
- *Universal Copyright Convention 1952.*
- *WIPO Copyright Treaty (WCT) 1996*, and

- *Marrakesh Treaty to Facilitate Access to Published Works for Persons Who are Blind, Visually Impaired or Otherwise Print Disabled 2013* (Marrakesh Treaty).

Important conventions dealing specifically with the related rights are:

- *International Convention for the Protection of Performers, Producers of Phonograms and Broadcasting Organizations (Rome Convention) 1961.*
- *Convention for the Protection of Producers of Phonograms Against Unauthorized Duplication of Their Phonograms (Phonograms Convention) 1971.*
- *WIPO Performances and Phonograms Treaty (WPPT) 1996*, and
- *The Beijing Treaty on Audiovisual Performances 2012.*

Members of the World Trade Organization (WTO) are additionally subject to the *Agreement on Trade-Related Aspects of Intellectual Property Rights of 1994* (TRIPS Agreement), including the EU,[1] regulating both types of rights and intellectual property law generally.

From among these instruments the EU is, as a union, an independent signatory of the WCT and WPPT[2] and the Marrakesh Treaty.[3] Although the EU is not an independent signatory of the Berne Convention, the substantive provisions of the Convention are incorporated through the WCT and TRIPS Agreement, making it also relevant in the EU legal context.[4] The Court of Justice of the European Union (CJEU) has in this respect been called upon to interpret the Berne Convention.[5]

With the proliferation of legal issues resulting from the rise of digital technology in general and the Internet in particular, the World Intellectual Property Organization (WIPO) copyright treaties are today still likely the two most important instruments as they strive to provide adequate solutions that such developments have carried forward,[6] having been adopted in a very different technological environment than exists today. One type of provision is particularly worth highlighting. Under Article 11 WCT and Article 18 WPPT the Contracting States are required to introduce protection and legal remedies against the circumvention of technological protection measures (TPMs) used by rightholders in the exercise of their exclusive rights. While the treaties set minimum standards of protection, technology has made it possible to enforce copyright *ex ante*, without the need to resort to the courts competent to review the rules of

1. Council Decision of 22 December 1994 concerning the conclusion on behalf of the European Community, as regards matters within its competence, of the agreements reached in the Uruguay Round multilateral negotiations (1986–1994) [1994] OJ L 336/1.
2. Council Decision of 16 March 2000 on the approval, on behalf of the European Community, of the WIPO Copyright Treaty and the WIPO Performances and Phonograms Treaty [2000] OJ L 89/8.
3. Council Decision (EU) 2018/254 of 15 February 2018 on the conclusion on behalf of the European Union of the Marrakesh Treaty to Facilitate Access to Published Works for Persons who are Blind, Visually Impaired, or otherwise Print Disabled [2018] OJ L 48/1.
4. Even though reference is sometimes expressly made to the Berne Convention instead of the adopted instruments, for example, in Art. 6(3) Computer Programs Directive in relation to the 'three-step test' which is also present in Art. 13 TRIPS Agreement and Art. 10 WCT 1996.
5. *See*, for example, Case C-138/16 *AKM* v *Zürs.net Betriebs* ECLI:EU:C:2017:218.
6. *See* to this effect the Preamble to WCT.

copyright, and virtually extending protection to cover exclusive control of *access* to works and the *consumption* of such works, despite that copyright law does not prima facie award such exclusive rights.

CHAPTER 2

Copyright in the EU Legal Framework

§2.01 INTRODUCTION

Copyright is today of great importance for the EU market economies and often a prerequisite for the dynamic development of culture, technology and wealth in the EU Member States. While the modern copyright system has never been as strong and effective as it is today, it is heavily criticised. It is understandable that rightholders wish to benefit from the economic value of their rights, but at the same time many hold the view that the balance in the system has shifted too much in favour of rightholders.

General economic and technological development is affecting the development of copyright law. New information technology, in particular digital technology, has in recent years had a considerable influence on EU copyright law and the EU has made legislative efforts to harmonise and adapt the legal framework to the demands of new technology. In the late 1980s and early 1990s, copyright was at the centre of attention in the EU. In 1988 the European Commission (EC) published its proposals for copyright protection within the Community.[7] The Commission's efforts led *inter alia* to the adoption of the first EU copyright directive, Directive 91/250/EEC on the legal protection of computer programs (superseded by Directive 2009/24/EC). Today copyright is very important in the EU, both because of its economic importance and its impact on communication technology, such as TV and Internet; however, it also expresses the desire of a common cultural policy and development. Significant harmonisation has been carried out in this area; however the legislative bodies of the EU are currently working on further legislation in the area of copyright law.[8]

7. *See* Commission, 'Green Paper on Copyright and the Challenge of Technology – Copyright Issues Requiring Immediate Action' COM(88) 172 final and the 'Follow-up to the Green Paper – Working Programme of the Commission in the Field of Copyright and Neighbouring Rights' COM(90) 584 final.
8. *See* §2.03 below.

§2.02 THE IMPACT OF DIFFERENT LEGAL SYSTEMS ON EU LAW

There are two different major traditions, or schools of thought, in copyright law – either a copyright framework will belong to the *droit d'auteur* (authors' rights) school, treating as its point of departure the personal connection that an author has with the work that they have created and using that as a universal reference point for protection or the *copyright* school, focusing instead on the commercial exploitability of the creation and the interests that exist therein. Consequently, the former school has been hesitant in awarding protection to corporations, and moral rights (*droit moral*) play therefore a more significant role than in the latter in which they have historically been attributed less attention or elsewhere than in copyright law or have been non-existent. Another important difference is that whereas in the authors' rights systems the catalogue of creations which may enjoy copyright protection is open, in the copyright systems a creation must usually fall within an enumerated and defined category of work to be protected.

The relevant school of thought often correlates with the type of legal system – common law countries such as the United Kingdom (UK), Ireland or, outside the EU, the USA, are examples of the copyright school, while civil law[9] countries such as France (*droit d'auteur*), Germany (*Urheberrecht*), Italy (*diritto d'autore*), Poland (*prawo autorskie*) are examples of authors' rights countries. The Scandinavian countries, while not entirely belonging to the civil law system, represent the authors' rights school, for example, Sweden (*upphovsrätt*) or Denmark (*opphavsrett*).

The internationalisation and Europeanisation of copyright law has to some extent lessened the importance of these two traditions within the EU as the end result will often be the same regardless of copyright tradition; nevertheless, despite that copyright laws of most EU Member States emerge from the authors' rights tradition, some convergence has occurred in the formation of the EU copyright law framework. For example, while EU copyright law does not prescribe a finite list of types of creations that may be protected, rights to computer programs created in employment are attributed to the employer, rather than the actual author (creator) – the employee – affecting, therefore, the default position for rights ownership.

§2.03 EXISTING EU COPYRIGHT LEGISLATION

The following legal instruments make up the EU copyright framework:

- *Computer Programs Directive*: Directive 91/250 of 14 May 1991 on the legal protection of computer programs (now replaced by the codifying Directive 2009/24 of 23 April 2009). The directive instructs the Member States to grant copyright protection to computer programs and harmonises the rules of protection, which the Member States are obliged to uphold in their national copyright legislation.

9. Otherwise called the Roman-Germanic system.

- *Rental and Lending Rights Directive*: Directive 92/100 of 19 November 1992 on rental right and lending right and on certain rights related to copyright in the field of intellectual property, now replaced by the codifying Directive 2006/115 of 12 December 2006. The directive instructs the Member States to introduce uniform provisions on the scope of the exclusive right to authorise and prohibit rental and lending of protected material. Also, the directive harmonises to some extent related rights concerning performing artists, producers of phonograms, producers of films and broadcasting organisations.
- *SatCab Directive*: Directive 93/83 of 27 September 1993 on the coordination of certain rules concerning copyright and rights related to copyright applicable to satellite broadcasting and cable retransmission. The directive instructs the Member States to uphold provisions concerning transmission of television and radio programmes containing protected material by satellite, and cable retransmission of programmes containing protected material and which originate from other Member States.
- *Term Directive*: Directive 93/98 of 29 October 1993 on harmonising the term of protection of copyright and certain related rights, replaced by the codifying Directive 2006/116 of 12 December 2006, amended by Directive 2011/77 of 27 September 2011 amending Directive 2006/116/EC. The directive harmonises the provisions on the term of protection of copyright and related rights.
- *Database Directive*: Directive 96/9 of 11 March 1996 on the legal protection of databases. While the directive introduces sui generis protection of databases, it also harmonises copyright protection of databases.
- *InfoSoc Directive*: Directive 2001/29 of 22 May 2001 on the harmonisation of certain aspects of copyright and related rights in the information society. In many ways this directive is the most important copyright directive. It harmonises the norms on what it means to have copyright protection, the scope of economic rights and the admissible limitations and exceptions to copyright (concerning, for example, quotation and private use). The directive also requires the introduction of rules which prohibit persons who seek to gain access to protected material without permission from the rightholder to circumvent technological protection measures such as access codes, copy protection measures etc., and to alter rights-management information.
- *Enforcement Directive*: Directive 2004/48/EC of 29 April 2004 on the enforcement of intellectual property rights. While concerning intellectual property rights generally and not affecting the substantive rules of copyright exclusivity, the directive aims to approximate the laws of the Member States in the context of enforcement of rights to ensure a high, equivalent and homogeneous level of protection in the internal market.
- *Resale Rights Directive*: Directive 2001/84 of 27 September 2001 on the resale right for the benefit of the author of an original work of art. The directive instructs the Member States to introduce provisions according to which authors of certain types of original works of art are entitled to a royalty when the work is resold.

- *Orphan Works Directive*: Directive 2012/28 of 25 October 2012 on certain permitted uses of orphan works. The directive provides that libraries, educational establishments and certain other cultural institutions are to some extent allowed to publish orphan works[10] without permission.
- *CRM Directive*: Directive 2014/26 of 26 February 2014 on collective management of copyright and related rights and multi-territorial licensing of rights in musical works for online use in the internal market. The directive regulates the activities of collective management organisations which manage copyright on behalf of authors and other rightholders.
- *Streaming Regulation:*[11] Regulation 2017/1128 of 14 June 2017 on cross-border portability of online content services in the internal market. The Regulation, being the first legal instrument of its kind in the EU copyright framework, requires of providers of online content services, such as streaming, to provide access to such services when consumers are temporarily present in a Member State other than their Member State of residence.
- Directive 2017/1564 of 13 September 2017 on certain permitted uses of certain works and other subject matter protected by copyright and related rights for the benefit of persons who are blind, visually impaired or otherwise print-disabled and amending Directive 2001/29/EC on the harmonisation of certain aspects of copyright and related rights in the information society. This directive is accompanied by Regulation 2017/1563 of 13 September 2017 on the cross-border exchange between the Union and third countries of accessible format copies of certain works and other subject matter protected by copyright and related rights for the benefit of persons who are blind, visually impaired or otherwise print-disabled.

In addition to the above-mentioned instruments, the E-Commerce Directive[12] contains important provisions relating to the non-liability of different intermediaries, such as Internet Service Providers (ISPs) and content sharing platforms, for the content shared by customers/users and prohibits the introduction of a general monitoring obligation requiring the active discovery and prevention of infringements by customers or users. The Conditional Access Directive,[13] and the Audiovisual Media Services Directive,[14] also constitute significant sector-specific legislation that can be relevant in the copyright context, especially in the broadcasting and media sector.

10. Orphan works are works whose authors (or other relevant rightholders) are unknown or difficult to locate.
11. Also known as Portability Regulation.
12. Directive 2000/31/EC of 8 June 2000 on certain legal aspects of information society services, in particular electronic commerce, in the internal market.
13. Directive 98/84/EC of 20 November 1998 on the legal protection of services based on, or consisting of, conditional access.
14. Directive 2010/13/EU of 10 March 2010 on the coordination of certain provisions laid down by law, regulation or administrative action in Member States concerning the provision of audiovisual media services. The Directive is currently under review; *see* Commission, 'Proposal for a Directive amending Directive 2010/13/EU on the coordination of certain provisions laid down by law, regulation or administrative action in Member States concerning the provision of audiovisual media services in view of changing market realities' COM/2016/0287 final.

Moreover, other copyright legislation is being considered.[15] Of these the proposal for a Directive on copyright in the Digital Single Market (DSM) Directive[16] has received the most attention. The DSM Directive, and especially the proposed Article 11 introducing a completely new *press publication right*[17] and Article 13 requiring of content sharing platforms to conclude agreements with rightholders for the use of their works or the introduction of effective content recognition technologies, has undergone substantive academic scrutiny.[18]

Other important proposals, for which the legislative process is still ongoing but is much slower, are the SatCab Regulation[19] aiming to ensure the cross-border availability of online broadcasts and retransmissions by addressing difficulties related to rights clearance, and the Digital Content Supply Directive[20] concerning contractual arrangements for the supply of digital content, essentially aiming to create a framework comparable to the rules on the sale of (tangible) goods to consumers, but applying instead to digital content.[21]

§2.04 THE ROLE OF THE CJEU AND INTERPRETATION OF EU LAW

The national courts of the EU Member States are required to ensure that EU law is properly applied. Given the number of legal frameworks and traditions represented by

15. *See* generally Commission, 'A Digital Single Market Strategy for Europe' (Communication) COM(2015) 192 final, and Commission, 'Promoting a fair, efficient and competitive European copyright-based economy in the Digital Single Market' (Communication) COM(2016) 592 final.
16. Commission, 'Proposal for a Directive on copyright in the Digital Single Market' COM(2016) 593 final.
17. With its own scope and term of protection, and separate from potential copyright protection of journalistic articles or copyright-protected works being part of such articles.
18. *See*, for example, European Copyright Society, 'General Opinion on the EU Copyright Reform Package' 24 January 2017, available at https://europeancopyrightsocietydotorg.files.wordpress.com/2015/12/ecs-opinion-on-eu-copyright-reform-def.pdf. *See also* Ricolfi, M., Xalabarder, R., van Eechoud, M., 'A Statement from EU Academics on Proposed Press Publishers' Right', 24 April 2018 available at: https://www.ivir.nl/academics-against-press-publishers-right/. Non-European scholars have also voiced concerns; *see*, for example, Samuelson, P., 'The EU's Controversial Digital Single Market Directive – Part I: Why the Proposed Internet Content Filtering Mandate Was so Controversial' Kluwer Copyright Blog, 10 July 2018 and 'The EU's Controversial Digital Single Market Directive – Part II: Why the Proposed Mandatory Text- and Data-Mining Exception is Too Restrictive' Kluwer Copyright Blog, 12 July 2018. *See* however von Lewinski, S., 'Comments on Article 13 and Related Provisions in the JURI Committee Report for a Directive on Copyright in the Digital Single Market' Kluwer Copyright Blog, 3 September 2018.
19. Commission, 'Proposal for a Regulation laying down rules on the exercise of copyright and related rights applicable to certain online transmissions of broadcasting organisations and retransmissions of television and radio programmes' COM(2016) 594 final.
20. Commission, 'Proposal for a Directive on certain aspects concerning contracts for the supply of digital content' COM(2015) 634 final.
21. This last proposal, if adopted, will fill an important lacuna as current EU consumer protection law does not apply as such to the purchase of digital content. Offering, or 'sale' of, such content remains largely unregulated compared to other commodities, tangible or not. *See* Directive 1999/44/EC on certain aspects of the sale of consumer goods and associated guarantees. *See* however Council Directive 93/13/EEC on unfair terms in consumer contracts and Directive 2011/83/EU on consumer rights. Among the EU Member States, it is only the UK that has introduced specific legislation regulating rights and obligations for the sale/purchase of digital content. *See* ss 33–47 Consumer Rights Act 2015.

the Member States, different interpretations of what EU law requires are inevitable. This is furthered by the fact that the bulk of the EU copyright framework is made up of *directives*, a legal instrument which often specifies the result to be achieved while leaving the means of achieving the results to the Member States. Different interpretations relating to EU law may therefore not only occur because a specific provision of EU law is ambiguous, but, when seen from the complete legal framework of a Member State, may give rise to questions which would not have arisen in another Member State, either as such or because of the way in which it has been implemented in the relevant Member State.

Under Article 267 TFEU, a court of a Member State may refer questions of interpretation or validity of EU law or, as the case may be international law which has become part of EU law, to the CJEU. This is known as *a reference for a preliminary ruling*. The substantive content of such references varies, depending both on the factual and legal circumstances of the case. For example, instead of directly asking for an interpretation of a specific provision, a national court may instead phrase its questions in a way that seeks to determine the compatibility of a national provision with EU law, alternatively whether a specific factual circumstance in the case is compatible with EU law. This does not, however, mean that the CJEU is bound to directly answer the question as it has been asked or indeed answer it at all if it finds it inadmissible.

Under a long time, mainly during the 1990s and the beginning of the twenty-first century, the Court had very few cases concerning copyright. But the increasing importance of copyright for companies based in the EU as well as for the functioning of the internal market, resulting *inter alia* from the growing amount of legislation concerning copyright law, the number of decisions is rapidly increasing and the CJEU has already played, and continues to play, an important role in forming the EU copyright framework.

§2.05 HUMAN RIGHTS AND EU COPYRIGHT LAW*

The EU has not formally acceded to the European Convention on Human Rights (ECHR).[22] Despite this, the Convention has played an important role in the jurisprudence of the CJEU, which has reiterated a number of times that:

> Fundamental rights form an integral part of the general principles of law the observance of which the Court ensures, and that, for that purpose, the Court draws inspiration from the constitutional traditions common to the Member States from the guidelines supplied by international treaties for the protection of human rights

* This section is based on the author's ongoing research in Szkalej, K., 'Consumption of digital works – an analysis of EU copyright law within the framework of lawful acquisition and use of protected content', pp. 291–357.

22. Convention for the Protection of Human Rights and Fundamental Freedoms 1950. *See* Art. 6(2) first sentence TEU stating that the EU shall accede to the Convention. *See* further CJEU Opinion 2/13 of 18 December 2014 essentially concluding that the agreement on EU's accession to the ECHR will affect the EU's competencies as defined in the Treaties and is therefore not compatible with Art. 6(2) TEU.

on which the Member States have collaborated or to which they are signatories. The ECHR has special significance in that respect.[23]

However, on 7 December 2000 in Nice the Charter of Fundamental Rights of the European Union (EU Charter) was signed and proclaimed by the Commission, the Council and European Parliament, prescribing civil, political, economic and social rights. While a policy document at the time,[24] with the entry into force of the Lisbon Treaty[25] on 1 December 2009 the EU Charter received binding treaty status within the EU legal framework.[26] Effectively, therefore, legislation must be interpreted in accordance with the EU Charter.[27]

While the precise contours of its application and relation to the EU copyright framework are yet to be determined by the CJEU, the Charter is playing an increasingly important role in copyright cases which require the balancing of different interests, whether or not those interests directly originate from copyright law. Most obviously such balancing may be required in the context of the application of limitations and exceptions to copyright protection. In *Deckmyn*[28] the CJEU held that in applying the parody exception under Article 5(3)(k) InfoSoc Directive a fair balance must be struck between on the one hand the interests and rights of rightholders, and the freedom of expression of the person who is relying on the parody exception on the other hand.[29] Such balancing must, according to the Court, take into account all circumstances of the case.

The EU Charter has however also been applied outside the context of the application of limitations and exceptions. In *Scarlett*[30] the CJEU determined that the issuing of an injunction against an ISP, whose customers where infringing copyright by reproducing and communicating works to the public, requiring the ISP to filter content, such filtering essentially amounting to a general monitoring obligation, would impair the ISPs freedom to conduct a business protected under Article 16 EU Charter, as well

23. Case C-479/04 *Laserdisken* v *Kulturministeriet* ECLI:EU:C:2006:549, para. 61. *See also* Case C-112/00 *Schmidberger and Internationale Transporte und Planzüge* v *Republik Österreich* ECLI:EU:C:2003:333, para. 71 and case law cited therein. This follows now expressly from Art. 6(3) TEU.
24. The Commission decided however to scrutinise any proposal for legislation and draft instrument to be adopted by it for compatibility with the Charter. *See* Commission, 'Application of the Charter of Fundamental Rights of the European Union' (Memorandum) SEC(2001) 380, and Commission, 'Compliance with the Charter of Fundamental Rights in Commission Legislative Proposals. Methodology for systematic and rigorous monitoring' (Communication) COM(2005) 172 final. *See also* recital 32 Enforcement Directive 'respecting' fundamental rights and 'observing' the principles recognised by the Charter. The CJEU has also applied the Charter in the copyright context before its binding status. *See* Case C-275/06 *Promusicae* v *Telefónica de España* ECLI:EU:C:2008:54.
25. Treaty of Lisbon amending the Treaty on the European Union and the Treaty establishing the European Community.
26. TEU, Art. 6(1). Without however extending the competencies of the Union as defined in the Treaties – Art. 6(1) para. 2. *See also* Art. 51(2) EU Charter.
27. This originates from the primary character of the legal source. *See also* Art. 6(1) para. 3 TEU and Arts 51–54 EU Charter.
28. Case C-201/13 *Deckmyn and Vrijheidsfonds* v *Vandersteen and Others* ECLI:EU:C:2014:2132.
29. C-201/13 *Deckmyn*, paras 27–28.
30. Case C-70/10 *Scarlett Extended* v *SABAM* ECLI:EU:C:2011:771.

as the customers freedom of expression (freedom to receive and impart information) and right to protection of personal data.[31] By contrast, subsequently in *UPC Telekabel,*[32] which instead concerned an injunction requiring an ISP to block access to a website that the ISPs customers were accessing (the infringements having been only alleged in respect of the website in question), the CJEU determined that an injunction which leaves it to the ISP to choose which measures to implement will not impair the ISPs freedom to conduct a business. The Court also stated that in choosing the relevant measures, which must be strictly targeted, it is the ISP that *must* ensure compliance with its customers' freedom of information.[33]

Most recently in *Bastei Lübbe*[34] the CJEU has been asked to clarify whether the requirements of Article 8(1)-(2) InfoSoc Directive and Article 3(2) Enforcement Directive, which require 'effective and dissuasive sanctions for infringement' and 'effective measures for enforcement' respectively, are still met when an owner of an Internet connection which has been used to infringe copyright cannot be held liable to pay damages under national law because it cannot be determined whether that person or instead anyone else from an exhaustive list of persons (two other family members) has conducted the relevant infringement. Although reference to fundamental rights is not present in the literal wording of the referred questions, owing to the particular circumstances of the case Advocate General Maciej Szpunar has noted in his opinion that in answering the referred question two aspects must be examined - the scope of the provisions in question on the one hand, and the application of those provisions in a way that is compatible with fundamental rights on the other hand, which according to the Advocate General concern foremost respect for private and family life protected by Article 7 EU Charter,[35] as well as Article 20 concerning equality before the law and Article 54 prohibiting abuse of rights recognised in the Charter.[36] The Advocate General has essentially reached the conclusion that Article 7 EU Charter concerning respect for private and family life cannot be applied in a way that deprives rightholders of all real possibilities to protect their intellectual property in accordance with Article 17(2) EU Charter, if the application of that Article is made exclusively to escape liability.

In another recent reference for a preliminary ruling, the CJEU has been asked more directly about the role of the EU Charter in the copyright framework and in particular with regards to the exceptions and limitations. In *Spiegel Online*[37] two of the five questions asked by the German Supreme Court expressly concern the Charter:

- In which way are the fundamental rights of the Charter of Fundamental Rights of the European Union to be taken into account when determining the scope of the exceptions or limitations provided for in Article 5(3) of Directive 2001/29/EC to the exclusive right of authors to reproduce (Article 2(a) of

31. C-70/10 *Scarlett*, paras 48 and 50.
32. Case C-314/12 *UPC Telekabel Wien* v *Constantin Film and Wega* ECLI:EU:C:2014:192.
33. C-314/12 *UPC Telekabel Wien*, paras 55–57.
34. Case C-149/17 *Bastei Lübbe* v *Strotzer*.
35. C-149/17 *Bastei Lübbe*, Opinion of AG Szpunar, para. 34.
36. C-149/17 *Bastei Lübbe*, Opinion of AG Szpunar, paras 42 and 43, respectively.
37. Case C-516/17 *Spiegel Online* v *Beck*. *See also* pending Case C-476/17 *Pelham and Others* v *Hütter and Schneider-Esleben*.

Directive 2001/29/EC) and communicate to the public their works, including the right to make their works available to the public (Article 3(1) of Directive 2001/29/EC)?

- Can the fundamental rights of freedom of information (second sentence of Article 11(1) of the Charter) or freedom of the media (Article 11(2) of the Charter) justify exceptions or limitations to the exclusive rights of authors to reproduce (Article 2(a) of Directive 2001/29/EC) and communicate to the public their works, including the right to make their works available to the public (Article 3(1) of Directive 2001/29/EC), beyond the exceptions or limitations provided for in Article 5(3) of Directive 2001/29/EC?

The answer to the second question will arguably have most impact on the EU copyright framework because the German Court is essentially asking whether fundamental rights, in particular freedom of information alternatively freedom of the media, can operate as an external constraint on copyright exclusivity justifying exceptions and limitations beyond the list of exceptions and limitations in Article 5(3) InfoSoc Directive, despite that the entire list in Article 5 is exhaustive.[38]

[A] Balancing Rights

Whenever fundamental rights concerns are raised, courts must engage in a difficult task of balancing the different rights which are at stake. In copyright law this ought to almost always be the case because intellectual property is expressly protected under Article 17(2) EU Charter as property, while any exploitation of copyright-protected works and subsequent attempts by rightholders to enforce the exclusive rights may implicate freedom of expression and information, right to respect for private life and many others. In this context the Court has made it clear that the right to (intellectual) property is not inviolable and must be absolutely protected.[39]

Member States must, when transposing directives, rely on an interpretation which allows a fair balance to be struck between various protected fundamental rights, and when implementing measures transposing such legislation, the national authorities and courts must, except interpreting national law in a manner consistent with such legislation, also make sure that they do not rely on an interpretation which would be in conflict with those fundamental rights or with the other general principles of EU law, such as the principle of proportionality.[40] In the context of determining the appropriateness of a sanction, the Court has stated that national authorities and courts must strike a fair balance between the protection of copyright and the protection of the fundamental rights of individuals who are affected by measures adopted to protect

38. InfoSoc Directive, recital (32). *See* further on limitations and exceptions below.
39. C-70/10 *Scarlett Extended*, para. 43, Case C-314/12 *UPC Telekabel Wien*, para. 61.
40. C-275/06 *Promusicae*, para. 68, C-314/12 *UPC Telekabel Wien*, para. 46. *See also* C-201/13 *Deckmyn* paras 25–27.

copyright holders.[41] Hence, even if the applicability of an exception or limitation is not raised, a balancing act is required.

The seemingly unlawful character of exploitation does not as such preclude a balancing act to occur. In fact, it is precisely in such situations that it may most be required. To this extent it is worth noting that in *Neij and Kolmissoppi*,[42] which was a case before the European Court of Human Rights (ECtHR), in which the operators of The Pirate Bay, having been criminally convicted in Sweden for contributory infringement of copyright by operating the platform, alleged unjustified interference with their freedom of expression guaranteed under Article 10 ECHR, the ECtHR did agree that the operation of a platform such as The Pirate Bay falls within the scope of Article 10. While the ECtHR concluded, given the relevant facts of the case, that the interference with the freedom of expression was prescribed by law, pursued a legitimate aim and was necessary in a democratic society and should, therefore, be allowed, the Court observed, in accordance with its previous case law, that the Internet plays an important role in enhancing access to news and facilitating sharing and dissemination of information generally, and that Article 10 not only applies to the content of the information but also to the means of transmission or reception of information, requiring therefore that the interference be justified in accordance with Article 10(2) ECHR.[43]

The CJEU's approach in striking a fair balance is however not always easy to follow. For example, in *Deckmyn* the Court, while underlining that the application of the parody exception in Article 5(3)(k) InfoSoc Directive must strike a fair balance between the rightholders on the one hand, and freedom of expression of the parodist on the other hand, simply held that where a parody conveys a discriminatory message which has the effect of associating the protected work with such a message attention must be drawn to the principle of non-discrimination based on race, colour and ethnic origin,[44] and that therefore rightholders have *in principle* a legitimate interest in ensuring that the work protected by copyright is not associated with such a message.[45] This seems to imply that a parody, even if squarely falling within the definition of a parody and the wording of Article 5(3)(k),[46] might nevertheless not be allowed because

41. C-70/10 *Scarlett Extended*, para. 44.
42. Application No. 40397/12.
43. Interestingly, in Case C-610/15 *Stichting Brein* v *Ziggo and XS4ALL Internet* ECLI:EU:C:2017:456 (*Stichting Brein II*) which *inter alia* concerned primary liability of the operators of The Pirate Bay under EU law (communication of works to the public), no such considerations were made, but on the basis of the EU Charter instead, by the CJEU in its judgement. Admittedly, the operators of The Pirate Bay were not a party in the proceedings, given the substance of the case, but the combined effect of the growing body of case law appears to be that a court must in any event consider fundamental rights when different interests are at stake in the process of applying at least secondary EU legislation.
44. Defined in Directive 2000/43/EC of 29 June 2000 implementing the principle of equal treatment between persons irrespective of racial or ethnic origin (OJ 2000 L 180, p. 22), and protected by Art. 21(1) EU Charter.
45. C-201/13 *Deckmyn*, para. 31.
46. *See* C-201/13 *Deckmyn*, paras 20–24 for definition of a parody. Article 5(3)(k) InfoSoc Directive provides laconically that 'use for the purpose of caricature, parody or pastiche' may be excepted from reproduction or communication not the public.

the rightholder may have an overriding interest that is not originating from copyright law.[47] The Court does not, however, specify in its judgement any conditions under which the principle of non-discrimination should prevail over the freedom of expression or vice versa, in a situation where the use in question is evidently parodical. Nor does the Court expressly apply the Charter's own provisions concerning the rules under which limitations to the rights and freedoms may be made.

According to Article 52(1) EU Charter limitations on the exercise of the rights and freedoms provided by the Charter must be provided for by law and respect the *essence* of the relevant rights and freedoms. Moreover, subject to the principle of proportionality, limitations may be made 'only if they are necessary and genuinely meet the objectives of general interest recognised by the Union or the need to protect the rights and freedoms of others'.

Here too the CJEU has not shed much light on the particular scope of the provision or the individual requirements when limiting or balancing the rights at stake in a copyright context. For example, in limiting the freedom to conduct a business in *UPC Telekabel* the CJEU, while noting that that freedom includes the right to be able to freely use, within the limits of its liability for its own acts, the economic, technical and financial resources available to it[48] and recognising that the open-ended injunction that the rightholders were applying for would restrict that freedom by constraining the ISP in a manner which restricts the free use of the resources available at the ISP's disposal because it obliges them to take measures which may represent a significant cost, have a considerable impact on the organisation of activities or require difficult and complex technical solutions,[49] stated that such an injunction makes it possible to choose to put in place measures which are best adapted to the resources and abilities available to the ISP (yet in selecting the measures the ISP must ensure compliance with the fundamental rights of Internet users) and that such an injunction allows the ISP to avoid liability by proving that all reasonable measures have been taken.[50] On the basis of these, three, considerations the CJEU arrived at the rather startling conclusion that such an injunction 'does not seem to infringe the very substance of the freedom'[51] and is therefore not precluded by EU law.

This reasoning may be difficult to reconcile with the earlier *Scarlett Extended* judgement in which the Court reached the opposite conclusion. Additionally, the Court requires ISPs to assess the compatibility of measures which it can select but must introduce, which may or may not satisfy the requirement of reasonableness at the time of implementation, with fundamental rights of Internet users, which, traditionally and by virtue of the Court's case law, is a matter for national authorities and courts to do. Nevertheless, recognising that protection of intellectual property is not absolute and that a measure may not lead to a complete cessation of infringement, the Court ultimately approaches the question of the effectiveness of the measures pragmatically

47. For the sake of completeness, it is worth mentioning that EU copyright law does not harmonise moral rights. *See* recital 19 InfoSoc Directive.
48. C-314/12 *UPC Telekabel Wien*, para. 49.
49. C-314/12 *UPC Telekabel Wien*, para. 50.
50. C-314/12 *UPC Telekabel Wien*, paras 52–53 read together with 55.
51. C-314/12 *UPC Telekabel Wien*, para. 51.

for it states that such measures 'must have the effect of preventing unauthorised access to protected subject matter, or at least, making it difficult to achieve and of seriously discouraging Internet users from such access'.[52] This rather flexible approach was subsequently applied by the CJEU in *McFadden* concerning the provision of free unprotected Wi-Fi.[53]

In the most recent case dealing with copyright and the EU Charter, the Court seems to have backed a few steps relative to its rather progressive approach to the EU Charter. In *Land Nordrhein-Westfalen,*[54] a case concerning the publication on a school website of a pupil's presentation for a language workshop that included on the first page a photograph taken from an online travel portal on which it was lawfully published and without any restrictions, the CJEU, while comprehensively explaining the scope of the communication to the public right and arguably making a very broad interpretation of the *new public* criterion,[55] restricted itself to noting the appellant's argument that account must be taken of the right to education under Article 14 EU Charter and that the action of the pupil is covered by the exercise of that right. Without addressing the substance of this argument, the Court held that 'the findings (...) relating to the concept of 'new public', are not based on whether the illustration used by the pupil for her school presentation is educational in nature, but on the fact that the posting of that work on the school website made it accessible to all the visitors to that website' and merely observed that 'the pursuit of a balance between the right to education and the protection of the right to intellectual property' is provided in Article 5(3)(a) InfoSoc Directive which enables Member States to 'provide for exceptions or limits [sic] to the rights (...) so long as it is for the sole purpose of illustration for teaching or scientific research and to the extent justified by the non-commercial purpose to be achieved',[56] implying that it is not applicable and finding that a communication to the public had occurred.

Educational establishments of all levels play a crucial role in society as they are the carriers of knowledge, within and outside their physical confines. Like any other sector of society, schools adapt to new environments and become increasingly more digitised and find new ways to perform the duties they are tasked with. Impeding innovative efforts of schools affects not only the dissemination of knowledge and skills-learning, but it also risks discouraging creative efforts of their students. While the literal wording of Article 14 EU Charter does indeed provoke reasonable questions as to its applicability to the facts of the case, since it appears to foremost concern *access* to education as such, as opposed to Article 5(3)(a) InfoSoc Directive, the circumstances of the case may instead be seen as a conflict between the protection of intellectual

52. C-314/12 *UPC Telekabel Wien*, paras 61–63.
53. Case C-484/14 *McFadden* v *Sony Music Entertainment* ECLI:EU:C:2016:689, paras 95–96 read together with 99–100.
54. Case C-161/17 *Land Nordrhein-Westfalen* v *Renckhoff* ECLI:EU:C:2018:634.
55. The case only concerned potential infringement of the communication to the public right under Art. 3(1) InfoSoc Directive, and, surprisingly, not also the reproduction right under Art. 2 InfoSoc Directive. *See* further below on communication to the public where this point is discussed further.
56. C-161/17 *Land Nordrhein-Westfalen*, paras 42–43.

property on the one hand, and freedom of expression on the other hand. Admittedly, the German Supreme Court did not ask about the scope of either Article 5(3)(a) InfoSoc Directive or Article 14 EU Charter, nor indeed the freedom of expression under Article 11 EU Charter. Such a circumstance does not, however, preclude the Court from making an assessment on matters which are seemingly relevant to the circumstances of the case.[57] The noteworthy circumstances of the publication of the work and the form it took, which were neither commercial in nature nor harmful to the rightholder since it had been commercially published on a travel portal and freely available, warrant at least a different and more substantive treatment of the provisions of the EU Charter and the required balancing act, especially in light of the Court's judgements in *Scarlett Extended* and *UPC Telekabel* which too did not concern an exception or limitation. Ultimately, by limiting the judgement to the narrow question of the reference, *Land Nordrhein-Westfalen* was a missed opportunity for the CJEU to cast light on the difficult intersection of education, freedom of expression and copyright protection as well as the scope of Article 5(3)(a) InfoSoc Directive.

§2.06 HOW DO THE COPYRIGHT DIRECTIVES AFFECT NATIONAL LAW IN THE MEMBER STATES?*

[A] Full Harmonisation and Partial Harmonisation? Terminological Questions

As can be seen from the list of existing EU copyright legislation above in section 3, harmonisation of EU copyright law has mainly been carried out on the basis of EU directives. Article 288 TFEU describes the difference between directives and regulations as follows:

> A regulation shall have general application. It shall be binding in its entirety and directly applicable in all Member States.
>
> A directive shall be binding, as to the result to be achieved, upon each Member State to which it is addressed, but shall leave to the national authorities the choice of form and methods.

Therefore, regulations are valid and applicable internally in the Member States, essentially, in the same way as the statutes which have been issued by the Member States' own legislator. directives, on the other hand, are not immediately valid in the Member States. Rather, directives oblige the Member States to introduce and uphold certain legal norms in their legal systems. To put it in another way, regulations are directly applicable in the Member States, while directives, on the other hand, are not.

57. *See*, for example, Case C-265/16 *VCAST* v *RTI* ECLI:EU:C:2017:913.

* This section is based on, and re-uses text from, the article *Dansk ophavsret til EU-retligt serviceeftersyn* written by Rosenmeier, M., Blomqvist, J., Riis, T., Schovsbo, J., Schwemer, S., Udsen, H., published in Nordiskt immateriellt rättsskydd (NIR) 2018 vol. 3 (*forthcoming in print*). The relevant parts of the article are written by Morten Rosenmeier. The other authors as well as NIR consent to the reuse below.

As a starting point it is up to the Member States to decide how to implement directives. Among other things, in some instances it is possible to conduct a non-statutory implementation of directives by relying on the understanding that the norms which a directive aims to impose already exist in national legislation, national case law, or both. Often, however, the Member States must modify or renew their legislation in order to live up to the obligations imposed on them by EU directives.

The *extent* to which national law must correspond with EU law before the former is a correct implementation of the latter is an important question. A directive which intends to impose on the Member States an obligation to introduce certain legal norms, neither more nor less, is sometimes said to reflect 'full harmonisation' (or 'maximum harmonisation'). On the other hand, if a directive only imposes minimum standards, such a directive is often said to reflect 'minimum harmonisation'.[58]

One might ask whether the copyright directives constitute full harmonisation directives or minimum harmonisation directives. It is difficult to answer this question in a precise manner. No clear EU law principles exist as to when directives fully harmonise an area or when they harmonise it only on a minimum level.

It is, however, important to observe that the traditional full harmonisation/minimum harmonisation terminology is in fact *immensely inaccurate* because it is unclear what full harmonisation actually entails. How much freedom of choice an EU law provision provides Member States can become apparent in several, different ways.

In order to understand to what extent copyright directives leave Member States a freedom of choice, it is *not* enough to ask whether the provision reflects full harmonisation or minimum harmonisation; it is more relevant to instead ask the following questions:

- To what extent must the Member States interpret words and concepts in copyright directives in a uniform EU law manner?
- To what extent are the Member States allowed to supplement the provisions of a copyright directive with provisions of their own which concern the same topic as the directive?
- To what extent are the Member States allowed to concretise abstractly worded provisions in copyright directives?

[B] The Extent to Which Member States Must Interpret Words and Concepts in Copyright Directives in a Uniform EU Law Manner

The words and concepts which become part of a legal provision can be more or less sharp. Some words and concepts are so concrete that they must refer to a certain, specific thing. What that thing is must then be decided through *interpretation*. Other provisions are worded in such a general, abstract manner that they necessitate some

58. *See*, for example, Case C-5/11 *Donner* ECLI:EU:C:2012:370, Opinion of AG Niilo Jääskinen, paras 24–25.

level of *discretion*. The difference between interpretation and discretion is grounded in the freedom of choice that the one tasked with applying the provision is given. If a provision is to be interpreted, those applying the provision must find out the 'legally correct meaning' of it, including what the body that created the provision intended it to mean. If, on the other hand, a provision necessitates discretion it is essentially up to those applying the provision to decide the meaning.

Many words and concepts, however, create doubt as to whether they must be interpreted or whether they leave discretion to those applying them. Frequently, the reason is that the provisions are of a general nature without being completely capacious. Often it is therefore difficult to decide whether such provisions necessitate discretion and to what extent they may do so. When it comes to provisions of EU law, another question transpires, namely who is to carry out the interpretation or the discretionary estimation of what the provision conveys – the Member States or the CJEU.

Within areas regulated by EU law – including copyright law – it has therefore been a recurring question who should decide how to understand words and notions in the EU directives and to what extent the Member States have a freedom of choice in this regard. A directive contains a certain word, the question is what the word means. Who should decide this? The Member States or the EU? It is a question to which EU law has not always provided a clear answer. It has been dealt with on a case-to-case basis, and there have been many instances where the Member State and/or the EU authorities believed that the Member States had a freedom of choice in relation to the understanding of words and concepts of EU directives. In this regard it has probably been of significance that according to Article 288 TFEU directives, as opposed to regulations, are not directly applicable and that the former leaves it to the national authorities to choose 'forms and methods' for the implementation. When it comes to the copyright directives, it may also have mattered that the Berne Convention and other copyright treaties leave a substantial degree of discretion to the Contracting States. Furthermore, the Berne Convention reflects minimum harmonisation in the sense that Article 19 allows Contracting States to grant more protection than required by the Convention. Perhaps there can be other explanations as well. In any case, with respect to copyright law, as well as other areas, it has traditionally been assumed that the Member States have had some reasonable freedom of choice during the implementation of the words and notions in the directives in their national systems.

Nevertheless, this starting point is no longer valid. It follows from a number of decisions that the Member States must interpret words and concepts in EU directives in common, uniform ways unless something else is stated in the directives. This principle is valid within all areas of EU law, and it has often been cited in copyright cases. For example, in *SGAE* v *Rafael Hoteles* concerning the notion 'communication to the public' in Article 3(1) InfoSoc Directive the CJEU observed that:

> [I]t should be noted that the need for uniform application of Community law and the principle of equality require that where provisions of Community law make no express reference to the law of the Member States for the purpose of determining their meaning and scope, as is the case with Directive 2001/29/EC, they must normally be given an autonomous and uniform interpretation throughout the

> Community [...] It follows that the Austrian Government cannot reasonably maintain that it is for the Member States to provide the definition of 'public' to which Directive 2001/29 refers but does not define.[59]

Some cases state that the Member States must not only conduct a uniform interpretation of specific *words and notions* but of *provisions* in general. For instance, in *UsedSoft* the Court made a general observation that:

> According to settled case law, the need for a uniform application of European Union law and the principle of equality require that the terms of a provision of European Union law which makes no express reference to the law of the Member States for the purpose of determining its meaning and scope must normally be given an independent and uniform interpretation throughout the European Union.[60]

There do however exist a number of EU law principles on how one should find the 'correct' EU law interpretation of words and notions in directives. For example, one must look at a word's 'usual meaning in everyday language, while also taking into account the context in which it occurs and the purposes of the rules of which it is part'.[61]

Hence, the starting point is that the Member States must interpret words and notions in EU directives in common, uniform ways unless something else is stated in the directives. In spite of this, rather, bombastic starting point, however, there are instances where the words and notions in EU directives are so abstract and capacious that they must necessarily require interpretation or discretion from the Member States, even though the directives do not expressly say so. This is also relevant when it comes to copyright directives. In this respect the Court has, for example, stated that the Member States are granted 'a degree of discretion' as to what is meant by 'in certain situations where the prejudice to the rightholder would be minimal' in recital 35 of the InfoSoc Directive.[62] Further, the Court has made it clear that the Member States have a broad discretion as regards the notion 'fair compensation' required for private copying under Article 5(2)(b) InfoSoc Directive:

> With regard to the answer to the question of the identification of the person who must be regarded as responsible for paying the fair compensation, the provisions of Directive 2001/29 do not expressly address the issue of who is to pay that

59. Case C-306/05 *SGAE* v *Rafael Hoteles* ECLI:EU:C:2006:764, para. 31. *See also* C-5/08 *Infopaq International* v *Danske Dagblades Forening* ECLI:EU:C:2009:465 paras 27 et seq. (on the notion 'reproduction in part' in Art. 2 InfoSoc Directive), Case C-510/10 *DR and TV2 Danmark* v *NCB* ECLI:EU:C:2012:244, paras 33 et seq. (on the meaning of 'by means of their own facilities' in Art. 5(2)(d) InfoSoc Directive), Case C-201/13 *Deckmyn and Vrijheidsfonds* v *Vandersteen and Others* ECLI:EU:C:2014:2132, paras 14 et seq. (on the notion 'parody' in Art. 5(3)(k) InfoSoc Directive) and Case C-128/11 *UsedSoft* v *Oracle International* ECLI:EU:C:2012:407, para. 40 (on the concept of 'sale' in Art. 4(2) Computer Programs Directive).
60. C-128/11 *UsedSoft* v *Oracle*, para. 39. *See also* C-5/08 *Infopaq International* v *Danske Dagblades Forening*, para. 27 and C-510/10 *DR and TV2 Danmark* v *NCB*, para. 33.
61. C-201/13 *Deckmyn and Vrijheidsfonds* v *Vandersteen and Others*, para. 19 and Case C-285/12 *Diakité* ECLI:EU:C:2014:39, para. 27 with further references.
62. Case C-463/12 *Copydan Båndkopi* v *Nokia Danmark* ECLI:EU:C:2015:144, paras 56 et seq.

compensation, meaning that the Member States enjoy broad discretion when determining who must discharge that obligation.[63]

Moreover, Member States are allowed to define 'the most relevant criteria' as to what constitutes an 'equitable remuneration' according to Article 8(2) Renal and Lending Rights Directive. In *SENA* the Court held that since there exists no Community definition of the notion of equitable remuneration it is up to 'the Member States alone to determine, in their own territory, what are the most relevant criteria for ensuring, within the limits imposed by Community law, and particularly Directive 92/100, adherence to that Community concept'.[64] This was subsequently affirmed in *Lagardère Active Broadcast* where Court reiterated it:

> has already held that there is no objective reason to justify the laying down by the Community judicature of specific methods for determining what constitutes uniform equitable remuneration, which would necessarily entail its acting in the place of the Member States, which are not bound by any particular criteria under Directive 92/100. It is therefore for the Member States alone to determine, in their own territory, what are the most relevant criteria [...].[65]

The Court has also explained when exceptions or limitations can be provided 'for the purpose of public security' under Article 5(3)(e) InfoSoc Directive.[66]

In some cases the Court has stated that if a directive does not clearly define the obligations which follow from the directive, Member States can determine the most relevant criteria to ensure compliance with the directive:

> In the absence of sufficiently precise Community criteria in a directive to delimit the obligations under the directive, it is for the Member States to determine, in their own territory, what are the most relevant criteria for ensuring, within the limits imposed by European Union law and in particular by the directive concerned, compliance with that directive.[67]

Further, in some cases the Court has held that if a notion is not defined in a directive, Member States enjoy a discretion if there is nothing that speaks against it:

> In the absence of any Community definition of equitable remuneration, there is no objective reason to justify the laying down by the Community judicature of specific methods for determining what constitutes uniform equitable remuneration, which

63. Case C-462/09 *Stichting de Thuiskopie* v *Opus Supplies Deutschland and Others* ECLI: EU:C:2011:397, para. 23. *See* further Joined Cases C-457/11 to 460/11 *VG Wort* v *Kyocera and Others* and *Fujitsu Technology Solutions and Hewlett-Packard* v *VG Wort* ECLI:EU:C:2013:426, para. 74. Cases C-521/11 *Amazon.com International Sales and Others* v *Austro-Mechana* ECLI: EU:C:2013:515 (para. 20) and C-463/12 *Copydan Båndkopi* v *Nokia Danmark* (para. 20) add that the broad discretion of the Member States also allow them to determine, *inter alia*, who must pay the compensation, and that they may establish the form and level of compensation and make detailed arrangements for collection.
64. Case C-245/00 *Stichting ter Exploitatie van Naburige Rechten (SENA)* v *Nederlandse Omroep Stichting (NOS)* ECLI:EU:C:2003:68, para. 34.
65. Case C-192/04 *Lagardère Active Broadcast* v *SPRE and GVE* ECLI:EU:C:2005:475, para. 48.
66. C-145/10 *Painer* v *Standard Verlags and Others* ECLI:EU:C:2011:798 paras 100 et seq.
67. C-521/11 *Amazon.com International Sales and Others* v *Austro-Mechana*, para. 21. *See* further C-36/05 *The Commission* v *Spain* ECLI:EU:C:2006:672 para. 33 and C-145/10 *Painer* v *Standard Verlags and Others*, para. 103.

> would necessarily entail its acting in the place of the Member States, which are not bound by any particular criteria under Directive 92/100 [...]. It is therefore for the Member States alone to determine, in their own territory, what are the most relevant criteria for ensuring, within the limits imposed by Community law, and particularly Directive 92/100, adherence to that Community concept.[68]

Added to this can be various other 'Member State-friendly' declarations. In *Copydan Båndkopi* the Court left it to the Member States to decide what is meant by 'In certain situations where the prejudice to the rightholder would be minimal' in recital 35 of the InfoSoc Directive and held that 'the objective of Directive 2001/29 is to harmonise only certain aspects of the law on copyright and related rights ...' and that:

> the general scheme of the directive is circumscribed by a number of its provisions which disclose the intention of the EU legislature to grant a degree of discretion to the Member States in the implementation of the directive, such as Article 5, which sets out a series of exceptions and limitations which the Member States are free to transpose into their national law. [...] In the same way that Member States may elect whether or not to adopt any of the exceptions set out in Article 5(2) [...], they also have the option, as confirmed by recital 35 [...], to provide – in certain cases covered by the exceptions which they have freely established – for an exemption from payment of fair compensation where the prejudice caused to rightholders is minimal. [...] For the reasons given [...], the setting of a threshold below which the prejudice may be classified as 'minimal', for the purpose of recital 35 [...], must also be within the discretion of the Member States, provided, inter alia, that the application of the threshold is consistent with the principle of equal treatment [...].[69]

Simultaneously, however, the Court has formulated a general rule according to which words and notions in directives must be interpreted in common, uniform ways by the Member States unless something else is stated in the directives. Such self-contradictions make it difficult to comprehend this legal area.

Member States are rarely allowed to participate in deciding how to understand words and notions in the directives. Rather the starting point of the Court is that Member States must interpret words and notions in EU directives in common, uniform ways. This is so even in situations where the words or notions in question are so abstract and capacious that they necessitate discretion for the Member States. However, even in the rare instances where the Member States enjoy discretion, the discretion is in no way unlimited. On the contrary, Member States, as it is often stressed by the Court, are typically only allowed to define the 'most relevant criteria'. Therefore,

68. C-245/00 *Stichting ter Exploitatie van Naburige Rechten (SENA)* v *Nederlandse Omroep Stichting (NOS)*, para. 34. *See also* C-192/04 *Lagardère Active Broadcast* v *SPRE and GVE*, paras 46 et seq., where the Court stresses, among other things, that 'is clear from its wording and scheme that Directive 92/100 provides for minimal harmonisation regarding rights related to copyright'. *See* further C-462/09 *Stichting de Thuiskopie* v *Opus Supplies Deutschland and Others*, para. 23. *See also* C-463/12 *Copydan Båndkopi* v *Nokia Danmark*, para. 20 and Joined Cases C-457/11 and 460/11 *VG Wort* v *Kyocera and Others* and *Fujitsu Technology Solutions and Hewlett-Packard* v *VG Wort*, para. 74, C-521/11 *Amazon.com International Sales and Others* v *Austro-Mechana*, para. 20 and C-145/10 *Painer* v *Standard Verlags and Others*, paras 100 et seq.
69. C-463/12 *Copydan Båndkopi* v *Nokia Danmark*, paras 57 et seq.

the Court itself can also define the criteria., and it does so with great enthusiasm. Normally, this substantially limits the discretion of the Member States.

In *SENA*, having explained the right of the Member States to determine themselves the most relevant criteria on the notion 'equitable remuneration' in Article 8(2) Rental and Lending Rights Directive, the Court observed that 'whether the remuneration, which represents the consideration for the use of a commercial phonogram, in particular for broadcasting purposes, is equitable is to be assessed, in particular, in the light of the value of that use in trade',[70] that its role was 'to provide the national court with the information it needs to assess whether the national criteria used for assessing the remuneration of performing artists and phonogram producers are such as to ensure that they receive equitable remuneration in a manner that is consistent with Community law', and that one must take into account 'the methods used in the other Member States'.[71] Additionally, the Court listed a large number of criteria which were relevant for the assessment, including the number of hours the phonograms were broadcast, the number of viewers and listeners, the tariffs set by the public broadcast organisations in the Member States bordering the Member State concerned etc.[72] In *Lagardère Active Broadcast* the Court stressed that the Rental and Lending Rights Directive only provides for minimal harmonisation and that it was up to the Member States to determine the most relevant criteria.[73] Subsequently, however, the Court added that the Member States must 'exercise their powers in this area within the limits laid down by Community law', and that they must, among other things, regard the circumstances set out in recital 17 of the Directive, the actual audience, the potential audience, the language version of the broadcast etc.[74]

In *Padawan* the Court stressed that the concept of 'fair compensation' within the meaning of Article 5(2)(b) InfoSoc Directive is an autonomous concept of EU law which must be interpreted in a uniform manner in all Member States, that the Member States were not at liberty to define its limits in an inconsistent and non-harmonised manner, and that they may charge persons who make copying equipment available for private users or who provide copying services for them etc.[75] That the notion of 'fair compensation' is an autonomous EU legal concept which must be interpreted in a uniform manner in the Member States was also stated in *Hewlett Packard Belgium*, in which the Court also put forward a number of instructions on the necessity to distinguish between different forms of copying etc.[76] In *Stichting de Thuiskopie* the Court granted Member States 'broad discretion' with regards to who must pay the compensation according to the InfoSoc Directive, yet made it nevertheless clear that it is the final user or persons who make the reproduction equipment, devices and media

70. C-245/00 *Stichting ter Exploitatie van Naburige Rechten (SENA)* v *Nederlandse Omroep Stichting (NOS)*, para. 37.
71. C-245/00 *Stichting ter Exploitatie van Naburige Rechten (SENA)* v *Nederlandse Omroep Stichting (NOS)*, para. 44.
72. C-245/00 *Stichting ter Exploitatie van Naburige Rechten (SENA)* v *Nederlandse Omroep Stichting (NOS)* para. 46.
73. C-192/04 *Lagardère Active Broadcast* v *SPRE and GVE*, paras 46 et seq.
74. C-192/04 *Lagardère Active Broadcast* v *SPRE and GVE*, paras 49 et seq.
75. C-467/08 *Padawan* v *SGAE* ECLI:EU:C:2010:620, paras 31 et seq.
76. C-572/13 *Hewlett Packard Belgium* v *Reprobel* ECLI:EU:C:2015:750, paras 35 et seq.

that becomes available to the final user.[77] Similarly in *Copydan Båndkopi* the Court, having noted the broad discretion of the Member States in relation to Article 5(2)(a) InfoSoc Directive, pointed to a number of complicated criteria.[78] Intensive intervention regarding whether the Member States may charge suppliers of various forms of equipment linked together occurred in *VG Wort* and *Fujitsu Technology Solutions*.[79]

Therefore, it can normally be assumed that the Member States must interpret words and notions in EU directives in common, uniform ways unless there are special reasons to believe otherwise. And even when that is the case, the discretion of the Member States is rather very narrow.

[C] Are the Member States Allowed to Supplement the Provisions of a Copyright Directive with Their Own National Provisions?

Copyright directives limit the freedom of the Member States in another way: if a directive aims to promote the internal market, its provisions are sometimes exhaustive in the sense that the Member States are not at liberty to have other, supplementing provisions *concerning the same topics as those dealt with by the directives*. This has in many situations been relevant especially within copyright law. For example, according to Article 3(1) Database Directive, Member States must grant copyright protection to compilations (databases) which can be considered original in a copyright sense. In *Football Dataco* the Court was asked if it was consistent with Article 3 to grant other sorts of copyright protection to databases than the protection which follows from the Directive. The Court ruled that is was not. It referred to the fact that the Directive aimed to:

> remove the differences which existed between national legislation on the legal protection of databases, particularly as regards the scope and conditions of copyright protection, and which adversely affected the functioning of the internal market, the free movement of goods or services within the European Union and the development of an information market within the European Union[80]

and that it 'precludes national legislation which grants databases, as defined in Article 1(2) of the directive, copyright protection under conditions which are different to those set out in Article 3(1) of the directive'.[81] Similarly in *Laserdisken* in relation to Article 4(2) InfoSoc Directive, which provides that 'The distribution right shall not be exhausted within the Community except where the first sale or other transfer of ownership in the Community [...] is made by the rightholder or with his consent', the question came up if the distribution right was also exhausted if a first sale etc. was

77. C-462/09 *Stichting de Thuiskopie* v *Opus Supplies Deutschland and Others*, paras 23 et seq.
78. C-463/12 *Copydan Båndkopi* v *Nokia Danmark*, paras 20 et seq. *See also* C-521/11 *Amazon.com International Sales and Others* v *Austro-Mechana*.
79. Joined Cases C-457/11 and 460/11 *VG Wort* v *Kyocera and Others* and *Fujitsu Technology Solutions and Hewlett-Packard* v *VG Wort*, paras 60 et seq.
80. Case C-604/10 *Football Dataco and Others* v *Yahoo! UK and Others* ECLI:EU:C:2012:115, para. 48.
81. C-604/10 *Football Dataco and Others* v *Yahoo! UK and Others*, para. 52.

made *outside* of the Community. The Court held that it was not. It referred to the fact that the Directive did not leave it open for the Member States to provide for a rule of exhaustion other than the Community-wide exhaustion rule in the Directive.[82] The Court emphasised that this was 'the only interpretation which is fully consistent with the purpose of Directive 2001/29 which [...] is to ensure the functioning of the internal market' and that '[a] situation in which some Member States will be able to provide for international exhaustion of distribution rights whilst others will provide only for Community-wide exhaustion of those rights will inevitably give rise to barriers to the free movement of goods and the freedom to provide services'.[83] In *Svensson* the Court was asked whether it was 'possible for a Member State to give wider protection to authors' exclusive right by enabling communication to the public to cover a greater range of acts than provided for in Article 3(1)' InfoSoc Directive. The Court answered that it was not. According to the Court a different result would lead to legislative differences and legal uncertainty which would undermine the objective pursued by the Directive and affect the function of the internal market.[84]

Although Member States are often not at liberty to have other, supplementing provisions concerning the same topics as those dealt with by the directives, there are instances where they may, in fact, introduce such provisions.

According to the InfoSoc Directive Member States must grant authors the exclusive right of reproduction, distribution and 'communication to the public', i.e., communication aimed towards persons not present at the place from which the communication originates, such as radio or TV broadcasts or situations where protected material is available over the Internet. On the other hand, the Directive does not say anything about whether authors should also be granted a right to display copies of the works or to perform the works for an attending audience. Nevertheless, some Member States, including the Nordic countries, grant authors such rights. The EU has not yet taken legislative action towards such exploitations. Until the countries are told otherwise, they, therefore, assume that it is acceptable.[85] In *Soulier* the Court indicated, however, that even though the InfoSoc Directive only grants copyright to authors, Member States are at liberty to grant certain rights to publishers and other third parties as long as it does not harm the rights which the Directive provides for authors.[86]

By way of another example, Article 3(1) InfoSoc Directive grants authors the exclusive right to communicate works to the public, including the making available to the public of their works in such a way that members of the public may access them from a place and at a time individually chosen by them. Article 3(2)(d) grants

82. C-479/04 *Laserdisken* v *Kulturministeriet*, para. 24.
83. C-479/04 *Laserdisken* v *Kulturministeriet*, para. 26. *See also* C-355/96 *Silhouette International Schmied GmbH & Co. KG* v *Hartlauer Handelsgesellschaft mbH* ECLI:EU:C:1998:374, paras 15 et seq. in relation to exhaustion in trademark law. *See also* Chapter 7.
84. Case C-466/12 *Svensson and Others* v *Retriever Sverige* ECLI:EU:C:2014:76, paras 34 et seq.
85. That some Member States have provisions regarding performance for an attending audience was acknowledged – and accepted by implication? – by the CJEU in Case C-283/10 *Circul Globus Bucureşti* v *UCMR – ADA* ECLI:EU:C:2011:772 and Joined Cases C-403/08 and C-429/08 *FAPL and Others* v *QC Leisure and Others* ECLI:EU:C:2011:631, paras 201 et seq.
86. Case C-301/15 *Soulier and Doke* v *Premier ministre and Ministre de la Culture et de la Communication* ECLI:EU:C:2016:878, para. 48.

broadcasting organisations a similar making available right as regards fixations of broadcasts but says nothing about whether broadcasting organisations should also enjoy an exclusive right to other types of communication to the public. In *C More Entertainment* the Court held that Member States are at liberty to extend the right of broadcasting organisations so that it includes a making available right, enabling them, having regard to the factual circumstances of the case, to take action against websites where it is possible to watch the broadcasts live as it is being transmitted. To this extent it is worth noting that recital 16 of the Rental and Lending Rights Directive expressly states that Member States 'should be able to provide for more far-reaching protection for owners of rights related to copyright than that required by the provisions laid down in this Directive in respect of broadcasting and communication to the public'. Interestingly, it was also acknowledged that the purpose of the InfoSoc Directive is to harmonise copyright and related rights as far as is necessary for the smooth functioning of the internal market, that it has harmonised copyright and related rights only in part, and that the Directive does not harmonise the extent of the protection according to Article 3(2)(d).[87]

The question of whether Member States are at liberty to supplement the provisions of a copyright directive with their own national provisions is thus a difficult one, which cannot be answered precisely in a general manner. It is rather a matter which must be dealt with on a case-by-case basis.

[D] Are the Member States at Liberty to Concretise Generally Worded Provisions in the Copyright Directives?

Finally, the question is whether the Member States are at liberty to *concretise and narrow down provisions in the copyright directives by supplementing any relevant requirements with additional requirements*. For example, under Article 5(3)(h) InfoSoc Directive Member States may provide for copyright exceptions concerning 'works, such as works of architecture or sculpture, made to be located permanently in public places'. In Denmark the provision has been implemented in § 24(2) Copyright Act, which states that 'Works of art may be depicted if they are durably placed at or next to a publicly accessible open space or road. The before-mentioned rule is not applicable if the artistic work is the main motive and the reproduction is being used commercially.' The question that may arise is whether the conditions in § 24(2) whereby the artistic work cannot be the main motive and that the reproduction must not be used commercially for the exception to apply are compatible with the InfoSoc Directive, given that such conditions are not mentioned in Article 5(3)(h).

When it comes to the *mandatory* provision on the exhaustion of the distribution right in Article 4(2) InfoSoc Directive, the Court has issued statements which suggest that the provision must be implemented in the exact manner in which it appears in the Directive. In particular, the Court has held that Article 4(2) 'does not leave it open to the Member States to provide for a rule of exhaustion other than the Community-wide

87. Case C-279/13 *C More Entertainment* v *Sandberg* ECLI:EU:C:2015:199, paras 29 et seq.

exhaustion rule'[88] and that it 'does not leave it open to the Member States to provide for an exhaustion rule other than that set out in that provision' since 'differences in the national laws governing exhaustion of the right of distribution are likely to affect directly the smooth functioning of the internal market'.[89] Perhaps the same ought to apply to the mandatory exception on temporary acts of reproduction in Article 5(1) InfoSoc Directive.

In relation to the facultative exceptions and limitations in Article 5(2)-5(4) InfoSoc Directive, the Member States *are* indeed at liberty to concretise the provisions by introducing conditions apart from those expressly provided, because of recital (44) InfoSoc Directive,[90] the so-called three-step test in Article 5(5),[91] and the general principle according to which provisions of a directive which derogate from a general principle established by that directive must be the subject of a narrow and strict interpretation[92] as long as such an interpretation does not substantially erode the exceptions and deprive them of their effectiveness.[93] Additionally, in *VG Wort* and *Fujitsu Technology* the Court observed the title of Article 5 InfoSoc Directive, 'Exceptions and limitations', and indicated the Member States can choose to either exclude a right altogether or merely limit it.[94]

These qualities suggest that Member States are at liberty to concretise and limit provisions which entail copyright exceptions. In spite of this default position, however, the line between cases concerning the question whether Member States may concretise a provision and cases concerning the interpretation of words and notions in a directive may not always be easy to draw and the circumstances may one type transition into the second type. Moreover, the circumstance that Member States must interpret words and notions in common uniform ways, compatible with the requirements of EU law unless

88. Case C-479/04 *Laserdisken* v *Kulturministeriet*, para. 24.
89. Case C-419/13 *Art & Allposters International* v *Stichting Pictoright* ECLI:EU:C:2015:27, para. 30.
90. According to which: 'When applying the exceptions and limitations provided for in this Directive, they should be exercised in accordance with international obligations. Such exceptions and limitations may not be applied in a way which prejudices the legitimate interests of the rightholder or which conflicts with the normal exploitation of his work or other subject-matter. The provision of such exceptions or limitations by Member States should, in particular, duly reflect the increased economic impact that such exceptions or limitations may have in the context of the new electronic environment. Therefore, the scope of certain exceptions or limitations may have to be even more limited when it comes to certain new uses of copyright works and other subject-matter.'
91. The three-step test is a general copyright principle according to which exceptions to copyright apply only in *certain special cases* (step 1) which do not *conflict with a normal exploitation of the work or other subject-matter* (step 2) and which do not *unreasonably prejudice the legitimate interests of the rightholder* (step 3). *See* further Chapter 5. On the principle *see*, for example, Case C-117/13 *Technische Universität Darmstadt* v *Ulmer* ECLI:EU:C:2014:2196, paras 48 et seq.; C-5/08 *Infopaq International* v *Danske Dagblades Forening*, paras 56 and 58; Case C-527/15 *Stichting Brein* v *Wullems* ECLI:EU:C:2017:300, paras 62 et seq.; and C-265/16 *VCAST* v *RTI*, paras 31 et seq. That the three-step tests influences the interpretation of Art. 5(2)(b) InfoSoc Directive was made clear in C-572/13 *Hewlett Packard Belgium* v *Reprobel*, para. 59.
92. *See*, for example, C-5/08 *Infopaq International* v *Danske Dagblades Forening*, para. 56. *See* further Chapter 5.
93. C-145/10 *Painer* v *Standard Verlags and Others*, paras 129 et seq; *see also* para. 133.
94. Joined Cases C-457/11 and 460/11 *VG Wort* v *Kyocera and Others* and *Fujitsu Technology Solutions and Hewlett-Packard* v *VG Wort*, paras 33 et seq. Cf. C-145/10 *Painer* v *Standard Verlags and Others*, paras 101 et seq.

something else is stated in the directives, may in some cases erode the possibility for Member States to concretise copyright exceptions.

The following examples provide an illustration.

It is a basic copyright principle that it is no copyright infringement to parody protected works or subject them to satire and so on. The InfoSoc Directive recognised this in Article 5(3)(k) which allows Member States to introduce an exception concerning use 'for the purpose of caricature, parody or pastiche'. In a number of Member States it has been submitted that parodies are only allowed if they aim to ridicule the very work used in them and that it is, therefore, not lawful to use a protected work in a parody which aims to ridicule something else than the protected work, for example, political opponents etc. In *Deckmyn*[95] the Court made it clear that no such requirement exists. The Court held that the essential characteristics of a parody are, first, to evoke an existing work while being noticeably different from it, and, second, to constitute an expression of humour or mockery, and that it is of no significance for copyright whether a parody concerns the work which it uses or something else. The traditional assumption that parodies must aim to ridicule the very works which are part of the parody is therefore not relevant for the applicability of the exception. This is so regardless of whether one perceives the understanding that parodies must ridicule the very works which go into them as something which follows from the notion of parody as such or as something which follows from a supplementing, concretising requirement. The Member States cannot introduce such a requirement.

The Court was aware that exceptions must be interpreted strictly,[96] but it reached its conclusion because, among other things, 'The interpretation of the concept of parody must [...] enable the effectiveness of the exception thereby established to be safeguarded and its purpose to be observed.'

Similarly, in *Painer* the Court made it clear in relation to the quotation exception in Article 5(3)(d) InfoSoc Directive that the quoted passage need not be incorporated into something that must be considered a new copyright-protected *work*, explaining that it would otherwise make the exception ineffective.[97] Member States cannot, therefore, require that quotations be incorporated into something constitutes a work in itself, even if such a requirement does, in fact, reflect a concretising, strict interpretation of Article 5(3)(d) InfoSoc Directive.

Provisions which derogate from a general principle established by a directive must be the subject of a narrow and strict interpretation. When it comes to provisions which *do not* reflect exceptions to main rules, the question is more difficult. On the one hand there exists an EU law principle according to which EU provisions must be interpreted in common, uniform ways, which are compatible with the requirements of EU law, unless something else is stated in the directives,[98] but at the same time, as explained above in [B], there exists another, somewhat unclear EU law principle that

95. C-201/13 *Deckmyn and Vrijheidsfonds* v *Vandersteen and Others.*
96. C-201/13 *Deckmyn and Vrijheidsfonds* v *Vandersteen and Others*, para. 22.
97. C-145/10 *Painer* v *Standard Verlags and Others*, para. 133.
98. *See*, for example, C-128/11 *UsedSoft* v *Oracle International*, para. 39, C-5/08 *Infopaq International* v *Danske Dagblades Forening*, para. 27, C-34/10 *Oliver Brüstle* v *Greenpeace e.V.* ECLI:EU:C:2011:669, para. 25, C-510/10 *DR and TV2 Danmark* v *NCB*, para. 33.

if a directive does not clearly define the obligations which follow from it, Member States can determine 'the most relevant criteria' to ensure compliance with the directive. This must mean that, unless the provisions of a directive appear to be unclear and abstract, Member States are, as a default point, not at liberty to supplement the requirements of a provision with new requirements, unless the directives say otherwise or unless the provisions reflect exceptions to the main rule.

[E] What Do the Principles Mean in Practice?

What is said above means that the Member States normally have very little freedom of choice during the implementation of the copyright directives:

- Member States must interpret words and notions in EU directives in common, uniform ways, which are compatible with the requirements of EU law unless something else is stated in the directives (*see* above [B]).
- To a certain extent the Member States are not at liberty to supplement the provisions of a directive with national provisions concerning the same topics as those dealt with by the directive (*see* above [C]).
- When it comes to clear and concrete provisions which do not reflect exceptions to main rules, Member States are not at liberty to supplement the requirements in the provisions with new requirements (*see* above [D]).

These aspects are not only relevant in relation to how the Member States should construct the wording which implements the copyright directives. The above-mentioned principles are also relevant for national courts which must interpret national provisions that implement the directives. It is a basic premise that national rules must, as far as possible, be interpreted in a manner which conforms with the requirements of EU law. However, it is clear that in cases between private parties national courts are not obliged to apply an interpretation of EU law if it will contradict clear national provisions. The Court expressed this view by saying that in cases between individuals the obligations of national courts to interpret national law in accordance with EU law cannot serve as the basis for an interpretation of national law *contra legem*.[99] But apart from such cases not only the legislature but also the courts and other national bodies are obliged to interpret national legal rules in a way which brings national law in conformity with the requirements of EU law.

99. *See*, for example, C-351/12 *OSA* v *Léčebné lázně Mariánské Lázně* ECLI:EU:C:2014:110, para. 45 with further references.

Chapter 3
Copyright and Related Rights

§3.01 INTRODUCTION

Subject matter protected by copyright and subject matter falling under related rights is protected automatically and protection is granted without any formalities such as registration. This important quality has its foundation in the Berne Convention. Automatic protection arises as soon as a work is created and rights are granted irrespective of how the creation has been expressed – it does not matter whether the creation has been printed on paper or exists only digitally.[100] Certain states, such as the UK, however require that the expression be fixed and therefore possess a certain degree of permanence or materiality.[101] Such a fixation requirement is however expressly permitted in the Berne Convention.[102] If a work is being created in several stages – sketches, models, drafts etc. – copyright protection can also subsist in such conceptual creations, if they independently satisfy the requirements of protection and can be considered 'works'.

§3.02 SUBJECT MATTER

Copyright protects *literary* and *artistic* works. The terms can however be misleading as these two types encapsulate a very broad range of different subject matter, such as poems, novels, scientific papers, reports, classical music, heavy metal music, expressionistic paintings, cubist paintings, sculptures, buildings, photographs, science-fiction films, documentaries, television commercials, and even computer programs. The variety of creations that can be protected reaffirm the notion that copyright does not concern itself with what is aesthetically pleasing, but with the intellectual effort that

100. *See* Art. 2(1) and 5(2) Berne Convention.
101. Copyright, Designs and Patents Act 1988, s. 3(2) concerning literary, dramatic and musical works.
102. Berne Convention, Art. 2(2).

has been expended by the creator. On the other hand, creators of subject matter falling within the ambit of related rights are awarded protection for their creations not so much for the intellectual originality as the organisational and financial effort that has been expended in creating such subject matter. Hence, related rights can protect performances, phonograms (sound recordings), and broadcasts, or even simple photographic pictures (that do not possess the required level of originality, such as passport photographs, photographs used by the press, such as 'snapshots', amateur photographs etc.)

[A] Literary and Artistic Works

Under the Berne Convention the Contracting Parties – which include all the EU Member States – must provide copyright protection to *literary and artistic works,* which includes:

> every production in the literary, scientific and artistic domain, whatever may be the mode or form of its expression, such as books, pamphlets and other writings; lectures, addresses, sermons and other works of the same nature; dramatic or dramatico-musical works; choreographic works and entertainments in dumb show; musical compositions with or without words; cinematographic works to which are assimilated works expressed by a process analogous to cinematography; works of drawing, painting, architecture, sculpture, engraving and lithography; photographic works to which are assimilated works expressed by a process analogous to photography; works of applied art; illustrations, maps, plans, sketches and three-dimensional works relative to geography, topography, architecture or science.[103]

At *EU level* no such open list is enunciated, instead the framework harmonises to a limited extent what specific creations must be protected by copyright. By virtue of Article 1 Computer Programs Directive Member States must protect computer programs as literary works, under Article 3 Database Directive Member States must grant copyright protection to original databases, while under Article 6 Term Directive Member States must grant copyright protection to original photographs. Moreover, the very existence of the resale right under the Resale Right Directive means indirectly that Member States must protect certain kinds of visual art.[104] Apart from this, the EU copyright framework does not expressly say what works must be protected by copyright in the Member States, and so the question has come up whether the taste of cheese can be protected.[105]

[B] Computer Programs

Both at European and international level attention has been drawn to the question of the legal definition of computer programs. Internationally, it is apparent from Article

103. Berne Convention, Art. 2(1).
104. *See* Resale Right Directive, Art. 2(1) together with recitals (1) and (4).
105. Case C-310/17 *Levola Hengelo* v *Smilde Foods* (pending).

10(1) TRIPS Agreement that the source and object code of computer programs should be protected as literary works, while Article 4 WCT states that computer programs should be protected as literary works regardless of the way or form in which they are expressed. However, neither international treaties nor the Computer Programs Directive contain a legal definition of the term 'computer program'. Article 1(1) Computer Programs Directive only states that computer programs shall be protected and that the term includes the preparatory design material. At EU level it has not been considered necessary, or appropriate, to legally define these terms.[106] This provides the necessary space to interpret and adapt the term in line with technological developments, however, the lack of a definition does not mean that the term is unambiguous. Before the Computer Programs Directive the following legal definition of the term was given in 1978 in WIPO's Model Provisions on the Protection of Computer Software:

> A 'computer program' is a set of instructions expressed in words, codes, schemes or in any other form, which is capable, when incorporated in a machine-readable medium, of causing a 'computer' – an electronic or similar device having information-processing capabilities – to perform or achieve a particular task or result.

This definition has been repeated in several international and national contexts. In the preparatory works of the Computer Programs Directive a similar but simplified definition has been expressed:

> A computer program is a set of instructions the purpose of which is to cause an information processing device, a computer, to perform its functions.[107]

However, these descriptions are merely *simpler technical descriptions* of how a computer program is designed and what its function is, not a legal definition itself.

In the context of the Computer Programs Directive, recital 7 only states that the term 'computer program' refers to 'programs in any form', while protection is granted under Article 1(2) to 'any form of a computer program'. The central reason why the term computer program is not further defined in the Computer Programs Directive is that such a definition can quickly become obsolete as a result of future technical changes relating to the nature of computer programs.[108] Computer programs have a wide range of variations, and exist in many different forms and technologies – some are embedded in different products and mechanisms, while others are perceptible and controllable by end users. During the negotiations of the Computer Programs Directive it was considered appropriate to let the term be dynamic so that it could be adjusted in coherence with technical developments.[109]

---

106. *See also* Commission, 'Staff working paper on the review of the EC legal framework in the field of copyright and related rights' SEC(2004) 995, 19 July 2004, p. 8.
107. COM(88) 172 final p. 170 and Commission, 'Proposal for a Council Directive on the legal protection of computer programs' COM(88) 816 final – SYN 183, p. 3.
108. *See* COM(88) 816 final – SYN 183 p. 17. *See also* Commission, 'Report on the implementation and effects of Directive 91/250/EEC on the legal protection of computer programs' COM(2000) 199 final.
109. *See* COM(88) 816 final – SYN 183 p. 17. *See also* SEC(2004) 995, 19 July 2004 p. 8.

The term 'computer program' in the context of copyright should thus be interpreted free from technical criteria, but in a practical situation this will give little guidance. WIPO's simple technical description of the design and function of a computer program has been used by the CJEU in the delicate division of the protection of a computer program as such, as a literary work, and the independent protection of the program's graphical user interface (GUI).[110] Hence, in practice a distinction can, and should, be made between the protection provided for the computer program as such (*computer program protection*) and the protection provided for the content of the program, primarily the GUI and other objects displayed on the screen, that may or may not be part of it, or heard through the speakers. Furthermore, other interfaces, e.g., application programming interfaces (APIs), could possibly be protected as computer programs.

Where a number of persons are creating the computer program together, the computer program will become a work of joint authorship, in which case protection is shared among the different contributors. Alternatively, the constituent parts may themselves independently enjoy protection, in which case the end product may be covered by different copyrights of different authors or overlapping protection. Such joint authorship or overlapping rights can create difficulties for proper rights clearance relating to e.g., availability of programs, translations, permitted uses, amount of copies etc.

[1] The Code of the Program

Protection is limited to the literary form of the code of the computer program. According to the CJEU this is what the Computer Programs Directive intends to protect.[111] Thus, it is a relatively *narrow* protection, and the categorisation of the program as a *literary work* could be interpreted to mean that the concept of computer programs encompasses the writing of the program, i.e., protection of how the program's structure and functions have been designed in literary form. Protection has nothing to do with how simple or difficult the structure or function is as such, and it may also exist for programs that are adaptations of existing programs.

The literary form of a computer program is limited to the technical description and relates to those parts of a program that enables the computer to perform a task or a particular function. As the CJEU has pointed out the object of protection under Article 1(2) Computer Programs Directive is 'the expression in any form of a computer program which permits reproduction in different computer languages, such as the source code and the object code'[112] and 'this enables the computer to perform its task'.[113] In practice, this means protection in all forms that exist for the code, but not

110. *See* Case C-393/09 *BSA* v *Ministerstvo Kultury* ECLI:EU:C:2010:816. *See also* Case C-406/10 *SAS Institute* v *World Programming* ECLI:EU:C:2012:259.
111. *See* C-393/09 *BSA*, paras 34–35 and C-406/10 *SAS Institute*, para. 38.
112. C-393/09 *BSA*, para. 35.
113. C-393/09 *BSA*, para. 38.

for what is shown on the screen, even though this reflects the program's instructions to the computer.[114]

Recital 7 of the preamble to the Computer Programs Directive states that the term *computer program* refers to 'programs in any form'. Furthermore, it is apparent from Article 1(2) Computer Programs Directive that copyright protection should 'apply to the expression in any form of a computer program'. Consequently, all forms that a computer program can take enjoy protection, such as when it exists in written form (system descriptions, flowcharts etc.) and when it is available in machine-processable form (source or object code). It does not matter on what medium the program exists, whether it is easily perceptible and free-standing or when it is part of system software or hardware products.

[2] Function, File Format and Programming Language

In *SAS Institute* the developer had created a system for statistical analysis (the SAS system). In order for the users of the system to be able to customise it for processing their own data, they could write and run their own applications, so-called scripts. These scripts were written in the system programming language (the SAS language). World Programming developed a competing system (the WPS system), designed to imitate the SAS system's functions. The WPS system enabled those who developed scripts in the SAS language to run these within the WPS system. SAS Institute considered this to be an infringement of their copyright to the SAS system.

The CJEU held that a program's features, formats of data files and programming languages cannot be categorised as computer programs,[115] justifying it on the ground that, as Advocate General Yves Bot opined, it would otherwise 'make it possible to monopolise ideas, to the detriment of technological progress and industrial development',[116] and that protecting only the individual expression of the computer program 'leaves other authors the desired latitude to create similar or even identical programs provided that they refrain from copying'.[117]

[3] Interface

In *BSA* the CJEU considered whether the graphic user interface (GUI) of a program is part of the protection of computer programs under the Computer Programs Directive. The Court held that a GUI should be seen as an object that allows communication between the program and the user, and not as an expression of the computer program, and that use of the user interface is not a reproduction of the program itself but instead a tool for using the program's features; for which reasons it was not covered by the

114. *See* further below on user interfaces.
115. C-406/10 *SAS Institute*, para. 46.
116. C-406/10 *SAS Institute*, para. 40.
117. C-406/10 *SAS Institute*, para. 41.

Computer Programs Directive.[118] The Court pointed out however that the GUI may enjoy protection under the InfoSoc Directive.[119]

Regarding application programming interfaces (APIs), these might be protected under the Computer Programs Directive. The CJEU's judgement in the subsequent *SAS Institute* case seems to indicate the contrary,[120] despite that protection of computer programs under the Computer Programs Directive explicitly includes preparatory design material.[121]

[4] Video Games as Multimedia Works

In *Nintendo* the CJEU held in relation to video games that the InfoSoc Directive - and not the Computer Programs Directive - should in some cases be applied to the work as a whole, at least regarding the rules governing technological protection measures.[122]

The case concerned legal protection of Nintendo's two-part protection measures, where one element was part of the game console, while the other part of the discs on which the video games were stored. This meant that games that did not have a recognition code could not be used on any of the Nintendo game consoles. PC Box had marketed Nintendo consoles in which the protection measure was deactivated. The main question in the case was whether the provisions of the InfoSoc Directive governing technological protection measures should apply or instead the Computer Programs Directive.

The CJEU stated that video games constitute complex multimedia products that include computer programs, images and sounds.[123] Although images and sounds have been encoded in programming languages, they have their own independent copyright protection. However, these parts cannot be separated in order to play the video game and the Court stated that when parts of a video game 'are part of its originality, they are protected, together with the entire work' and, under these circumstances, under the InfoSoc Directive.[124] This implies that when a product consists of a computer program and other copyright-protected subject matter that together form the actual product, the provisions of the general InfoSoc Directive will apply and not the specific provisions of the Computer Programs Directive. The judgement of the Court overcomes the lack of uniform regulation of copyright-protected works by applying an overreaching principle, allowing one copyright directive to apply instead of two. By this the CJEU has likely sought to resolve a difficult situation that would ensue for third parties, and since the rights to the computer program, and the remaining works, will likely belong to the same rightholder, the interests of rightholders are not impaired by applying this

118. C-393/09 *BSA*, paras 40–42.
119. C-393/09 *BSA*, paras 45–46.
120. C-406/10 *SAS Institute*, para. 39. *See also* COM(88) 816 final - SYN 183 p. 12.
121. On this term *see* further below.
122. Case C-355/12 *Nintendo and Others* v *PC Box and 9Net* ECLI:EU:C:2014:25. *See also* Case C-458/13 *Grund (SR-Tronic and Others)* v *Nintendo and Nintendo of America* ECLI: EU:C:2014:589 (Nintendo II).
123. C-355/12 *Nintendo*, para. 23.
124. C-355/12 *Nintendo*, para. 23.

overreaching principle. Regrettably, the Court did not explain the relationship between the InfoSoc Directive and the Computer Programs Directive, which, however, Advocate General Eleanor Sharpston did in her opinion.

The Advocate General opined on the basis of the Court's judgement in *UsedSoft* that the InfoSoc Directive does not affect the legal protection of computer programs under the Computer Programs Directive, because the Computer Programs Directive constitutes *lex specialis* in relation to the InfoSoc Directive.[125] However, according to the Advocate General, the Computer Programs Directive takes precedence over the InfoSoc Directive only 'when the protection object is entirely covered by the Computer Programs Directive', that is to say, only if the subject matter of the dispute would be a computer program that does not contain any other copyright-protected works. Because computer games are complex products that in addition to the program code include sounds, pictures, movies and animations, etc. which cannot be separated, the Advocate General also believed that the InfoSoc Directive should apply in this case. Such an outcome would also take into consideration the stronger protection that the InfoSoc Directive provides for copyrighted-protected works compared to the Computer Programs Directive. The Advocate General pointed out that if EU law is interpreted differently, rightholders would not be given protection for the other subject matter, to which they are entitled under the InfoSoc Directive.[126] The Advocate General also opined that both directives may apply in a particular situation if the game company has separate technological measures for the protection of the computer programs and of the other subject matter.[127] In such a situation, the Computer Programs Directive would apply to the computer program, whereas the InfoSoc Directive would apply to the other works.

[5] Preparatory Design Material

The preparatory design material of a computer program, i.e., the material from the earlier stages of development of a program, is considered to fall within computer program protection since it falls within the definition of a computer program.[128] Protection ensured by the Computer Programs Directive is more extensive in this respect than the protection of computer programs under Article 10(1) TRIPS and Article 4 WCT as these instruments do not include such material.

The preparatory design material should, however, be regarded as an 'independent' program, rather than being part of the developed computer program because of the material differences that may be present. While referring to the preparatory material as a program is somewhat exaggerated, it is primarily a question of ensuring that preparatory design material falls within the same protection framework.

125. *See* C-355/12 *Nintendo*, Opinion of AG Eleanor Sharpston, para. 34.
126. *See* C-355/12 *Nintendo*, Opinion of AG Eleanor Sharpston, para. 35.
127. *See* C-355/12 *Nintendo*, Opinion of AG Eleanor Sharpston, para. 34.
128. Computer Programs Directive, Art. 1(1).

There is no legal definition of the concept, however common understanding is that preparatory design materials comprise material from the earlier stages of development of a program. Material that is produced when the program is ready should therefore not be classified as preparatory design material.[129] It is also apparent from recital 7 Computer Programs Directive that a computer program ought to result from such material *at a later stage*.

Already in 1988 the EC stated that the term should refer to *necessary* preparatory design materials, such as flow charts and descriptions of the program that can lead to the creation of a computer program.[130] Similarly, the CJEU has held that the term *computer program* should include such preparatory design material that is capable of leading 'to the reproduction or the subsequent creation of such a program'.[131] Hence it is material that is linked to the actual design of the program's tasks, i.e., associated with the program's logic (structure). For example, it can be technical documentation or design documents with descriptions of programs, program ideas and how they can be implemented in terms of design and functions, which can be used to create a program. However, in order to be categorised as preparatory design material, it should have reached such a stage of development that a program can be created without difficulty. As Advocate General Yves Bot stated in his opinion in *BSA*, the material should be capable of being 'rewritten to source code or object code' in order for it to be categorically classified as a computer program,[132] which usually embodies detailed flowcharts, drawings, program specifications, algorithms, formulas, etc. This means, in effect, that the rightholder should have reached a point when the sequence, structure and organisation of the program are complete, but the individual series of instructions have not yet been coded. Such kind of subject matter is usually perceived as literary works, as they are descriptive, which makes it consistent with the premise that computer programs constitute literary works. However, a literary work of a descriptive nature can also enjoy independent protection as an artistic work and, in this capacity, should not be covered by the Computer Programs Directive, but by its own independent protection, under the InfoSoc Directive. For such subject matter there appears to be overlapping copyright protection.

Consequently, the term *preparatory design material* does not include other, more instructive materials, such as manuals (support material), which can be used by the user to understand the program. Support material, on the other hand, may similarly enjoy independent copyright protection. However, if essential elements of a computer program (the code) are reproduced in the material, these parts are covered by computer program protection.[133] Since the distance between preparatory design materials and user manuals and other support materials may be small and sometimes overlap, difficult differentiation problems may arise when assessing whether all or part of a material should be included in the term preparatory design material or categorised

129. *See* Case T-201/04 R *Microsoft* v *Commission* ECLI:EU:T:2004:372, para. 172.
130. *See* COM(88) 816 final – SYN 183 p. 17.
131. C-393/09 *BSA*, para. 37 and C-406/10 *SAS Institute*, para. 37.
132. C-393/09 *BSA*, Opinion of AG Yves Bot, para. 63.
133. *See* COM(88) 816 final – SYN 183 p. 17.

as a different type of work. This can be of practical importance because preparatory design materials enjoy (preferential) copyright protection as computer programs.

Nevertheless, most of these uncertainties will hopefully soon be clarified, as the CJEU has recently been asked about the meaning of the term. In particular, in *Dacom*[134] the Swedish Patent and Market Court of Appeal has asked the following three questions in relation to the term:

> 1.1 What criteria are to determine whether material constitutes such preparatory design material as is referred to in Article 1(1) of [Computer Programs Directive]? Can documents which set out the requirements as to the functions which are to be performed by a computer program and the result which the computer program must achieve, for example, detailed descriptions of investment principles or risk models for asset management including mathematical formulae to be applied in the computer program, constitute such preparatory design material?
>
> 1.2 Must material, in order to constitute preparatory design material within the meaning of the directive, be so complete and detailed that in practice it requires no independent choices on the part of the person who actually writes the code of a computer program?
>
> 1.3 Does the exclusive right to preparatory design material within the meaning of the directive mean that the computer program in which the preparatory design material subsequently results is to be regarded as an adaptation of the preparatory design material and therefore a dependent work for the purpose of copyright (Article 4(1)(b) of [Computer Programs Directive]), or that the preparatory design material and software are to be regarded as different forms of expression of the same work, or that they are two independent works?

[C] Databases

The Database Directive instructs the Member States to grant protection to databases. Article 1 of the Directive defines a database as 'a collection of independent works, data or other materials arranged in a systematic or methodical way and individually accessible by electronic or other means'. As it follows from this definition, protection must be granted not only to electronic databases but also to paper-based analogue databases such as, for example, a traditional encyclopaedia.

Databases that are *original* are however to be seen as *copyright-protected works*. The originality requirement is defined in Article 3(1) Database Directive, which states that:

> databases which, by reason of the selection or arrangement of their contents, constitute the author's own intellectual creation shall be protected as such by copyright. No other criteria shall be applied to determine their eligibility for that protection.

134. C-313/18 *Dacom* v *IPM*.

The required originality can both lie in the way the contents of the database are selected, and in the way they are being put together. To put it in another way, a database can be original because of the selection as well as the arrangement.

To compile all data on a specific topic will not qualify as an original selection. Nor is it an original arrangement to arrange something numerically, chronologically or alphabetically. However, a database will fulfil the originality requirement as long as there is either originality in the selection or in the arrangement. Therefore, there will be copyright in a compilation which reflects original selection, even if the arrangement is not original, and vice versa.

If the elements compiled in a database are in themselves original, they will in themselves be protected by copyright. This can be relevant in connection to, for example, a collection of short stories or an encyclopaedia. The originality of such elements, however, is of no significance as to whether the database is protected by copyright as such. If, for example, one makes a work by creating a number of elements which are being put together in a creative way, the originality which went into the creation of the elements does not make the database as such original.[135] However, the inclusion of original works in a database will affect the exploitability of the database as the reproduction, communication or distribution of those elements is subject to copyright exclusivity resting with the respective authors.

Since numerical, chronological or alphabetical arrangement or the compilation of all data on a topic does not qualify as original, many databases are left without copyright protection. However, databases may also be protected by sui generis protection under Article 7 Database Directive, which instead of originality requires *substantial investment* in either 'the obtaining, verification or presentation of the contents ...'. The sui generis protection is, however, weaker both in terms of scope and duration,[136] but it may apply concurrently with copyright protection.[137]

[D] Photographs

According to recital 16 and Article 6 Term Directive Member States must grant copyright protection to photographs which are original 'in the sense that they are the author's own intellectual creation'.

Photographs are pictures created through a process where light sensitive materials are being subjected to light. The protection not only includes photographs taken by means of traditional film but also digital photographs, x-rays, infrared pictures, holograms, etc. Most likely, protection also comprises still pictures stored magnetically on video tape. Pictures created with the aid of off-set techniques, however, probably cannot be considered photographs. The same probably goes for photocopies and pictures created digitally by means of drawing software. The latter may, however, enjoy protection as an artistic work, similarly to paintings.

135. *See* Case C-604/10 *Football Dataco and Others* v *Yahoo! UK and Others*.
136. *See* Database Directive, Arts. 7(1)-(2) and 10.
137. Database Directive, Art. 7(4).

[E] Related Rights

The above-mentioned subject matter is protected by copyright if it satisfies the originality requirement. However, there exist a number of subject matter that cannot – or cannot always – be qualified as original works, but which need protection nevertheless.

A number of international conventions make it obligatory for the Contracting Parties to grant related rights protection in their copyright legislation. The most important conventions are the Rome Convention, WPPT, TRIPS Agreement, Beijing Treaty on Audiovisual Performances, and the Phonogram Convention.

Related rights subject matter is harmonised by EU law in a similar vein as copyright subject matter – Member States must grant related rights protection to the following:

- performances of performing artists.[138] Performing artists are, for example, singers, musicians, and actors. Their performances are typically not works – if a singer performs a musical work the copyright in the song remains with the composer of the music and the author of the text. The performing artist is however entitled to protection of the performance;
- sound recordings as such.[139] Protection is granted regardless of the content of the recording, i.e., irrespective of whether the content is, in itself, protected by copyright. Therefore, record companies have an exclusive related right in their records. The distinction could be made that whereas copyright protects the *content*, related rights protect the *signal;*
- fixations of films.[140] The film itself can enjoy copyright protection.[141] The InfoSoc Directive states that protection is given to 'the producers of the first fixations of films, in respect of the original and copies of their films'.[142] Copying (recording) a film shown in the cinema or broadcast on television does not afford the copier new and independent related rights protection of that copy;
- fixations of radio and television broadcasts.[143] Often the contents of the broadcasts will also be protected by copyright.

---

138. *See* Rental and Lending Directive, Art. 3(1)(b), InfoSoc Directive, Arts 8, 2(b) and 3(2)(a), and Term Directive, Art. 3(1).
139. *See* Rental and Lending Directive, Art. 3, InfoSoc Directive, Arts 8, 2(c) and 3(2)(b), and Term Directive, Art. 3(2).
140. *See* Rental and Lending Directive, Art. 3(d), InfoSoc Directive, Arts 2(d) and 3(2)(c), and Term Directive, Art. 3(3).
141. One notable exception among the Member States is the UK. *See* s .1(1) Copyright, Designs and Patents Act 1988, listing 'film' as a separate category together which sound recordings and broadcast and not requiring originality, together with together with s. 5B(1) defining a film as a 'recording on any medium from which a moving image may by any means be produced'.
142. *See*, for example, InfoSoc Directive, Art. 2(d).
143. *See* Rental and Lending Directive, Art. 7(2), InfoSoc Directive, Arts 2(e) and 3(2)(d), and Term Directive, Art. 3(4).

§3.03 QUALIFICATION OF PROTECTION

It follows from EU law that Member States are obliged to grant copyright protection to computer programs, databases and photographs, and related rights protection to the performances of performing artists, sound recordings, fixations of radio and television broadcasts. The question remains, however, what criteria must be met for protection to be granted.

[A] Copyright Protection of Works

As mentioned above, copyright protection of works is independent of formalities. Hence, protection is granted as soon as the work is created, and there can be no requirements of, say, registration, deposition or use of the © symbol. The use of the latter used to be a requirement in US copyright law but this has changed after the US signed the Berne Convention which states in Article 5(2) that the enjoyment and the exercise of copyright shall not be subject to any formality.

A basic copyright principle, that has materialised in, for example, Article 2 WCT and Article 9(2) TRIPS, is that 'Copyright protection extends to expressions and not to ideas, procedures, methods of operation or mathematical concepts as such.' This refers to the *idea-expression dichotomy* and means that abstract parts of a work, the idea underlying the work, fall outside copyright protection. Copyright does not protect the idea as such, but the way in which that idea has been *expressed*. Consequently, there is no copyright in, for example, the morale of a novel, the atmosphere of a song, the idea to build a house out of certain material etc.

The dividing line between the idea and expression of the idea is not however always easy to draw. For example, could the inclusion of one minute of silence as a separate track in a music album infringe any rights in a composition consisting of four minutes and thirty-three seconds of silence?[144] This question presumes the existence of copyright protection, but even this may be difficult to establish. Can it be a musical work, and if not that, could it be a literary or dramatic work? It is only after establishing that protection exists that infringement may potentially occur.

For copyright protection to be granted, the created works must be *original*. The requirement is somewhat misleading in the sense that the threshold for protection is not that the creation must never have been created before, but that it reflects some level of creativity. The originality requirement stems back to the nineteenth century and applied in the Member States long before the EU was established. The originality requirement also applies under EU law. With regards to computer programs, databases, and photographs the originality requirement is referred to in recital 8 and Article 1(3) Computer Programs Directive, Articles 3(1) and 6 Database Directive, and recital 16 Term Directive. Here it is set out that protection is granted if the work in question is

144. *See/listen* to The Planets, 'A One Minute Silence' credited as 'Batt/Cage', on 'Classical Graffiti' (2002), and John Cage's composition '4'33 (1952).

the 'author's own intellectual creation' and that no other criteria shall be applied to determine its eligibility for that protection.

Further, when it comes to types of works other than computer programs, databases and photographs, the CJEU has set out in a number of decisions that the InfoSoc Directive only applies for works which are original in the above-mentioned sense.[145]

According to the CJEU the author's own intellectual creation means that the author was able to make creative choices.[146] In this context, the Court has stated that:

> copyright is liable to apply only in relation to a subject-matter, such as a photograph, which is original in the sense that it is its author's own intellectual creation. [...] As stated in Recital 17 in the preamble to Directive 93/98, an intellectual creation is an author's own if it reflects the author's personality. [...] That is the case if the author was able to express his creative abilities in the production of the work by making free and creative choices.[147]

Some Member States have traditionally interpreted the originality requirement differently with regards to different types of works by applying a lower threshold of originality in relation to some works and a higher threshold of originality in relation to other works. For example, in some countries, including Germany and the Nordic countries, it has been the general norm only to protect works of applied art if the works reflect a high and obvious degree of originality. The question is whether this is consistent with EU law. Works of applied art are not only protected by copyright but can also be protected by design law. European design law is harmonised through the Design Directive which provides in Article 17 that:

> A design protected by a design right registered in or in respect of a Member State in accordance with this Directive shall also be eligible for protection under the law of copyright of that State as from the date on which the design was created or fixed in any form. The extent to which, and the conditions under which, such a protection is conferred, including the level of originality required, shall be determined by each Member State.

The question is whether this means that the originality requirement falls outside of EU harmonisation when it comes to works of applied art. If this is the case the Member States are free to apply such a threshold of originality as they see fit in connection to such works. The CJEU is however expected to finally answer this question in the upcoming *Cofemel* case.[148]

145. *See* Case C-5/08 *Infopaq International* v *Danske Dagblades Forening* ECLI:EU:C:2009:465 (*Infopaq I*), paras 36–37; *see also* paras 33 et seq.; C-393/09 *BSA*, paras 44 et seq.; Joined Cases C-403/08 and C-429/08 *FAPL and Others* v *QC Leisure and Others* ECLI:EU:C:2011:631, paras 96 et seq.; Case C-145/10 *Painer* v *Standard Verlags and Others* ECLI:EU:C:2011:798, paras 87 et seq.; C-406/10 *SAS Institute*, paras 45 and 65; and C-335/12 *Nintendo*, para. 21. *See* further C-604/10 *Football Dataco*, decided according to the Database Directive, paras 37 et seq.
146. *See* C-145/10 *Painer*, paras 87 et seq.
147. *See* further C-5/08 *Infopaq I*, para. 40.
148. Case C-683/17 *Cofemel* v *G-Star Raw*.

[B] Related Rights

The Member States are obliged to grant related rights protection to performing artists, sound recordings, fixation of films and broadcasts. The protection is independent of formalities, i.e., there are no requirements of deposition, registration or the like. However, no originality requirement applies in connection to related rights protection of the above-mentioned subject matter, which in practice means that protection is afforded immediately upon performance or fixation.

§3.04 AUTHORSHIP AND OWNERSHIP

Copyright protection is granted to the author of the work. This raises some questions in the context of employment relationships, especially since employees receive a salary for the performance of their duties. The initial position is that rights are attributed to the actual creator of the work, who in an employment relationship will be the employee. What therefore becomes crucial for determining ownership of rights (alternatively the possibility of exploitation and commercialisation) and the scope of such ownership is the existence of rights transfer clauses in the collective agreement and/or the individual employment contract regulating the employment relationship.

Remarkably this is an area that remains outside the EU copyright framework, with one notable exception.

The EU copyright framework deals only with copyright in computer programs created in an employment context, specifically in Article 2 Computer Programs Directive.[149] The Article deals with authorship of programs, collective works and employees' programs.

Article 2(1) Computer Programs Directive sets out that the author of a computer program is the natural person or group of natural persons who have created the program or, where the legislation of the Member States permits, the legal person designated as the rightholder. Where collective works are recognised by national legislation the person considered by the laws of such Member State to have created the work will be deemed its author.

From Article 2(2) Computer Programs Directive it follows that where a computer program is created by a group of natural persons working together, the exclusive rights will be owned *jointly*. Member States not allowing corporations to be authors nor recognising the concept of collective works does not have to amend their laws to implement this. Article 2(3) of the Directive contains a mandatory requirement on employees' programs. Under the provision the employer shall exclusively be entitled to exercise *all* economic rights in an employee's computer program, where the program is created in the execution of the employee's duties or where the employee is following instructions given by the employer.[150] Hence, there occurs an automatic legal transfer

149. The only other provisions expressly dealing with IP created in an employment context is Art. 14(3) Community Design Regulation, and Art. 3(2)(a) Semiconductor Products Directive.

150. *See* Art. 3(2)(a) Semiconductor Products Directive (which is a non-mandatory provision regarding employees' chips).

of the copyright in computer programs. However, if the parties agree, the employee-author can recover the rights through a specific clause in the employment contract or a separate agreement on the exploitation of that computer program. Hence the default position for the attribution of rights in computer programs is instead reversed.

Article 2(3) Computer Programs Directive was inspired by the employer provision in the Semiconductor Products Directive[151] and the original proposal for the provision also mirrored the wording.[152] The European Economic and Social Committee proposed, however, that the chosen formulation should be amended so as to only apply to such computer programs created by employees whose duty is to develop programs. The European Parliament argued, on the other hand, that the employer should be entitled to more than that, and it was this proposal that eventually formed the basis of the formulation of Article 2(3) Computer Programs Directive. One reason to widen the scope of the provision could have been that computer programs are created by various types of employees and it would have been inappropriate if the presumption only applied to some employees. The employer has, therefore, in comparison to the original proposal, received a broad right to their employees' computer programs which has come to be expressed in the laws of the Member States.[153]

A similar provision to Article 2(3) Computer Programs Directive was included in the first draft of the Database Directive. However, it was deleted from the final version of the Directive and recital 29 only states that nothing prevents Member States from stipulating in national laws that where a database is created by an employee in the execution of the duties or following the instructions given by the employer, the employer shall exclusively be entitled to exercise the rights in the database so created.

One difficulty in harmonising the legal framework is attributable to the differences between the various national models within the Member States. During the early 2000s the EC, however, announced as regards ownership of employees' copyright that:

> At this point, it would seem advisable to analyse the issue further and, in particular, identify specific situations where harmonisation would yield added value and address Internal Market needs.[154]

The challenge is that it may at present not be possible to overcome national differences in legislation as they are, after all, based on different legal traditions. The interest to realise the internal market may, however, become relevant for harmonisation efforts even in this area in order to facilitate cross-border trade. This makes legislative action on an EU level a real possibility.

In any event, the more general question of ownership of works created in employment is, with the exception of computer programs, left to the different national solutions. In some countries, such as in the Netherlands and the UK, national copyright acts regulate employees' copyright. In other countries, such as Germany, France and the Nordic countries, a transfer from the employee to the employer follows from

151. *See* COM(88) 172 final p. 196.
152. *See* COM(88) 816 final - SYN 183 p. 34.
153. *See* further COM(2000) 199 final.
154. SEC(2004) 995, 19 July 2004, p. 14.

general principles of law. Nevertheless, all Member States have included in their national copyright laws provisions implementing the mandatory requirement on employees' computer programs contained in Article 2(3) Computer Programs Directive.[155]

§3.05 TERM OF PROTECTION

The international framework created by the Berne Convention sets a minimum protection period of fifty years after the death of the author. However, the Convention provides for shorter minimum periods for certain types of works, including for cinematographic works, photographic works and works of art.

In the EU the term of protection is harmonised. The applicable term depends on whether the subject matter is protected by copyright or by related rights, and if the latter – what specific type it constitutes.

Literary and artistic works are protected for the duration of the author's life and for seventy years after their death, irrespective of the date when the work was published in the sense of lawfully having been made available to the public.[156] This is set out in Article 1(1) Term Directive. The same applies to the so-called artist's resale right.[157] For a work of joint authorship, the term shall be calculated from the death of the last surviving author. However, for anonymous or pseudonymous works the term of protection runs instead for seventy years after the work is lawfully made available to the public.[158] While the duration of protection of cinematographic works specifically is the same as for the remaining types of works, the Directive recognises, arguably, the collective effort required to create such a work and provides that the term of protection expires seventy years after the death of the last of the following persons to survive: the principal director, author of the screenplay, author of the dialogue, or composer of the music specifically created for the use in the work, regardless of whether any of these persons are regarded as co-authors under national rules.[159]

To streamline the calculation process Article 8 Term Directive provides that the calculation of terms provided for in the directive shall occur from the first day of January of the year following the relevant event (publication, death etc.). The same applies to subject matter protected by related rights.

In so far as the duration of related rights is concerned, the following terms apply. Rights of *performers* to their performances expire fifty years after the date of the

155. *See* further, COM(2000) 199 final.
156. The need to harmonise the term of protection was highlighted already in Case C-341/87 *EMI Electrola* v *Patricia Im-und Export and Others* ECLI:EU:C:1989:30 and in practice, there was only one reasonable solution – to harmonise the term upwards to seventy years for copyright-protected works because Germany as well as France, in case of musical works, had already had such protection for some time.
157. Resale Right Directive, Art. 8(1), together with Term Directive, Art. 1.
158. Term Directive, Art. 1(2)-(3).
159. Term Directive, Art. 2(2). The Directive only designates the principal director as the author of a cinematographic work, in Art. 2(1), but leaves it to the Member States to also designate co-authors. This gives room to question whether in fact the collective effort is recognised as only one person is designated author, and therefore rightholder.

performance, unless the performance has been recorded (fixed) (but is not a sound recording) and lawfully published or 'communicated to the public' during this period, in which case the rights will instead expire fifty years after the first publication or communication to the public, whichever is earlier.[160] Where the fixation of the performance is instead a sound recording, a recorded musical performance, the rights will expire seventy years after the date of first publication or communication of the recording to the public, whichever is earlier.[161]

Rights of *producers* of sound recordings expire fifty years after the fixation (recording) is made, unless, similarly as above, the recording has been lawfully published within this period, in which case the rights expire seventy years after the first lawful publication or communication to the public.[162]

The practical effect is that performers, alternatively rightholders, are entitled to remuneration for the exploitation of their rights each time the relevant subject matter is played on the air and in public places such as bars and clubs under a period of seventy years. Simultaneously, record producers will receive revenue from the sale of records in shops and on the Internet or through streaming services.

Rights of producers of first fixation of films expire fifty years after fixation, alternatively fifty years after publication, while rights of broadcasting organisations expire fifty years after the first transmission of the broadcast.[163]

160. Term Directive, Art. 3(1).
161. Term Directive, Art. 3(2) as amended by Art. 1(2) Directive 2011/77/EU. The term of protection for performers and sound recordings was extended in 2011 to align related rights protection with copyright protection.
162. Term Directive, Art. 3(2) as amended by Directive 2011/77/EU.
163. Term Directive, Art. 3(4)-(5).

CHAPTER 4

Exclusive Economic and Moral Rights

§4.01 INTRODUCTION

Copyright law grants authors exclusive economic and moral rights.

Economic rights concern the author's right to decide over the making available of the work and its reproduction (copying). The economic rights enable the author to secure revenue from the exploitation of the work. The author has full freedom with respect to the economic rights and can transfer all or parts of their rights for a limited or an unlimited period of time.

Moral rights aim at protecting the author's personality which is expressed through the work. Moral rights entail, first of all, the right of the author to be named as the author of the work (paternity right). There are no uniform rules for providing the name of the author. This will depend on the type of work in question and how the name is usually provided for such a work. Second, the author may object to the distortion or derogatory treatment of the work (integrity right). Normal cropping or alteration in the production process is however permitted. In most Member States moral rights cannot be assigned, but can only be waived to a limited extent, if at all.

In EU law, the economic rights can be found in the InfoSoc Directive, the Computer Programs Directive, the Rental and Lending Rights Directive and the SatCab Directive. Moral rights are not regulated by EU law and are instead to be found in international instruments, such as the Berne Convention,[164] and in the national laws of the Member States.

164. *See* Berne Convention, Arts 6*bis*.

§4.02 ECONOMIC RIGHTS

[A] Literary and Artistic Works

What it means to have copyright protection is set out in several directives. When it comes to literary and artistic works, apart from computer programs and databases, the relevant provisions are set out in the InfoSoc Directive, the Rental and Lending Rights Directive and the Satellite and Cable Directive. The directives instruct the Member States to grant authors the following exclusive rights:

- Reproduction (copying).
- Distribution of the original or copies thereof, including rental and lending.
- Communication to the public.

[1] The Reproduction Right

By virtue of Article 2 InfoSoc Directive:

> Member States shall provide for the exclusive right to authorise or prohibit direct or indirect, temporary or permanent reproduction by any means and in any form, in whole or in part:
>
> (a) for authors, of their works;
>
> ...

To reproduce a work means to make copies of it. Copies are, *inter alia*, books, sheets of music, posters, and electronic files containing protected works stored on storage media such as CDs, DVDs, USB storage devices, hard disks etc. The fact that the author is granted an exclusive reproduction right means that as a starting point permission from the author is required to make such copies. The wording of the provision is intentionally so broad to cover everything from printing a book or a poster, to transferring the protected work to a storage device etc.

Pictures of protected works, such as a photograph of a protected painting or a drawing of a protected sculpture, are considered copies of the works which they depict. Therefore, as a starting point, if one wishes to use a picture of, say, a sculpture on a post card permission from the sculptor will have to be obtained (or from whomever they might have transferred this right to).

As mentioned above it is also considered copying to save a protected work to a digital storage device. Moreover, when computers render protected works they save the work or parts of it in the computer memory, the RAM, or store it in the 'cache' for faster loading. If, for example, one listens to a song through Spotify on the smartphone the latter constantly saves small parts of the music in the RAM memory for faster rendering. In the same way, if one watches a film on the Internet the computer will continuously transfer data to the RAM memory for viewing. This is considered reproduction in a copyright sense. However, such reproduction will be considered temporary reproductions, which constitute an excepted use under Article 5(1) InfoSoc

Directive. A device may also store data in the 'cache' for more efficient rendering of content that has already been rendered; for example, when visiting a webpage the web browser will not download the entire webpage every time but will store some data in the cache for faster viewing. Data stored in the cache is not necessarily temporary in the same sense as data transferred to RAM.

It would seem intuitive to hold that the display of a protected work on a screen like a computer monitor is a communication to the public as opposed to a reproduction since this follows by implication from the CJEU case concerning the use of televisions at hotels and restaurants and the like.[165] Nevertheless, the CJEU held in *PRCA* that the viewing of websites on a computer constitutes a temporary reproduction in the sense of Article 5(1) InfoSoc Directive.[166]

[2] Distribution, Rental and Lending

Member States must also grant authors the exclusive rights to distribute copies of their works to the public. In general, distribution of works involves the *dissemination of protected works to others*. For example, it is distribution to sell a copy or to give it away.

In a number of Member States, such as the Scandinavian countries, distribution constitutes an umbrella term incorporating different forms of dissemination of works, such as *sale*, but also *rental* and *lending*. In the EU copyright framework rental and lending is however governed separately by Article 2 Rental and Lending Rights Directive, which does not apply to buildings or works of applied art.[167]

The general distribution right follows in Article 4 InfoSoc Directive, according to which:

> Member States shall provide for authors, in respect of the original of their works or of copies thereof, the exclusive right to authorise or prohibit any form of distribution to the public by sale or otherwise.

The distribution right only concerns distribution to the *public*. Thus, distribution in the private sphere is not covered by the distribution right.

Regarding *lending* the rule follows from the definition of lending in Article 2(1)(b) Rental and Lending Rights Directive which states that lending 'means making available for use, for a limited period of time and not for direct or indirect economic or commercial advantage, when it is made through establishments which are accessible to the public'. On the other hand no such reservation is built into the definition of *rental* in Article 2(1)(a) which defines rental as 'making available for use, for a limited period of time and for direct or indirect economic or commercial advantage'. It is arguable however whether making available of a work for a limited time within the private sphere should be considered a rental. While it is certainly ambiguous, the definition requires that the making available for a limited time is done for the purpose of receiving

165. Case C-306/05 *SGAE* v *Rafael Hoteles* ECLI:EU:C:2006:764. Cf. C-393/09 *BSA*.
166. *See* Case C-360/13 *Public Relations Consultants Association* v *Newspaper Licensing Agency and Others* ECLI:EU:C:2014:1195, paras 14, 20, 36 et seq, 55 and 60 et seq.
167. *See* Rental and Lending Rights Directive, Art. 3(2).

(direct or indirect) economic or commercial *advantage*. This implies a commercial (or economic) nature of the activity on a market. The original proposal referred to 'for profit-making purposes'[168] but was subsequently changed to 'economic or commercial advantage' with a view of providing a more precise definition.[169] The degree to which this may have been achieved is, however, questionable.

With regards to the types of acts that fall within the exclusive right of *distribution* under Article 4(1) InfoSoc Directive, the CJEU held in *Peek & Cloppenburg* that distribution *by sale or otherwise* means that there must be a transfer of ownership in the copy.[170] This raised doubts as to the conformity with EU law of national legislation of Member States, such as Germany and the Nordic countries, that defined distribution in such a way that the mere offering for sale of a copy was to be considered distribution to the public. The CJEU has however confirmed that this conforms with EU law. The Court has held that the concept of distribution to the public in Article 4 InfoSoc Directive must be interpreted in accordance with Article 6 WCT and that distribution to the public occurs not only where a contract of sale and dispatch has been concluded but also when a legally binding offer of a contract of sale is directed towards 'a member of the public' or if there is advertising directed towards 'members of the public'.[171]

[3] Communication to the Public

Member States must also grant authors the exclusive right to communicate works to the public.

The concept of communication to the public is well-established in international and EU copyright law. Apart from being provided under Article 3 InfoSoc Directive, Article 8 Rental and Lending Rights Directive, Articles 1 et seq. SatCab Directive, Article 5 Database Directive, it is also provided in a number of provisions in the Berne Convention, Article 14(1) and (3) TRIPS Agreement, Article 8 WCT, Article 6(i) and Article 15 WPPT as well as Article 7(1)(a) Rome Convention.

Communication to the public essentially means to transfer a work to an audience which is located elsewhere than the place from which the communication is originating. Among other things it is considered a communication to the public to broadcast protected works through radio or television. Further, it is considered a communication to the public to upload works to the Internet or similar public networks so that the audience can choose when to access the works. This sort of communication is called 'making available on demand' and the relevant exclusive right is sometimes referred to

---

168. Commission, 'Proposal for a Council Directive on rental rights, lending right and on certain rights related to copyright' COM(90) 586 final – SYN 319 OJ C 53/35.
169. Commission, 'Amended Proposal for a Council Directive on rental right and lending right and on certain rights related to copyright in the field of intellectual property' COM(92) 159 final – SYN OJ C 128/8, p. 8.
170. Case C-456/06 *Peek & Cloppenburg* v *Cassina* ECLI:EU:C:2008:232, para. 33. *See also* paras 30–32.
171. *See* Case C-516/13 *Dimensione Direct Sales and Labianca* v *Knoll International* ECLI:EU:C:2015:315, paras 23 et seq., Case C-5/11 *Donner* ECLI:EU:C:2012:370, paras 23 et seq., and Case C-98/13 *Blomqvist* v *Rolex and Manufacture des Montres Rolex* ECLI:EU:C:2014:55, para. 28.

as the 'making available right'. It is also considered a communication to the public to participate in file sharing in peer-to-peer networks. In this connection it is not only the file sharers who are considered to communicate protected subject matter to the public but also the operators of websites which facilitate such file sharing by indexing information about where the relevant files may be obtained. Up-to-date examples of such websites are *Popcorn Time* and *The Pirate Bay*.[172] Moreover, even the sale of multimedia players which contain pre-installed links to websites on which copyright-protected works have been made available to the public without the consent of the right holders constitutes communication to the public.[173]

In national copyright legislation it is common to grant authors the right to perform their works for an audience which is located in the same place, such as performances in front of an audience in theatres, concert halls etc. The right to such performances – referred to in some Member States as 'direct performances' – is not harmonised by EU law.[174]

It is a basic premise in copyright law that persons who transmit to the public communications initiated by others thereby undertake an exploitation which in itself requires permission from the author. For example, it follows from the SatCab Directive that the notion *communication to the public* includes cross-border transmission of broadcasts which others have initiated.[175] In the same way it is common for restaurants which play radio or television for the customers to obtain permission from rightholder organisations such as PRS, SACEM, STIM, etc. One would think that the exploitation which takes place in such restaurants must be considered 'direct performance' rather than 'communication to the public', since the audience seems to be located in the same place as the one in which the exploitation takes place, i.e., the restaurant. However, the CJEU has made it clear that such exploitation constitutes communication to the public.[176] The Court bases its assessment on the fact that the audience is located in a place other than the one from which the first communication is originating.[177] In light of this it must be considered a communication to the public, rather than direct performance, to transmit works from the Internet to an audience such as where a

172. On file sharing *see C-610/15 Stichting Brein II.*
173. *See* Case C-527/15 *Stichting Brein* v *Wullems* ECLI:EU:C:2017:300.
174. *See* Case C-283/10 *Circul Globus Bucureşti* v *UCMR – ADA* ECLI:EU:C:2011:772 and C-403/08 *FAPL*, paras 201 et seq.
175. *See*, e.g., Joined Cases C-431/09 and C-432/09 *Airfield and Canal Digitaal* v *SABAM* and *Airfield* v *Agicoa Belgium* ECLI:EU:C:2011:648.
176. *See* Case C-306/05 *SGAE* v *Rafael Hoteles* ECLI:EU:C:2006:764 (television in hotel rooms), Case C-136/09 *Organismos Sillogikis Diacheirisis Dimiourgon Theatrikon kai Optikoakoustikon Ergon* v *Divani Akropolis Anonimi Xenodocheiaki kai Touristiki Etaireai* ECLI:EU:C:2010:151 (OSDD) (TV in hotel rooms), Case C-162/10 *Phonographic Performance (Ireland)* v *Ireland and Attorney General* ECLI:EU:C:2012:141 (radio, television sets, and cd-players in hotel rooms), C-403/08 and C-429/08 *FAPL* (television in restaurants), Case C-151/15 *Sociedade Portuguesa de Autores* v *Ministério Público and Others* ECLI:EU:C:2015:468 (radio in restaurants), Case C-117/15 *Reha Training* v *GEMA* ECLI:EU:C:2016:379 (television in training rooms and waiting rooms at rehabilitation centres). *See also* Case C-135/10 *SCF* v *Del Corso* ECLI:EU:C:2012:140 on the use of radio in a dental clinic.
177. *See* C-403/08 *FAPL*, paras 200 et seq. Compare Art. 8(3) Rental and Lending Rights Directive and Art. 13(d) Rome Convention.

teacher shows their students a YouTube film or if a shop plays music or films from streaming services such as Spotify or Netflix for its customers.[178]

Communication of works only requires permission from the author if it is directed towards the *public*. The CJEU has dealt with this term in a large number of cases. Some cases concern the interpretation of Article 3 InfoSoc Directive while others concern Article 8(2) Rental and Lending Rights Directive and the SatCab Directive.[179]

These decisions led to the following conclusions:

• *The Communication Must Be Directed to an Indeterminate Number of Potential Recipients, and Whether this Is the Case Is to Be Assessed 'Cumulatively'*

Public means 'an indeterminate number of potential recipients'.[180] This means that the work must be made 'perceptible [...] to "persons in general" rather than to specific individuals belonging to a private group'.[181] The persons in question must constitute 'a fairly large number of persons'.[182] It follows that the concept of *public* encompasses a '"certain *de minimis* threshold", which excludes from the concept groups of persons which are too small, or insignificant'.[183] The crucial factor is whether the work is made available to the public in such a way that persons forming the public may access it,

178. In this regard *see* C-610/15 *Stichting Brein II*, para. 34.
179. For the moment the decisions are the following: Case C-192/04 *Lagardère Active Broadcast* v *SPRE and GVL* ECLI:EU:C:2005:475 (on the notion 'communication to the public by satellite' in Arts 1 et seq. Satellite and Cable Directive), C-306/05 *SGAE*. *See also* C-136/09 *OSDD* (Art. 3(1) InfoSoc Directive), C-403/08 and C-429/08 *FAPL* (Art. 3(1) InfoSoc Directive), C-431/09 and C-432/09 *Airfield* (Arts 1 et seq. Satellite and Cabel Directive), C-135/10 *SCF* (Art. 3(1) InfoSoc Directive and Art. 8(2) Rental and Lending Rights Directive), C-162/10 *Phonographic Performance (Ireland)* (Art. 8(2) Rental and Lending Rights Directive), Case C-607/11 *ITV Broadcasting and Others* v *TVCatchup* ECLI:EU:C:2013:147 (Art. 3(1) InfoSoc Directive), C-466/12 *Svensson and Others* v *Retriever Sverige* (Art. 3(1) InfoSoc Directive), Case C-351/12 *OSA* v *Léčebné lázně Mariánské Lázně* ECLI:EU:C:2014:110 (Art. 3(1) InfoSoc Directive), Case C-348/13 *BestWater International* v *Mebes and Potsch* ECLI:EU:C:2014:2315 (Art. 3(1) InfoSoc Directive), C-151/15 *Sociedade Portuguesa de Autores* (Art. 3(1) InfoSoc Directive), Case C-325/14 *SBS Belgium* v *SABAM* ECLI:EU:C:2015:764 (Art. 3(1) InfoSoc Directive), C-117/15 *Reha Training* (Art. 3(1) InfoSoc Directive and Art. 8(1) Rental and Lending Rights Directive), Case C-160/15 *GS Media* v *Sanoma Media Nethelands and Others* ECLI:EU:C:2016:644 (Art. 3(1) InfoSoc Directive), C-527/15 *Stichting Brein* (Art. 3(1) InfoSoc Directive), C-610/15 *Stichting Brein II* (Art. 3(1) InfoSoc Directive), C-138/16 *AKM* (Art. 3(1) InfoSoc Directive), Case C-265/16 *VCAST*, paras 40 et seq. (Art. 3(1) InfoSoc Directive), and Case C-161/17 *Land Nordrhein-Westfalen* v *Renckhoff* ECLI:EU:C:2018:634 (Art. 3(1) InfoSoc Directive). Some cases which do not concern the concept of communication to the public nevertheless contribute to the interpretation of the said concept, *see* Case C-89/04 *Mediakabel* v *Commissariaat voor de Media* ECLI:EU:C:2005:348, C-314/12 *UPC Telekabel* paras 38 et seq., Case C-117/13 *Technische Universität Darmstadt* v *Ulmer* ECLI:EU:C:2014:2196, para. 41, compare also Case C-202/12 *Innoweb* v *Wegener ICT Media and Wegener Mediaventions* ECLI:EU:C:2013:850, paras 51–52, Case C-641/15 *Verwertungsgesellschaft Rundfunk* v *Hettegger Hotel Edelweiss* ECLI:EU:C:2017:131, paras 17 et seq. and C-301/15 *Soulier and Doke* v *Premier ministre and Ministre de la Culture et de la Communication*.
180. *See*, for example, C-117/15 *Reha Training*, para. 41 and C-160/15 *GS Media*, para. 36.
181. *See*, for example, C-117/15 *Reha Training*, para. 42.
182. *See*, for example, C-117/15 *Reha Training*, para. 41 and C-160/15 (GS Media) para. 36.
183. *See*, for example, C-117/15 *Reha Training*, para. 43.

irrespective of whether they avail themselves of that opportunity.[184] For example, it is considered communication to the public to install television sets in hotel rooms regardless of whether the guests switch them on or not.[185] However, in *SCF* the CJEU held that it was not a communication to the public to play radio in a dental clinic, partly because the communication was not directed towards 'persons in general' and partly because the clinic did not have room for more than a very limited number of patients.[186]

Cross-border satellite broadcasts are only considered communication to the public if the broadcast signal can be received by an indefinite number of recipients. A satellite transmission where an encrypted signal is being sent up and can only be taken down by a specific receiver with the use of professional equipment, therefore, is not a communication to the public.[187]

In some Member States, including Germany and the Nordic countries, it has traditionally been submitted that communications must be assessed in isolation when one is to determine whether such communications are directed towards the public and that several private communications of the same work do not cumulatively constitute a communication to the public. Under EU law, on the other hand, one must instead consider the cumulative effect of a communication when one determines the size of the audience.[188] Accordingly, one must take into consideration not only the number of persons who have access to the work at the same time but also how many persons have access to the work consecutively. A communication is therefore not only public when a protected work is communicated one time to a significant number of persons; it can also be considered public if a protected work is communicated several times to persons who constitute a significant number of persons when put together. In *SGAE*, for example, the Court held that it is a communication to the public to transmit television programs in a hotel to television sets installed in the hotel rooms[189] because, not only must one consider the number of guests who are simultaneously present in a hotel but also take into account that hotel customers quickly succeed each other.[190] Unfortunately, the Court did not shed light on its seeming assumption that the different guests were watching the same programs. Perhaps the Court assumed that some of them were re-run. On the other hand, in *SCF* the Court concluded that it was not a communication to the public as provided for in Article 8(2) Rental and Lending Rights Directive when a dentist had the radio turned on in their dental clinic, since there was only room for a few patients at the same time and the successive patients did not listen to the same sound recordings broadcast on the radio.[191] That different and successive hotel guests

184. *See*, for example, C-466/12 *Svensson*, paras 18 et seq. and C-527/15 *Stichtin Brein*, para. 36 with further references.
185. *See*, for example, C-306/05 *SGAE*, para. 43.
186. *See* C-135/10 *SCF*, paras 95 et seq.
187. *See* C-192/04 *Lagardère Active Broadcast*, paras 29 et seq.
188. *See*, for example, C-306/05 *SGAE*, para. 39, C-351/12 *OSA*, para. 28 and C-527/15 *Stichting Brein*, para. 44.
189. C-306/05 *SGAE*.
190. C-306/05 *SGAE*, para. 38. *See also* C-351/12 *OSA* concerning the use of television sets at spa establishments.
191. C-135/10 *SCF*, paras 95 et seq.

watch the same programs on television while different and successive patients in a dental clinic do not hear the same phonograms on the radio is a circumstance upon which more light should have been cast by the CJEU.

• *The Communication Must Be Deliberate, Although Negligence Is Sufficient*

According to the CJEU a communication is only directed towards the public if the person behind the communication initiates it deliberately.[192] On the other hand, it does not constitute a communication to the public to deliver the technical means for a communication initiated by somebody else. However, a hotel's transmissions of television programs to the hotel rooms must be considered a communication to the public since, among other things:

> The transmission of the broadcast work [...] is not just a technical means to ensure or improve reception of the original broadcast in the catchment area. On the contrary, the hotel is the organisation which intervenes, in full knowledge of the consequences of its action, to give access to the protected work to its customers. In the absence of that intervention, its customers, although physically within that area, would not, in principle, be able to enjoy the broadcast work.[193]

In *SBS Belgium* the criterion was instead a contributory act – if a broadcasting organisation transmits broadcasts to distributors which send them to the subscribers, then it is the latter, and not the broadcasting organisation, that carries out a communication to the public.[194] Things are different, however, if the distributors are not independent in relation to the broadcasting organisation, in which case the distributors' intervention is only a technical means for a communication to the public initiated by the broadcasting organisation. In *GS Media* the criterion led the Court to decide that the posting of hyperlinks which lead to works put on the Internet without permission from the rightholders, or which allow the user to circumvent *restrictions* put in place to protect the work, is considered a communication to the public if the person posting the hyperlinks knew or ought to have known that the hyperlinks provide access to copyright infringing material.[195] Hence, there is no communication to the public if the linker does not know, or cannot reasonably know, that the work was uploaded without permission. The justification is that in such situations the communication is not deliberate.[196] However, if linking is carried out for profit it is presumed that he person responsible for linking knows or ought to have known that the work that was linked to was infringing.[197]

Originally it followed from the decisions of the CJEU that there is only a communication to the public if the person responsible for the communication has 'full knowledge' of the consequences of their actions (intervention).[198] In *GS Media*,

192. *See*, for example, C-160/15 *GS Media*, para. 35.
193. C-306/05 *SGAE*, para. 42.
194. C-325/14 *SBS Belgium*.
195. C-160/15 *GS Media*, paras 49–50.
196. C-160/15 *GS Media*, paras 47–48.
197. *See* C-160/15 *GS Media*, paras 48 et seq.
198. *See*, for example, C-306/05 *SGAE*, para. 42.

however, the Court implied instead that it is sufficient that the linker 'knows or ought to have known' of, on the facts of the case, the illegality of the works.[199] This was subsequently echoed in *Stichting Brein (Filmspeler)*.[200] Consequently, for an act to be deemed a communication, where knowledge is a prerequisite for determining the existence of a communication, it is sufficient that the person ought to have known about the consequences of their conduct.

• *The Communication Must, in Some Cases, Be Directed to a New Public*

As mentioned earlier some types of communication are characterised by the circumstance that someone continues a communication which was originally initiated by someone else. An example is if a restaurant plays radio or television content for the guests or if a teacher shows their students a film from YouTube. According to the CJEU such activities constitute, in themselves, a communication to the public, as opposed to a direct performance. Furthermore, the Court has held that such secondary communication can only be considered a communication to the public if it is either transmitted by other technical means than the initial communication or, failing that, if it is directed towards a *new public*,[201] i.e., 'a public which was not taken into account by the authors of the protected work when they authorised its use by communication to the original public'.[202] Based on the new public criterion the CJEU has considered it to be a communication to the public when:

- a hotel transmits radio and television programs to the hotel rooms;[203]
- a hotel offers CD-players and CDs in the hotel rooms;[204]
- a restaurant allows the guests to watch television;[205]
- a satellite package provider transmits television programs broadcast by others;[206]
- a spa establishment transmits radio and television programs to the patients' rooms;[207]
- a rehabilitation centre has television sets in waiting rooms and training rooms;[208]

199. C-160/15 *GS Media*, para. 49. But *see* para. 55, in which the Court instead refers to the *lack* of knowledge, or reasonable lack of knowledge, as opposed to *presence* of knowledge, or the duty to possess knowledge ('ought to have known').
200. C-527/15 *Stichting Brein*, para. 49. The Court pointed out however that the sale of the multimedia player was made 'in full knowledge' of the fact that the pre-installed add-ons contained links to unlawfully published works (para. 50).
201. *See*, for example, *C-607/11 ITV Broadcasting*, para. 39 and C-466/12 *Svensson*, para. 24.
202. Quoted from C-162/10 *Phonographic Performance (Ireland)*, para. 49.
203. *See* C-306/05 *SGAE* and C-162/10 *Phonographic Performance (Ireland)*.
204. *See* C-162/10 *Phonographic Performance (Ireland)*.
205. *See* C-403/08 and C-429/08 *FAPL*.
206. *See* C-431/09 and C-432/09 *Airfield*.
207. *See* C-351/12 *OSA*.
208. *See* C-117/15 *Reha Training*.

- one sells multimedia devices containing pre-installed links to illegal material;[209]
- one operates a website which indexes metadata relating to protected content, but does not store the content in question and helps users to share files illegally;[210]
- a protected work which has been placed on a website by or with the permission of the author is subsequently placed on another website without such permission.[211]

Furthermore, the Court has held that linking to works, although constituting a *communication* regardless of the type of link used, is not directed to a *new public* and is therefore not a communication to the public within the meaning of Article 3 InfoSoc Directive, when the works that are linked to have been uploaded to the website by, or with the permission of, the rightholder.[212] This will however not be the case if the link *circumvents* a protection measure which restricts access to a (lawfully) uploaded work, nor when the link refers to an unlawfully uploaded work but on condition that the linker did not have reasonable grounds to know about the status of the copy.[213]

However, in so far as subject matter protected by related rights is concerned, in particular broadcasts, the communication to the public right may be broader. In *C More*, a case which originally was a linking case but in which the linking questions where withdrawn following the Court's judgement in *Svensson*, the Court held that Member States are entitled to extend the scope of the communication to the public right provided in Article 3(2) InfoSoc Directive, provided that such extension does not undermine protection of copyright.[214]

Regrettably, the description of the circumstances of the case in paragraphs 12–13 of the judgement does not fully embrace the factual circumstances. The website from which the hockey matches were (lawfully) communicated was openly available in the same sense as the 'digital lockers' in the subsequent *GS Media* case – i.e., anyone with the link would have received access. The paywall that the CJEU mentions in paragraph 12, intended to protect access, did not immediately protect access to the 'webcast' but to another website, therefore making the webcast unprotected. This was later rectified as follows from paragraph 14, and the webcast was no longer accessible through the links in question. Unfortunately, in *GS Media* the Court did not address the relevance of the circumstance whereby the provision of hyperlinks 'makes it much easier to find those works, given that the website on which they are available is not easily findable by the general internet public'.[215] Since *C More* concerned linking to lawful content

209. *See* C-527/15 *Stichting Brein*.
210. *See* C-610/15 *Stichting Brein II*.
211. *See* C-161/17 *Land Nordrhein-Westfalen*. One might argue, however, that the new public criterion is only applicable in cases where a communication carries (or *retransmits*) a communication initiated by someone else, and that this was de facto not the situation in the case.
212. C-466/12 *Svensson*, paras 20 and 27–30. *See also* C-348/13 *BestWater*.
213. C-466/12 *Svensson*, para. 31 and C-160/15 *GS Media*.
214. C-279/13 *C More Entertainment* v *Sandberg* ECLI:EU:C:2015:199. *See also* paras 20–21.
215. *See* C-160/15 *GS Media*, para. 54 last sentence together with para. 26.

which was de facto available without a technical restriction, such linking would have had to be allowed on the basis of *Svensson*, which might very well explain the question that was eventually left for the Court to answer. In any event, by retracting its linking questions, it was a missed opportunity for the Swedish Supreme Court to request the CJEU to clarify complex aspects relating to the new public criterion and circumvention, or rather the *effectiveness*, of technical restrictions intended to protect streamed content.

The new public criterion appears to necessitate an evaluation of what the authors and other rightholders understood, or did not understand, when they gave their initial permission. The way in which the CJEU applies the criterion, however, can hardly be said to reflect realistic judgments. This makes it difficult to foresee the results of cases in which the new public criterion is relevant. Sometimes the application of the new public criterion leads to surprising results. For example, it follows from *AKM* that if somebody receives broadcasting signals sent out from a country's national broadcasting corporation and retransmits them within the same country, then there is no new public if the rightholders, when they gave their permission to the national broadcasting corporation, took into account that the broadcasts could be seen by everybody in the country.[216] However, it is a basic premise in copyright that retransmission requires permission from the author[217] and the *AKM* decision, therefore, threatens to derail enormously valuable financial flows in many of the Member States. As noted above, the new public criterion is only relevant in cases where the subsequent communication (transmission) is effected with *the same technical means* as the initial communication. This was expressly made clear in *ITV Broadcasting*, in which the live retransmission of free-to-air television broadcasts over the Internet was considered a communication to the public since it was carried out with different technical means.[218] In *AKM*, however, while the Court concluded that the cable retransmission was made with technical means different from those used for the initial broadcast transmission, which, the Court noted, allowed the Court to find that a communication was taking place, nevertheless proceeded to applying the new public criterion and, not surprisingly, concluded that the retransmission was not directed to a new public,[219] and that it, therefore, was not a communication to the public within the meaning of Article 3(1) InfoSoc Directive. This decision is difficult to follow and reconcile with *ITV Broadcasting* since the circumstances are virtually identical in material aspects. In that case, the retransmission was made from a free-to-air broadcast to an Internet platform to which users received access after having confirmed that they were entitled to watch the broadcast on television. Such entitlement came with the payment of the TV-licence fee, which is a legal, and not a technical restriction, the practical consequence of which was that although anyone who owned receiving equipment may have received the signal, only those who had paid the TV-licence fee were legally entitled to do it. The platform

216. C-138/16 *AKM*.
217. *See* to this effect, for example, C-117/15 *Reha Training*, para. 39.
218. *See* especially C-607/11 *ITV Broadcasting*, paras 37 et seq. *See also* C-466/12 *Svensson*, para. 24, C-348/13 *BestWater*, para. 14, C-160/15 *GS Media*, para. 37, C-527/15 *Stichting Brein*, para. 33 and C-610/15 *Stichting Brein II*, para. 28.
219. C-138/16 *AKM*, paras 26–27.

(TVCatchup) limited access to only those users who could evidence the payment of that fee, therefore limiting the retransmission to persons entitled to watch the initial broadcast transmitted by the original technical means.

The general approach has been that the new public criterion is only relevant in relation to acts done on a communication initiated by someone else, such as retransmissions or linking. In *VCAST* the new public criterion was not applied. The case concerned an Internet cloud service allowing customers to record television programmes for later viewing (digital time-shifting) which were then made available to them through the cloud service. The CJEU found that the original transmission of the broadcasts and the subsequent making available of recorded content to specific customers, which it considered to be a communication to the public, were different communications to different publics and that the new public criterion was therefore irrelevant.[220] The Court's judgement is somewhat perplexing because the referring Italian court asked about the scope of Article 5(2)(b) (reproduction for private use) and how it relates to cloud computing services such as VCAST, while the Court focused the judgement on the scope of the communication to the public right instead.[221] Although this is not made clear in the judgement, the Court's assessment appears to be that although the service was indeed capturing the initial broadcast, the creation of a (non-transient) copy of the broadcast broke the dependence on the initial broadcast, the result of which was that any subsequent act on the recorded broadcast would be a new, independent act. This would explain why the Court, possibly in light of the *AKM* judgement,[222] felt obliged to state that it was thus not necessary to consider whether the communication of the recorded broadcasts was directed to a *new* public. This consideration would arguably not have been necessary anyway in light of *ITV Broadcasting*, since in *VCAST* the service was also digitising terrestrial broadcasts and, therefore, communicated with different technical means, however the cases are not identical because the former case concerned direct *retransmissions* of broadcasts and this dependence on the initial broadcast was therefore sustained. Similarly, and subsequently, in *Land Nordrhein-Westfalen,*[223] regarding the facts of the case, the dependence on the original communication was broken by the making of a copy by downloading a photograph lawfully published on a website and subsequently uploading it to another webpage, which resulted in a new and independent communication.

The complexity of, an almost abundant amount of, cases concerning the communication to the public right and the amount of different factors that may, or may not, become relevant in establishing whether a communication to the public has taken place might also be a reason why the Court feels itself obliged to refer to, or justify the non-application of, the new public requirement, and why national courts may feel it necessary to continue asking about the new public requirement, even in seemingly uncomplex cases such as *Land Nordrhein-Westfalen*. The Court's judgement in this case has, regrettably, added another layer of questions because not only did it proceed

220. C-265/16 *VCAST*, paras 49–50.
221. Cf. C-265/16 *VCAST*, Opinion of AG Maciej Szpunar.
222. Which it did not refer to, as opposed to AG Maciej Szpunar.
223. C-161/17 *Land Nordrhein-Westfalen* v *Renckhoff* ECLI:EU:C:2018:634.

to assessing the existence of a *new* public, contrary to its earlier approach in *VCAST*, but the Court reached the rather surprising conclusion that the work was indeed communicated to a new public and limited henceforth the scope of the public from any Internet user to the specific visitors of the website;[224] a conclusion which may be difficult to reconcile with *GS Media* and *Svensson*[225] and one which must preclude potential visitors of a website. Potential visitors of a website cannot be included as they are simultaneously potential visitors of the other website. While the Court's intention might have been to emphasise the different target groups of either websites as the work was lawfully published on a travel portal, but was subsequently included in a school pupil's presentation made for a language workshop that was made available on the school website, such a conclusion cannot be inferred from its assessment.[226] Moreover, limiting the public to actual visitors of the website or alternatively creating further groups of visitors[227] provides significant room for questioning whether that group of persons still constitutes an '*indeterminate* number of recipients', and therefore *public*. Requiring the application of the new public criterion in such situations also raises the question about the definition of a website and forces a dangerously narrower approach, for example:

- Is the entire YouTube platform a website?
- Will a work that has been *re-uploaded* to a video-sharing service be communicated to a *new* public (a public which the rightholder did not have in mind) when the original work is still available on that service?
- Does the answer to this question depend on whether the service presents a new webpage for each uploaded video, such as YouTube, or alternatively dynamically shows content on the same webpage, which requires the user to 'scroll down' to view other videos, such as Facebook?
- In any event, if it must be presumed that the rightholder considered exclusively the visitors of the specific webpage (or part of the webpage) on which their work is available, should the assessment of whether the communication of the re-uploaded video occurs to a new public include the potential viewers of that re-uploaded video?

The liability of the services is another matter, which will be governed by the provisions of the E-Commerce Directive, under which no liability ensues as long as the service is unaware of the infringing activity, and removes or disables access to the content once it becomes aware of it.[228]

224. C-161/17 *Land Nordrhein-Westfalen*, para. 35.
225. C-160/15 *GS Media*, 42 and C-466/12 *Svensson*, para. 26; *see* especially last sentence.
226. C-161/17 *Land Nordrhein-Westfalen*, paras 26–34.
227. Such as potential visitors of the original website on the one hand, and potential visitors of the other website on the other hand who are simultaneously not potential visitors of the original website.
228. E-Commerce Directive, Art. 14. *See also* Arts 12, 13 and 15. *See* however Art. 13 in the proposed DSM Directive, COM(2016) 593 final.

• *The Profit-Making Intention of the Communication Is Relevant*

In a number of decisions, the CJEU has stated that although it is not decisive whether the communication takes place for profit it is, however, not irrelevant. In *SCF* this profit criterion, together with other factors, led the Court to conclude that it was not a communication to the public under the Rental and Lending Rights Directive that a dentist played radio in his dental clinic. Among other things the Court referred to the fact that one does not go to the dentist in order to listen to music and that the communication, therefore, was not of a profit-making nature since it neither resulted in, nor allowed the dentist to, raise the prices.[229]

On the other hand this criterion has been used to find the existence of a communication to the public in cases concerning the showing of protected subject matter on television sets in restaurants[230] and rehabilitation centres[231] as well as in cases concerning the use of radios and television sets in hotel rooms.[232] The underlying reasoning is that such acts of communication contribute to the status of recreation centres' standing and attractiveness, thereby giving them a competitive advantage,[233] increases the number of guests in restaurants,[234] and make it possible for hotel owners to charge more for the rooms.[235] The profit criterion is also of significance for Internet hyperlinking to protected subject matter which is uploaded without permission from the rightholders; in particular, the profit-making intention of linking in such circumstances imposes on the linker the burden of proving that it was carried out without knowledge of the unlawful status of the subject matter. Failing such proof will mean that there was a communication to the public, in accordance with the principle that the communications must be deliberate.

The scope of the profit-making criterion was previously somewhat unclear. In some decisions the CJEU indicated that the criterion applies both in cases concerning communication to the public under Article 3(1) InfoSoc Directive and in cases concerning communication to the public under Article 8(2) Rental and Lending Rights Directive.[236] In *OSA*, on the other hand, the Court seemed to indicate that the profit-making criterion only applies in cases concerning Article 8(2) Rental and Lending Rights Directive, but not in cases concerning Article 3(1) InfoSoc Directive.[237] However, in *Reha Training* the CJEU finally determined that the profit criterion applies

229. C-135/10 *SCF*, paras 90–97 et seq.
230. C-403/08 and C-429/08 *FAPL*.
231. C-117/15 *Reha Training*.
232. C-306/05 *SGAE* and C-162/10 *Phonographic Performance (Ireland)*.
233. C-117/15 *Reha Training*, para. 63.
234. C-403/08 and C-429/08 *FAPL*, para. 205.
235. C-306/05 *SGAE*, para. 44 and C-162/10 *Phonographic Performance (Ireland)*, para. 44.
236. *See* C-306/05 *SGAE*, para. 44, C-403/08 and C-429/08 *FAPL*, para. 205, and C-607/11 *ITV Broadcasting*, para. 42.
237. *See* C-351/12 *OSA*, paras 34 et seq. Perhaps precursors to this view are perhaps reflected in C-135/10 *SCF*, paras 76 ff. and C-162/10 *Phonographic Performance (Ireland,)* paras 29 et seq. according to which a so-called 'individual interpretation of the concept of communication to the public' must be made in connection to Art. 8(2) Rental and Lending Rights Directive. Cf. C-607/11 *ITV Broadcasting*, para. 22.

in relation to both directives.[238] The Court stresses that it is understood that the public which is the subject of the communication is both targeted by the user and receptive, in one way or another, to that communication and not merely caught by chance.[239]

[B] Computer Programs

By virtue of Article 4(1)(a) Computer Programs Directive, rightholders have an exclusive right to the 'permanent or temporary reproduction of a computer program by any means and in any form, in part or in whole'.[240] Loading, displaying, running, transmission or storage of the computer program, falls within the right, to the extent that they necessitate a reproduction. Moreover, under subparagraph (b) adaptations and other alterations of a computer program are also exclusive to the rightholder.

Article 4(1)(c) Computer Programs Directive contains a right of distribution, including rental. This right is not limited to the distribution of tangible media, instead it refers to 'any form' of distribution, suggesting that downloadable copies may be distributed, and consequentially, resold under Article 4(2). This has however been resolved by the CJEU in *UsedSoft*,[241] which is further discussed below in relation to exhaustion.

[C] Databases

The rights that Member States must grant authors of copyright-protected databases are set out in Article 5 Database Directive which provides that authors shall have the exclusive right to carry out or authorise:

(a) temporary or permanent reproduction by any means and in any form, in whole or in part;
(b) translation, adaptation, arrangement and any other alteration;
(c) any form of distribution to the public of the database or of copies thereof [...]
(d) any communication, display or performance to the public;
(e) any reproduction, distribution, communication, display or performance to the public of the results of the acts referred to in (b).

It is important to underline that these rights concern the *expression* of the database, not the contents as such, as it is not the originality of the *content* that makes up a database under copyright law.[242]

238. C-117/15 *Reha Training*, paras 33–34, compare paras 22 et seq. The criterion was later cited in C-160/15 *GS Media*, C-527/15 *Stichting Brein*, and C-610/15 *Stichting Brein II* concerning Art. 3(1) InfoSoc Directive.
239. C-117/15 *Reha Training*, para. 48. *See also* C-135/10 *SCF*, para. 91, C-162/10 *Phonographic Performance (Ireland)*, para. 37.
240. Cf. InfoSoc Directive, Art. 2.
241. Case C-128/11 *UsedSoft* v *Oracle International* ECLI:EU:C:2012:407.
242. *See* above on the subsistence of database protection. There appears to be a difference for the sui generis database right. *See* further below.

[D] Related Rights and Sui Generis Protection of Databases

As described above Member States are obliged to grant related rights protection to the performances of performing artists, sound recordings, films, radio and television broadcasts. Databases, except enjoying protection under copyright law, may also enjoy special sui generis protection.

[1] Performing Artists

Performing artists are granted the following exclusive rights:

- Right to authorise or prohibit reproduction of fixations of their performances.[243]
- Right to authorise or prohibit rental and lending of fixations of their performances.[244] If they transfer or assign their rental right concerning a phonogram or an original or copy of a film to a phonogram or film producer, that author or performer shall retain an unwaivable right to obtain an equitable remuneration for the rental.[245]
- Right to make fixations of their performances available to the public by sale or otherwise.[246]
- Right to authorise or prohibit making available to the public, by wire or wireless means, in such a way that members of the public may access them from a place and at a time individually chosen by them.[247]
- Right to authorise or prohibit broadcasting by wireless means and the communication to the public of their performances, except where the performance is itself already a broadcast performance or is made from a fixation.[248]

Also, it follows from Article 8(2) Rental and Lending Rights Directive that Member States must ensure that a single equitable remuneration is paid by the user, if a phonogram published for commercial purposes, or a reproduction of such phonogram, is used for broadcasting by wireless means or for any communication to the public, and to ensure that this remuneration is shared between the relevant performers and phonogram producers.

Performing artists are also covered by the SatCab Directive according to which cross-border satellite transmission must be considered communication to the public.[249]

243. *See* InfoSoc Directive, Art. 2(b).
244. *See* Rental and Lending Rights Directive, Art. 3(1)(b).
245. *See* Art. 5(1)-(2) Rental and Lending Rights Directive.
246. *See* Art. 9(1)(a) Rental and Lending Rights Directive.
247. *See* Art. 3(2)(a) InfoSoc Directive.
248. *See* Art. 8(1) Rental and Lending Rights Directive.
249. *See* Art. 4 and paras 21 and 25 Satellite and Cable Directive.

[2] Sound Recordings

Producers of sound recordings (phonograms) are granted the following exclusive rights:

- Right to authorise or prohibit direct or indirect, temporary or permanent reproduction by any means and in any form, in whole or in part of their phonograms.[250]
- Right to authorise or prohibit rental and lending of their phonograms.[251]
- Right to make phonograms available to the public by sale or otherwise.[252]
- Right to authorise or prohibit making available to the public of phonograms, by wire or wireless means, in such a way that members of the public may access them from a place and at a time individually chosen by them.[253]

The single equitable remuneration applicable under Article 8(2) Rental and Lending Rights Directive and mentioned above also applies to phonogram producers.

Similarly to performing artists, producers of phonograms are also covered by the SatCab Directive according to which cross-border satellite transmission must be considered communication to the public.[254]

[3] Film Producers

Film producers of first fixations of films are granted the following exclusive rights:

- Right to reproduction in respect of the original and copies of the film.[255]
- Right to authorise or prohibit rental and lending of the first fixation of a film in respect of the original and copies of the film.[256]
- Right to make available to the public, by sale or otherwise, of the first fixation of a film in respect of the original and copies of the film.[257]
- Right to authorise or prohibit making available to the public, by wire or wireless means, of their films in such a way that members of the public may access them from a place and at a time individually chosen by them, i.e., on the Internet etc.[258]

250. *See* Art. 2(c) InfoSoc Directive.
251. *See* Art. 3(1)(c) Rental and Lending Rights Directive.
252. *See* Art. 9(1)(b) Rental and Lending Rights Directive.
253. *See* Art. 3(2)(b) InfoSoc Directive.
254. *See* Art. 4 paras 21 and 25 Satellite and Cable Directive.
255. *See* Art. 2(d) InfoSoc Directive.
256. *See* Art. 3(1)(d) Rental and Lending Rights Directive.
257. *See* Art. 9(1)(c) Rental and Lending Rights Directive.
258. *See* Art. 3(2)(c) InfoSoc Directive.

[4] Radio and Television Broadcasts

Broadcasting organisations are granted the following exclusive rights:

- Right to authorise or prohibit reproduction of fixation of their broadcasts.[259]
- Right to make fixations of their broadcasts available to the public by sale or otherwise.[260]
- Right to authorise or prohibit making available to the public fixations of their broadcasts, by wire or wireless means, in such a way that members of the public may access them from a place and at a time individually chosen by them, i.e., on the Internet etc.[261] The scope of this right is not necessarily identical with the exclusive right provided to authors in Article 3(1) InfoSoc Directive, because it is not fully harmonised and Member States may make it broader on condition that it does not undermine the protection of copyright.[262]

Radio and Television broadcasts are also covered by the SatCab Directive.

[5] Sui Generis Protection of Databases

Article 7(1) Database Directive provides an exclusive right to prevent *extraction* and *re-utilisation* of the whole or a substantial part of the contents of the database, to the maker of a database that is the result of a substantial investment in obtaining, verifying or presenting the contents. Extraction and re-utilisation are defined in Article 7(2) as follows:

(a) 'extraction' shall mean the permanent or temporary transfer of all or a substantial part of the contents of a database to another medium by any means or in any form;
(b) 're-utilisation' shall mean any form of making available to the public all or a substantial part of the contents of a database by the distribution of copies, by renting, by online or other forms of transmission. The first sale of a copy of a database within the Community by the rightholder or with his consent shall exhaust the right to control resale of that copy within the Community.

The provision also makes clear that public lending is not an act of extraction or re-utilisation. Moreover, the repeated and systematic extraction or re-utilisation of an *insubstantial* part of the contents of the database is not permitted.[263]

Similarly to the exclusive economic rights provided by copyright, the database right may be transferred, assigned or granted under a contractual licence.[264] The

259. *See* Art. 2(e) InfoSoc Directive.
260. *See* Art. 9(1)(d) Rental and Lending Rights Directive.
261. *See* Art. 3(2)(d) InfoSoc Directive.
262. *See* C-279/13 *C More Entertainment*, paras 29, 31 and 37. Cf. C-466/12 *Svensson*, paras 33-41.
263. Database Directive, Art. 7(5).
264. Database Directive, Art. 7(3).

exclusive right will, however, be contingent upon any rights existing in the *contents* of the database, as the case may be.[265]

The provisions of Article 7 Database Directive have been interpreted by the CJEU in *British Horseracing Board*, *Directmedia Publishing*, *Apis-Hristovich*, and *Innoweb*.[266] These decisions lead to the following conclusions:

- Whether something can be considered a 'substantial part' of a database must be evaluated either quantitatively or qualitatively. A *part* is to be considered *quantitatively substantial* if it represents a large part of the content of the entire database. Further, a *part* is to be considered *qualitatively substantial* if it is in itself the result of a substantial investment in the sense of the Database Directive.[267] What precisely is meant by *substantial investment* in the sense of the Database Directive is in itself ambiguous; although it is not completely arbitrary.[268]
- Article 7(5) on the repeated and systematic extraction and/or re-utilisation of insubstantial parts of the contents of a database is to be interpreted in such a way that the rightholder can only prohibit extraction or re-utilisation of insubstantial parts, if they in themselves reflect a substantial part of the database; i.e., they must in themselves reflect a substantial investment.[269]
- The concept of 'extraction' must be interpreted broadly and also includes manual recopying etc.[270] The very consultation of a database, however, cannot be considered extraction.[271] However the use of 'dedicated meta search engine' is to be considered re-utilisation of a database or a substantial part of it. Such search engines transfer the queries to the search engines of other databases and present the results in the same way as if the user had himself visited them.[272] In *Innoweb* a website with advertisements of second-hand cars contained a meta search engine which transferred the queries of the user concerning specific car models to the search engines of other websites with advertisements of second-hand cars. These search engines then searched the databases which formed the basis of these websites and transferred the search results to the search engine of website no. 1 which then presented the advertisements to the user. This way the user did not have to consult the

265. Database Directive, Art. 7(4).
266. Case C-203/02 *British Horseracing Board and Others* v *William Hill* ECLI:EU:C:2004:695, Case C-304/07 *Directmedia Publishing* v *Albert-Ludwigs-Universität Freiburg* ECLI:EU:C:2008:552, Case C-545/07 *Apis-Hristovich* v *Lakorda* ECLI:EU:C:2009:132, and C-202/12 *Innoweb*.
267. *See* C-203/02 *British Horseracing Board*, para. 82 and C-545/07 *Apis-Hristovich*, paras 61 and 66.
268. *See*, for example, recital 19 Database Directive specifying that the compilation of several recordings of musical performances falls outside the Directive because it *inter alia* does not represent a *substantial enough investment*. *See also* recital 7, noting that the making of databases requires the investment of *considerable* resources.
269. C-304/07 *Directmedia Publishing*, paras 59 et seq.
270. C-304/07 *Directmedia Publishing*, paras 34 et seq.
271. C-304/07 *Directmedia Publishing*, paras 51 et seq. and C-203/02 *British Horseracing Board*, para. 54. The exploitation of data from sui generis-protected topographic maps can constitute extraction. *See* Case C-490/14 *Freistaat Bayern* v *Verlag Esterbauer* ECLI:EU:C:2015:735.
272. *See* C-202/12 *Innoweb*, paras 24–26.

various websites themselves and this sometimes deprived the owners of income from web banner advertising. Essentially, the CJEU found that a dedicated meta search engine which transfers the query to the search function of a database re-utilises the database or a substantial part of it when the following conditions are satisfied:

(1) The meta search engine provides the end user with a search form which essentially offers the same range of functionality as the search form on the database site.
(2) The meta search engine *translates* queries from end users into the search engine for the database site in real time, so that all the information on that database is searched through; and
(3) The meta search engine presents the results to the end user using the format of its website, grouping duplications together into a single block item but in an order that reflects criteria comparable to those used by the search engine of the database site concerned for presenting results.

- It is irrelevant whether the contents taken from a protected database is being re-structured, for example, by being re-used in another database which structures the data in a different way.[273] Thus, databases protected by the sui generis right enjoy a more far-reaching protection than original databases protected by copyright, since this implies that protection is indeed given for the contents of the database.

§4.03 MORAL RIGHTS

Moral rights such as the right of paternity and the right of integrity are left outside the scope of the EU copyright framework and are therefore currently regulated by national provisions.[274] In Member States belonging to the *authors' rights tradition*, moral rights are considered to arise directly in the author and to be inalienable even by voluntary transfer (cession) of rights to an employer. On the other hand, in the Member States belonging to the *copyright tradition*, moral rights may be waived by an instrument in writing, and the right of paternity, and in some cases right of integrity, does not extend over anything done by the employer where copyright was first vested in the employer.[275]

273. C-304/07 *Directmedia*, paras 39 et seq. and C-545/07 *Apis-Hristovich*, para. 47.
274. InfoSoc Directive, recital 19. *See also* COM(88) 172 final, p. 197, Commission, 'Amended Proposal for a Council Directive on the legal protection of computer programs' COM(90) 509 final – SYN 183, p. 18, Commission, 'Copyright and related rights in the information society' (Green Paper) COM(95) 382 final 19 July 1995, pp. 65 et seq., and Commission, 'Follow-up to the Green Paper on copyright and related rights in the information society' (Communication) COM(96) 586 final, 20 November 1996, Chapter 3. *See also* Arts 6*bis* Berne Convention.
275. *See* for example s. 87 (regarding waiver) and ss 79(3) and 82 (regarding non-application of the paternity and integrity right) of the Copyright, Designs and Patents Act 1988 (UK).

§4.04 ARTIST'S RESALE RIGHT

The artist's resale right (*droit de suite*) is a hybrid kind of right because it entitles the author of an original work of art to a share of the resale price of their work and is, therefore, economic in character, however it is inalienable and unwaivable[276] and therefore possesses qualities of moral rights.

The resale right has been harmonised by the Resale Right Directive, under which:

> Member States shall provide, for the benefit of the author of an original work of art, a resale right (...) to receive a royalty based on the sale price obtained for any resale of the work, subsequent to the first transfer of the work by the author.

The right is not new as such, however it is discretionary under the Berne Convention, in which it is also broader because it includes original manuscripts, but a number of Member States had not introduced it.[277]

The types of works which fall under the resale right are works of graphic or plastic art, such as pictures, collages, paintings, drawings, engravings, prints, lithographs, sculptures, tapestries, ceramics, glassware and photographs, on condition that they are made by the artist or under their authority.[278] Hence, the resale right also applies to copies of such works, however these must originate directly from the author, and are in that sense original pieces, rather than replicas. The directive appears to indirectly require some form of authentication, as Article 2(2) informs, in relation to copies of works, that 'such copies will normally have been numbered, signed or otherwise duly authorised by the artist'.

The justification for the existence of the resale right, in the EU copyright framework, is primarily economic – it is meant to provide an incentive and reward successful creations:

> The resale right is intended to ensure that authors of graphic and plastic works of art share in the economic success of their original works of art. It helps to redress the balance between the economic situation of authors of graphic and plastic works of art and that of other creators who benefit from successive exploitations of their works.[279]

From the perspective of harmonisation, it is however intended to address issues relating to market competition:

> The application or non-application of such a right has a significant impact on the competitive environment within the internal market, since the existence or absence of an obligation to pay on the basis of the resale right is an element which must be taken into account by each individual wishing to sell a work of art. This right is therefore a factor which contributes to the creation of distortions of competition as well as displacement of sales within the Community.[280]

---

276. Resale Right Directive, Art. 1(1).
277. *See* Arts 14*ter* Berne Convention. *See also* recital 8 Resale Right Directive.
278. Resale Right Directive, Art. 2(1)-(2).
279. Resale Right Directive, recital 3.
280. Resale Right Directive, recital 9.

Member States are entitled to set a minimum sale price for the applicability of the right, however it may not be higher than EUR 3,000, while the maximum amount of payable royalty is EUR 12,500.[281] Article 4 sets the following thresholds for the royalty:

(a) 4% (optionally 5%) for the portion of the sale price up to EUR 50,000;
(b) 3% for the portion of the sale price from EUR 5,000,001 to EUR 200,000;
(c) 1% for the portion of the sale price from EUR 20,000,001 to EUR 350,000;
(d) 0.5% for the portion of the sale price from EUR 35,000,001 to EUR 500,000;
(e) 0.25% for the portion of the sale price exceeding EUR 500,000.

281. Resale Right Directive, Arts 3 and 4(1).

CHAPTER 5
Limitations and Exceptions

§5.01 INTRODUCTION

Except harmonising the exclusive rights of reproduction, communication of works to the public and distribution, the EU copyright framework also harmonises permissible uses which often reflect social and cultural values that should not be inhibited by copyright exclusivity and which therefore do not require rightholders' consent. Such uses are often described as limitations or exceptions (L&Es) to the exclusive rights or defences to copyright infringement. The EU framework does not categorise specific permissible uses in the InfoSoc Directive as either limitations or exceptions, arguably leaving instead such categorisation to the Member States in every case.[282] Whatever the appropriate categorisation, a common feature is that using the work in a manner or for the purpose described in the relevant provisions will normally not amount to infringement in the absence of consent. A number of L&Es are however contingent upon the payment of fair compensation.

Most L&Es are to be found in the InfoSoc Directive and concern literary and artistic works in general, but some are also contained in the specialised Computer Programs Directive and exclusively concern software, as well as the Orphan Works Directive. The Rental and Lending Rights Directive contains a few discretionary *limitations*, which however overlap with those present in the InfoSoc Directive and will therefore not be mentioned here.[283]

282. *See*, for example, Joined Cases C-457/11 to 460/11 *VG Wort* v *Kyocera and Others* and *Fujitsu Technology Solutions and Hewlett-Packard* v *VG Wort*, paras 33–38. *See also* title of Art. 5 InfoSoc Directive ('Limitations and Exceptions'), and recital 32 making clear that the list of exceptions and limitations 'takes due account of the different legal traditions in Member States…'.
283. *See* Art. 10(1)-(2) Rental and Lending Rights Directive.

§5.02 L&Es UNDER THE INFOSOC DIRECTIVE*

Article 5 InfoSoc Directive enumerates twenty-one different L&Es. Out of these only Article 5(1) concerning temporary reproduction is mandatory to implement, whereas the remaining ones in Article 5(2) concerning reproduction and Article 5(3) concerning reproduction and communication to the public are discretionary to implement. Article 5(4) also contains a discretionary rule permitting the introduction of limitations or exceptions to the distribution right in certain justified cases following from the other L&Es in Article 5.

[A] Scope and Rules of Interpretation

The Member States are only free to introduce into their national copyright law such limitations and exceptions as are expressly provided for in Article 5 because this list is exhaustive.[284] Although the discretionary character of almost all of the L&Es does put in question the effectiveness of the effort to harmonise this area of the law, as the Member States may implement only some, all, or, at least in theory, none of the discretionary L&Es, resulting in a variable array of permissible uses in each Member State, the entire catalogue of L&Es taken as a whole may create a flexible framework approaching its distant American fair use[285] cousin.

An important caveat attached to the applicability of the L&Es, apart from the individual requirements contained in each of the provisions separately which must be satisfied, is that they ought to be interpreted strictly. In particular, the CJEU restated in *Infopaq* that 'the provisions of a directive which derogate from a general principle established by that directive [i.e., the exclusive rights] must be interpreted strictly':[286] by contrast, the exclusive rights must be interpreted broadly.[287] This canon of interpretation may now arguably be put into question as courts are required to interpret EU legislation, and national legislation implementing it, in accordance with the EU Charter. This involves striking a fair balance between different fundamental rights that may be at stake.[288] While it does not necessarily mean that the L&Es have become enforceable rights, the L&Es, and especially those that specifically embody fundamental rights, certainly require different treatment than merely a strict interpretation.

* Parts of this section are based on the author's ongoing research in Szkalej, K., 'Consumption of digital works – an analysis of EU copyright law within the framework of lawful acquisition and use of protected content' (forthcoming 2019).

284. InfoSoc Directive, recital (32). This has however recently been questioned. *See* request for a preliminary ruling in C-516/17 *Spiegel Online*, question 3; and C-476/17 *Pelham and Others* v *Hütter and Schneider-Esleben* question 5, which instead concerns the question whether there is any latitude in implementation of the limitations and exceptions (as well as rights). *See also* COM(2016) 593 final, Arts 3–5 and 17(2)(a)-(b) of the proposed DSM Directive.
285. *See* 17 U.S.C. § 107.
286. C-5/08 *Infopaq*, para. 56.
287. *See* generally recital (21) InfoSoc Directive and specifically *Infopaq*, para. 43 for the reproduction right, and recital (23) and e.g., C-325/14 *SBS*, para. 14 for the communication to the public right.
288. *See* §2.05 above.

Similarly, however, the exercise of an L&E may become contingent upon the applicability of an overriding interest, resting instead with the rightholder, above and beyond the protection of intellectual property.[289] Nevertheless, the CJEU has observed that the interpretation of the conditions in the enumerated L&Es 'must enable the effectiveness of the exception thereby established to be safeguarded and permit observance of the exception's purpose as resulting in particular from recital 31 [InfoSoc Directive]'.[290] Although this necessarily permits the apprehension of a teleological approach when interpreting L&Es and using *the possibility of application* as a standard against which to interpret the scope of an L&E, L&Es are generally subject to another important prima facie restrictive rule.

Article 5(5) InfoSoc Directive states that:

> The exceptions and limitations provided for in [Arts 5(1)-(4)] shall only be applied in certain special cases which do not conflict with a normal exploitation of the work or other subject-matter and do not unreasonably prejudice the legitimate interests of the rightholder.

This provision is known as the three-step test. Its different incarnations are present in Article 9(2) Berne Convention, Article 10 WCT, Article 16 WPPT and Article 13 TRIPS Agreement,[291] the last of which Article 5(5) resembles the most in terms of wording. The InfoSoc three-step test works however very differently from its international counterparts. While in all of the three international instruments the three-step test works as a reference standard for the creation of L&Es, in the InfoSoc Directive it works instead as a supra rule for the applicability of any of the L&Es which are enumerated with noticeable specificity. That the InfoSoc three-step test should be layered onto the applicability of an L&E, and not, for example, be used as merely an interpretative tool for determining the scope of any of the L&Es has been made clear by the CJEU which has stated that the three-step test:

> does not therefore define the substantive content of the different exceptions and limitations set out in Article 5(2) of that directive but takes effect only at the time when they are applied by the Member States (...) [and that it is not intended to] either affect the substantive content of provisions falling within the scope of Article 5(2) (...) or, inter alia, to extend the scope of the different exceptions and limitations provided for therein.[292]

289. *See* C-201/13 *Deckmyn*.
290. C-403/08 and C-429/08 *FAPL*, para. 163, C-145/10 *Painer*, para. 133, C-201/13 *Deckmyn*, para. 23.
291. Articles 26(2) and 30 TRIPS Agreement also contain a three-step test for industrial designs and patents respectively, with an interestingly different scope. Both these provisions require instead that the legitimate interests of third parties be taken into account.
292. Case C-435/12 *ACI Adam and Others* v *Stichting de Thuiskopie and Stichting Onderhandelingen Thuiskopie* ECLI:EU:C:2014:254, paras 25–26. *See also* C-527/15 *Stichting Brein*, para. 63 'the exemption temporary reproduction must be interpreted in light of Art. 5(5) (...) under which that exemption is to be applied only in certain special cases which do not conflict with a normal exploitation of the work or other subject matter and do not unreasonably prejudice the legitimate interests of the right holder'. *See also* C-462/09 *Stichting de Thuiskopie* v *Opus Supplies Deutschland and Others*, paras 21 and 31, C-360/13 *Public Relations Consultants Association*, para. 53 and the subsequent methodical application of Art. 5(5) in 54–62. *See*

Therefore, to be able to apply a L&E, not only, would it appear, must the requirements of the specific L&E provision be satisfied and that provision be interpreted strictly, but the L&E can only be applied in certain special cases that do not conflict with the normal exploitation of the work and that simultaneously do not unreasonably prejudice the legitimate interests of the rightholder. This may create a difficult situation where a court is asked to strike a fair balance between different fundamental rights that may be at stake when applying an L&E. Should such balancing occur before the application of the three-step test, after it, or should the three-step test instead be part of the balancing act? While there is no express legal ground to justify the latter, especially in light of the fact that Article 5(5) only considers the legitimate interests of rightholders, normal exploitation, unreasonable prejudice and legitimate interests are standards which, given copyright's expansionist tendency, are bound to continuously expand rendering it therefore difficult to use as a balancing standard in such situations. The Court's approach does not however always appear to be consistent in such situations. In *Painer* the Court held in relation to Article 5(3)(d) (quotation) that it is intended to strike a fair balance between freedom of expression and the authors rights and implied that such a balance is struck within the provision as such,[293] while in *Deckmyn* the Court held in relation to Article 5(3)(k) (quotation) that the application of the provision must strike such a balance by taking into account all circumstances of the case,[294] but subsequently applied the three-step test in the former case (favouring a combined, umbrella approach),[295] even if very laconically and not as methodically as it subsequently did in *Public Relations Consultants Association*, whereas it did not consider it at all nor made any reference to it in the latter case.[296]

[B] Existing Limitations and Exceptions

The mandatory temporary reproduction provision is contained in Article 5(1) and requires that:

however Case C-302/10 *Infopaq International* v *Danske Dagblades Forening* ECLI: EU:C:2012:16 (*Infopaq II*), para. 56 in which the Court held that if the requirements for temporary reproduction in Art. 5(1) are fulfilled, then it must be held that such acts do not conflict with the normal exploitation of the work or unreasonably prejudice the legitimate interests of the rightholder.

293. C-145/10 *Painer*, paras 134–135. *See also* recital 31 InfoSoc Directive. Cf. C-145/10 *Painer*, para. 11 where the Court observes that Art. 5(3)(e), on the other hand, is only intended to ensure public security, rather than to strike a balance.
294. C-201/13 *Deckmyn*, paras 27–28.
295. C-145/10 *Painer*, paras 110–111 and 116, 137 read together with 130–136, and 149 read together with 139–148.
296. Admittedly the Belgian national court did not ask about Art. 5(5) in C-201/13 *Deckmyn*, as opposed to the Austrian court in C-145/10 *Painer*, which Advocate General Cruz Villalón noted in his opinion and remarked thus that the 'determination of whether or not each of those conditions is satisfied in the present case is a matter which, again, will fall to the national court' (para. 29). *See also* para. 42.

1. Temporary acts of reproduction referred to in Article 2, which are transient or incidental, which are an integral and essential part of a technological process and the sole purpose of which is to enable:[297]
   (a) a transmission in a network between third parties by an intermediary, or
   (b) a lawful use of a work or other subject-matter to be made, and which have no independent economic significance, shall be exempted from the reproduction right provided for in Article 2.[298]

In *Stichting Brein* the CJEU made it clear that an act of temporary reproduction resulting from viewing on a device of protected content which has been uploaded without consent of the rightholder, i.e., 'streaming' from unlawful sources, will not satisfy the requirements of point b) above and of the three-step test in Article 5(5),[299] for which reason it will amount to infringement of copyright.

The following limitations and exceptions may be introduced to the reproduction right exclusively (Article 5(2)):

(a) in respect of reproductions on paper or any similar medium, effected by the use of any kind of photographic technique or by some other process having similar effects, with the exception of sheet music, provided that the rightholders receive fair compensation;[300]

(b) in respect of reproductions on any medium made by a natural person for private use and for ends that are neither directly nor indirectly commercial, on condition that the rightholders receive fair compensation which takes account of the application or non-application of technological measures referred to in Article 6 to the work or subject matter concerned;[301]
    Although this does not follow from the express wording of the provision, reproductions for private use may only be made when the copy of the work is a lawful copy.[302] Hence, the act of downloading for private use (and any subsequent reproductions) of a copy of the work which has been unlawfully uploaded to a webpage or made available on a peer-to-peer sharing network

297. Corrigendum to Directive 2001/29/EC of the European Parliament and of the Council of 22 May 2001 on the harmonisation of certain aspects of copyright and related rights in the information society [2002] OJ L 6/70.
298. *See* C-5/08 *Infopaq*, C-403/08 and C-429/08 *FAPL*, C-302/10 *Infopaq II*, C-360/13 *Public Relations Consultants Association*, C-527/15 *Stichting Brein*.
299. C-527/15 *Stichting Brein*, para. 70.
300. *See* C-457/11 to C-460/11 *VG Wort*, C-117/13 *Technische Universität Darmstadt*, C-572/13 *Hewlett Packard Belgium* v *Reprobel*.
301. *See* C-467/08 *Padawan* v *SGAE*, C-462/09 *Stichting de Thuiskopie*, Case C-277/10 *Luksan* v *van der Let* ECLI:EU:C:2012:65, C-457/11-C-460/11 *VG Wort*, Case C-521/11 *Amazon.com International Sales and Others* v *Austro-Mechana*, C-435/12 *ACI Adam*, C-117/13 *Technische Universität Darmstadt*, C-463/12 *Copydan Båndkopi* v *Nokia Danmark*, C-572/13 *Hewlett Packard Belgium*, Case C-572/14 *Austro-Mechana* v *Amazon EU and Others* ECLI:EU:C:2016:286, Case C-470/14 *EGEDA and Others* v *Administración del Estado and Ametic* ECLI:EU:C:2016:418, Case C-110/15 *Microsoft Mobile Sales International and Others* v *MiBAC and Others* ECLI:EU:C:2016:717. *See also* C-265/16 *VCAST*.
302. C-435/12 *ACI Adam*, para. 41. Admittedly the CJEU refers to the unlawfulness of the *source*, as opposed to the *copy*. The same concerns Art. 5(2)(a). *See* C-572/13 *Hewlett Packard Belgium* v *Reprobel*, paras 64 and 57, also para. 56.

will not fall under this provision and will constitute an infringement; even though the applicability of the provision is conditioned upon the payment of 'fair compensation' for rightholder, which is a concept that has served the introduction of *private copying levies* on, for example, consumer electronics by almost all Member States.

(c) in respect of specific acts of reproduction made by publicly accessible libraries, educational establishments or museums or by archives, which are not for direct or indirect economic or commercial advantage;[303]

(d) in respect of ephemeral recordings of works made by broadcasting organisations by means of their own facilities and for their own broadcasts; the preservation of these recordings in official archives may, on the grounds of their exceptional documentary character, be permitted;[304]

(e) in respect of reproductions of broadcasts made by social institutions pursuing non-commercial purposes, such as hospitals or prisons, on condition that the rightholders receive fair compensation.[305]

The following limitations and exceptions may be introduced to the reproduction right and the communication to the public right (Article 5(3)):

(a) use for the sole purpose of illustration for teaching or scientific research, as long as the source, including the author's name, is indicated, unless this turns out to be impossible and to the extent justified by the non-commercial purpose to be achieved;[306]

(b) uses, for the benefit of people with a disability, which are directly related to the disability and of a non-commercial nature, to the extent required by the specific disability;[307]

(c) reproduction by the press, communication to the public, or making available of published articles on current economic, political, or religious topics or of broadcast works or other subject matter of the same character, in cases where such use is not expressly reserved and as long as the source, including the author's name, is indicated or use of works or other subject matter in connection with the reporting of current events, to the extent justified by the informatory purpose and as long as the source, including the author's name, is indicated, unless this turns out to be impossible;

(d) quotations for purposes such as criticism or review, provided that they relate to a work or other subject matter which has already been lawfully made available to the public, that, unless this turns out to be impossible, the source, including the author's name, is indicated, and that their use is

303. *See* C-117/13 *Technische Universität Darmstadt*.
304. *See* Case C-510/10 *DR and TV2 Danmark* v *NCB* ECLI:EU:C:2012:244.
305. *See* C-351/12 *OSA*.
306. *See* C-161/17 *Land Nordrhein-Westfalen*.
307. *See* C-351/12 *OSA*.

in accordance with fair practice, and to the extent required by the specific purpose;[308]

(e) use for the purposes of public security or to ensure the proper performance or reporting of administrative, parliamentary or judicial proceedings;[309]

(f) use of political speeches as well as extracts of public lectures or similar works or subject matter to the extent justified by the informatory purpose and provided that the source, including the author's name, is indicated, except where this turns out to be impossible;

(g) use during religious celebrations or official celebrations organised by a public authority;

(h) use of works, such as works of architecture or sculpture, made to be located permanently in public places;

(i) incidental inclusion of a work or other subject matter in other material;

(j) use for the purpose of advertising the public exhibition or sale of artistic works, to the extent necessary to promote the event, excluding any other commercial use;

(k) use for the purpose of caricature, parody or pastiche;[310]

(l) use in connection with the demonstration or repair of equipment;

(m) use of an artistic work in the form of a building or a drawing or plan of a building for the purposes of reconstructing the building;

(n) use by communication or making available, for the purpose of research or private study, to individual members of the public by dedicated terminals on the premises of establishments referred to in paragraph 2(c) of works and other subject matter not subject to purchase or licensing terms which are contained in their collections;[311]

(o) use in certain other cases of minor importance where exceptions or limitations already exist under national law, provided that they only concern analogue uses and do not affect the free circulation of goods and services within the Community, without prejudice to the other exceptions and limitations contained in this Article.[312]

§5.03 L&Es UNDER THE ORPHAN WORKS DIRECTIVE

The Orphan Works Directive provides two mandatory L&Es for the use of so-called orphan works, which are defined as works or phonograms for which 'none of the rightholders [are] (...) identified or, even if one or more of them is identified, none is located despite a diligent search for the rightholders having been carried out and

308. *See* C-145/10 *Painer*. *See also* Case C-476/17 *Pelham and Others* v *Hütter and Schneider-Esleben* (pending).
309. *See* C-145/10 *Painer*.
310. *See* C-201/13 *Deckmyn*.
311. *See* C-117/13 *Technische Universität Darmstadt*.
312. *See* C-138/16 *AKM*.

recorded'.[313] Article 6(1) enables the making available of such works, and their reproduction for the specific purpose of digitisation, making available, indexing, cataloguing preservation and restoration. It applies exclusively to libraries, educational establishments, museums, archives, film or audio heritage institutions and public service broadcasting organisations, who benefit from the two L&Es to the extent warranted by their public interest mission.[314] The institutions may, however, generate revenue but exclusively for the purpose of covering the costs of digitisation and the making available.[315]

If the rightholders 'put an end to the orphan status of their works or other protected subject-matter', i.e., identify themselves as the rightholders and thereby render the orphan status of a work obsolete, Member States must ensure that fair compensation is due for the uses made by the beneficiaries of the L&Es, the organisation of the payment of such compensation being left for the Member States to decide.[316]

§5.04 L&Es UNDER THE COMPUTER PROGRAMS DIRECTIVE

The Computer Programs Directive also contains a limited number of permissible uses. Needless to say, these are exclusively applicable to software, including in some instances video games. Interestingly, such uses are referred to in the Computer Programs Directive as *exceptions*.[317]

Under Article 5(1) Computer Programs Directive, a computer program may be reproduced or altered if such reproduction or alteration is necessary for the use of the computer program by the lawful acquirer[318] in accordance with its intended purpose, including for error correction. It seems, however, that such use may be prevented by contract, with the exception of the making of a backup copy.[319] This provision must be interpreted strictly.[320]

Moreover, under Article 5(3) a person having a right to use a copy of a computer program is entitled to observe, study and test the functioning of the program for the purpose of determining the ideas and principles which underlie any element of the program.[321]

Lastly, under Article 6 Computer Programs Directive decompilation of a computer program for the purpose of obtaining information necessary to achieve interoperability of another computer program created independently does not require authorisation from the rightholder, on condition that it is performed by a lawful user of the program (or on their behalf), the information necessary to achieve interoperability is

313. Orphan Works Directive, Art. 2(1).
314. Orphan Works Directive, Arts 1 and 6(2).
315. Orphan Works Directive, Art. 6(2).
316. Orphan Works Directive, Art. 6(5).
317. Which the CJEU has categorised as totally excluding the exclusive rights, albeit in relation to the InfoSoc Directive. *See* C-457/11-C-460/11 *VG Wort* para. 34.
318. This includes an acquirer of used software. *See* C-128/11 *UsedSoft*, paras 80–81.
319. *See* immediately below.
320. Case C-166/15 *Ranks and Vasiļevičs* v *Finanšu un ekonomisko noziegumu izmeklēšanas prokoratūra and Microsoft* ECLI:EU:C:2016:762, para. 42.
321. *See*, for example, C-406/10 *SAS Institute*.

not readily available to such persons, and that it is confined to those parts of the program which are necessary to achieve interoperability.

By virtue of Article 6(2) Computer Programs Directive the information which is obtained during such a process may however not be used for other purposes than achieving interoperability, be given to others, unless it is necessary to achieve interoperability, or be used for the development or marketing of a computer program which is substantially similar in its expression or for any other copyright infringing act.

The exceptions in the Computer Programs Directive are firmly entrenched in the framework, compared to the exceptions and limitations in the InfoSoc Directive, because the Directive expressly provides that the exceptions provided under Article 5(2) and 5(3), as well as decompilation under Article 6, cannot be contracted out. Such provisions are held to be null and void.[322]

322. Computer Programs Directive, Art. 8.

CHAPTER 6

Enabling Access to Digital Content*

§6.01 INTRODUCTION

European copyright law has not until recently expressly concerned itself with the availability of copyright-protected material. From an economic perspective this has not been necessary because unless the author publishes their work, they will not be able to benefit economically from the exploitation of the rights. Questions relating to access do not arise since this presumes that an author that has invested time and effort, and money, in creating a work will want to benefit from the economic exploitation of the rights. This presumption operates in line with the incentive-based theory of copyright law – the author receives exclusive rights in return for the creation of a work that they are able to use and profit on by making the work available, and will, for this reason, decide, or continue to, do so. At the same time, the concept of exclusivity of rights embeds the notion that it is the owner of the rights that decides when, how, and if at all, the work will be made available to the public (on the market). After all, copyright law affords protection also to unpublished works. This places copyright on a slightly different spectrum than other intellectual property rights, such as patents or trademarks, in which respectively the invention is published following a successful application or the mark, while also published, is required to be used for protection to remain.[323] Nevertheless, comparable requirements have existed in copyright law.[324]

---

* This chapter is based on the author's ongoing research in Szkalej, K., 'Consumption of digital works – an analysis of EU copyright law within the framework of lawful acquisition and use of protected content' (forthcoming 2019).

323. *See* for example Art. 98 European Patent Convention and Art. 16 Directive 2015/2436 to approximate the laws of the Member States relating to trademarks (Recast).

324. For example, under Art. 5(1) of the original text of the Berne Convention as agreed on 9 September 1886 the exclusive right of making or authorising a translation of a work expired ten years after publication of the original version. The subsequent Paris Act of 4 May 1886 changed the wording of Art. 5(1) but maintained a rule whereby that right will 'cease to exist' after the same period.

The dissemination of protected content has historically necessitated the involvement of commercial actors at various intervals in the process, such as book publishers, record labels, film producers, that create a finished product that can be transported to retail stores, broadcasting organisations, or cinemas. Because of such commercial actors' involvement in the product creation process and in the distribution chain, it has also not been necessary to encourage the dissemination of content – a publisher or record label that must invest in the creation and duplication of the product and potentially its marketing has an incentive to put a work on the market in a way akin to a pharmaceutical company that has invested in the creation of a medicinal product and seeks, firstly or supplementarily, to recoup the investments made.

The territorial nature of copyright protection and fragmented legal approaches in the Member States either generally or within specific sectors create sometimes challenges for various stakeholders to enter specific markets or simply make it not viable from a commercial perspective. The EU legislator, driven foremost by internal market considerations, has on numerous occasions taken steps to facilitate the making available of content, by primarily aiming to make the clearance of rights easier. In the early 1990s the SatCab Directive, in this context, except clarifying the legal status of satellite broadcasts, introduced an extended collective licensing mechanism by permitting Member States to allow a collective agreement between a broadcasting organisation and a collecting society to extend under certain circumstances to rightholders who are not represented by the collecting society, and mandating representation for cable retransmissions.[325] In 2014 the CRM Directive introduced an administrative framework for multi-territorial licensing of rights in musical works for online use in the internal market.[326] Other previous attempts, while slightly more direct, have either been limited to a specific type of work and for the benefit of specific institutions,[327] discretionary and limited to events of general public interest,[328] or required the *promotion* of access to European works and reservation of a proportion of the transmission time for such works, in both cases 'where practicable and by appropriate means', yet requiring that certain works are not transmitted outside periods agreed with rightholders, without regulating such agreements.[329]

325. SatCab Directive, Arts 3 and 9 respectively.
326. *See* especially Arts 23–24 and 29–31 CRM Directive.
327. Orphan Works Directive, Arts 1 and 6.
328. Audiovisual Media Services Directive, Art. 14.
329. Audiovisual Media Services Directive, Arts 13, 16, 17, and 8, respectively. The Directive is currently under review; *see* Commission, 'Proposal for a Directive amending Directive 2010/13/EU on the coordination of certain provisions laid down by law, regulation or administrative action in Member States concerning the provision of audiovisual media services in view of changing market realities' COM/2016/0287 final. *See also* Art. 7 of the current directive, *encouraging* the gradual making accessible of media services to persons with a visual or hearing disability. With regards to this, very important legislative steps have been taken to respond to the concerns and needs of persons with a disability. *See*, in particular, Directive 2017/1564 of 13 September 2017 on certain permitted uses of certain works and other subject matter protected by copyright and related rights for the benefit of persons who are blind, visually impaired or otherwise print-disabled, and Regulation 2017/1563 of 13 September 2017 on the cross-border exchange between the Union and third countries of accessible format copies of certain works and other subject matter protected by copyright and related rights for the benefit of persons who are blind, visually impaired or otherwise print-disabled.

Most of these legislative interventions are soft in the sense that they promote industry-led market developments and solutions - while a limited institutional framework is created, the industry is left to itself in the belief that market forces and competition will ultimately determine the best outcomes. Arguably, this has not always been working - most recently the European legislator has adopted a regulation to ensure access to online content services in the EU and in reaching this objective it attained a very different approach than previously within the copyright sector.

§6.02 CROSS-BORDER PORTABILITY OF CONTENT SERVICES: THE STREAMING REGULATION

In 2015 the Commission proposed as part of its *Digital Single Market Strategy*[330] the introduction of a *regulation* to ensure access to online content services in the EU. Passed approximately 1.5 years after the initial proposal,[331] and applicable since 1 April 2018,[332] the instrument is important for at least two reasons.

It is the first ever Regulation in the area of EU copyright law, the effect of which is its direct applicability in the Member States and binding character,[333] and the uniform interpretation and application of its provisions throughout the Union. From a legal hierarchical point of view, it places the rules above the InfoSoc Directive and the remaining directives where they may conflict, and it guarantees that rightholders and online service providers from different Member States are subject to the 'exact same rules',[334] in contrast to, for example, the discretionary framework of limitations and exceptions established by the InfoSoc Directive. To this extent it is worth noting that the only caveat made, in recital (34), concerns the application of the CRM Directive, which the Regulation does not affect.[335]

Second, but equally importantly, the Regulation directly regulates market relationships in the context of the provision of online content services by *obliging* market actors to provide under certain circumstances access to content and to have the same offering, and *preventing* rightholders as well as service providers from departing from this obligation by way of agreement. In this way the Regulation does to some extent affect the prerogatives ordinarily available to holders of exclusive rights, which too is a measure that European copyright law has generally avoided. In this sense, the Regulation constitutes an important sector-specific piece of legislation in what can be described as the area of *consumer copyright law*.[336]

330. COM(2015) 192 final.
331. Commission proposal, COM(2015) 627 final, published on 9 December 2015, adopted version signed by the European Parliament and Council on 14 June 2017.
332. Article 11(2). *See* Corrigendum to Regulation (EU) 2017/1128 on cross-border portability of online content services in the internal market [2017] OJ L 198/42.
333. *See* TFEU, Art. 288.
334. COM(2015) 627 final, p. 4.
335. As well as Arts 101 and 102 TFEU, concerning competition law (recital (33)).
336. *See also* Arts 5(1)(g)-(h), 6(1)(r)-(s) 9(2)(c), 16(m), and 17 Consumer Rights Directive, and generally Commission, 'Proposal for a Directive on certain aspects concerning contracts for the supply of digital content' COM(2015) 634 final.

For the sake of simplicity and for reasons explained below, *Streaming Regulation* constitutes a more appropriate and less equivocal short form and designation of the subject matter of the Regulation than *Cross-Border Portability of Online Content Services* (*Regulation*) or simply *Portability* (*Regulation*) and will, therefore, be used henceforth.

[A] Portability or Access?

The Streaming Regulation introduces a common approach to what it, rather oxymoronically, describes as 'cross-border portability of online content services'.[337] The main issue that the Regulation addresses is the potential lack of access to online services when consumers temporarily visit another Member State, an issue which is recognised in recital (3):

> Consumers increasingly enter into arrangements with service providers for the provision of online content services. However, consumers that are temporarily present in a Member State other than their Member State of residence often cannot continue to access and use the online content services that they have lawfully acquired the right to access and use in their Member State of residence.

Consequently, at its core, the Regulation requires that services lawfully provided in a Member State must be made available to the subscribers of such services when they are temporarily present in another Member State.[338] The underlying aim is, therefore, the management of reasonable expectations - consumers pay for access to content in their home Member State, travel to another Member State, for example, for holidays, and find out that they are not able to connect to the service or that the content which is available through the service in their home Member State is not available in the other Member State. The need to introduce an obligation such as this one for paid services seems rather counter-intuitive in the ubiquitous networked environment. Nevertheless, lack, or denial, of access for paid services was an issue that transpired early in the legislative process, which is all the more surprising since European markets provide access to over 500 million consumers. Prior to its initial proposal, the Commission launched in December 2013 a public consultation on the review of the EU copyright rules, which included a number of questions on cross-border access to online content.[339] The consultation generated a response amount of more than 9,500 replies to the consultation, of which 5,622 (58%) responses came from 'end users/consumers'.[340] According to the Commission Consultation Report, 'the vast majority' of end user/consumer respondents reported issues when attempting to access online services in other Member States:

337. Streaming Regulation, Art. 1(1).
338. Streaming Regulation, Arts 1(1) and 3(1).
339. Notably the first seven questions.
340. Commission, 'Report on the responses to the Public Consultation on the Review of the EU Copyright Rules', DG Internal Market and Services, July 2014 (Commission Consultation Report), p. 5.

> Many report seeking to view a video online via YouTube, but being blocked by a national collective management organisation for copyrighted content. Others signal the lack of access to popular video on demand services such as Netflix and the BBC iPlayer, which are currently only available to the residents of some EU Member States. Music services such as iTunes and Spotify are also criticised for either not being accessible in certain countries or only featuring a limited online catalogue compared to the one they offer in other countries. More generally, consumer [sic] report being frequently confronted with messages indicating that a given item of content/service is not available in their country. The experience is all the more frustrating, some say, when it happens to people seeking to view or listen to content from their home country when in another EU country.[341]

This highlights three relevant issues:

(A) the unavailability of a specific service for residents of a Member State,
(B) the unavailability of a specific service in a Member State for visiting residents of the Member State in which the service is ordinarily available,
(C) the lack of identical content in Member States in which the service is available and can be used either by residents of that Member State or another Member State. This can be divided into the following two related issues:
  (C1) the unavailability of specific content on a service provided in one Member State, but availability of that content on the same service in another Member State
  (C2) the unavailability of specific content to residents of a Member State in which the content is available when such residents access the service from a Member State in which the content is unavailable (C1).

The obligation to make content available to consumers is contained in Article 3 Streaming Regulation and requires that providers of paid online content services:

> enable a subscriber who is temporarily present in a Member State to *access* and *use* the online content service in the same manner *as in the Member State of residence*, including by providing access to the same content, on the same range and number of devices, for the same number of users and with the same range of functionalities [emphasis added].

Consequently, the Regulation deals with issue (B) and (C2) identified above, i.e., a service which is available to residents (subscribers) of a Member State must be made available to those residents when they are visiting another Member State, but not with issues (A) or (C1) which is also made clear at the end of recital (12):

> The concept of *cross-border portability of online content services* should be distinguished from that of *cross-border access by consumers to online content services provided in a Member State other than their Member State of residence*, which is not covered by this Regulation [emphasis added].

Moreover, recital (17) provides that:

> This Regulation should apply only to online content services which subscribers can effectively access and use in their Member State of residence without being limited to a specific location, as it is not appropriate to require providers of online

341. Commission Consultation Report, p. 6.

content services that do not offer portable online content services in the Member State of residence of a subscriber to do so across borders.

Hence, what constitutes *cross-border access by consumers to (ubiquitous) online content services provided in, or targeting, their Member State of residence*, the Regulation describes as *cross-border portability of online content services*. As suggested further below, there is an issue with important terms in the Regulation, however the *portable* nature of an online content service consists in the effective access and use of the online content service in the Member State of residence without being limited to a specific location,[342] i.e., it is infrastructurally not intended to be used solely in one location, as opposed to, for example, a television subscription service, which these days often delivers content over the Internet network (IPTV).[343] Hence, with reference to this conceptual framework, the Regulation concerns exclusively *cross-border access* to *portable online content services*.[344]

[B] Scope of Application: Streaming and Downloading?

While some provisions of the Regulation are to some extent self-explanatory, there is remarkably no unequivocal indication of the mode of content acquisition that the Regulation is intended to apply to, or not apply to. Instead, reference is made to access to, and use of, *online content services* throughout the Regulation. As indicated above, the underlying problem is, however, access to *content*, not the service as such. Having access to, and using, an online content service may very well occur already when a consumer has logged in to the service and is browsing the content catalogue, without necessarily consuming (viewing, listening to, reading, or as the case may be – playing) the content or having that possibility. After all, while some paid services require the payment of a subscription fee before the content catalogue can be viewed, others require payment of such a fee, or a one-time fee, once the consumer wishes to consume the content but allow the browsing of the content catalogue before the completion of a transaction. recital (15) states however that the Regulation:

> should apply to online content services that providers [having cleared the relevant rights] provide to their subscribers on the basis of a contract, by any means including *streaming, downloading,* through applications or *other technique which allows use of that content* [emphasis added].

As the Regulation does not define these terms nor place them in the context of the functionality of an online content service, it is useful to first briefly look at the different modes of content acquisition for the purpose of their subsequent consumption.

342. Streaming Regulation, Art. 2(6).
343. Where the same service offers however the possibility to view broadcast content on another device than the connected TV, it will be considered a *portable* service. This is sometimes referred to as Web TV.
344. But, since the concept 'portability' is part of the definition of 'online content service' in Art. 2(5), *cross-border access* to *online content services*.

[1] Modes of Content Acquisition

In the context of consumption of digital works two general forms of legal acquisition of content can be discerned.

On the one hand consumers can pay a one-time fee and download actual files to their device. The control and capacity to consume that a consumer is often understood to be able to exercise over such files is either permanent (indefinite) or time-limited. The nomenclature used to describe the initiation of such one-time fee transactions are usually '*Buy*' for seemingly permanent downloads, and '*Rent*' for time-limited downloads (rental downloads). In the case of the latter type of transaction usually special software is required for consumers to be able to read or watch the content, while in the former not necessarily; such software making the files unusable after the relevant rental period or removing the relevant files from the device. Current examples of major digital marketplaces allowing such acquisition of different types of content are the *Apple iTunes Store*, *Google Play Store* and *Microsoft Store*, as well as gaming console-specific stores, such as the *PlayStation Store*.[345] It ought to be noted that 'renting' does not always necessitate a download of a file in the sense as described here. This depends on the technological solution used by the supplier, the content in question, as well as the mode of accessing the content. For example, the supplier can make a rented film immediately available for watching, instead of requiring or allowing the downloading of the file,[346] or it may make a book available to the consumer in a closed environment on its servers without allowing the consumer to download the file. E-rentals can, therefore, be divided into the following two types:

rental downloads, which necessitate a download of the file; and

downloadable rentals, which cannot be downloaded, but may, if the supplier allows it.

Alternatively, consumers can pay a recurring fee, such as a monthly subscription fee, and instead receive access to a catalogue of content which they can consume without having to first download a copy of the file to their device; the access to such a catalogue being provided either as a standalone service or as part of a bundle of services.[347] This mode of content acquisition, and necessarily consumption, is popularly known as *streaming*. Current examples of major standalone streaming services are *Spotify*, *Tidal* and *Apple Music* for music, *Netflix*, *Amazon Prime* and *HBO Go* for videos, and *Storytel* for books.[348] Similar models exist for video games, for example, *PlayStation Now*, although due to the dynamic experience and amount of data, including audiovisual data, that is required for the experience, some amount of

345. And until October 2017 – *Xbox Games Store*.
346. Which is often the case when the digital content marketplace is accessed through a media box, such as AppleTV, connected to the TV, as opposed to accessing the same marketplace through the personal computer.
347. Such as in the example above, whereby a 'portable' Web TV service is offered as part of a non-'portable' IPTV contract.
348. That is e-books and audio books.

downloading is usually required for solely practical purposes. This is normally an act that the consumer cannot initiate or even prevent.

A similar categorisation was made in the Commission's Impact Assessment preceding the proposal for the Regulation, with reference however to the type of service, rather than the mode of consumption. According to the Assessment, *transactional services* incorporate purchases and rentals, while *subscription services* incorporate streaming.[349]

The difference between these two modes of content acquisition, except the type of payment and the á la carte or all-you-can-eat buffet character, relates to the degree of control that a consumer can usually exercise. When content is '*bought*' (purchased) for a one-time fee and necessarily downloaded to a device such as a computer, consumers often have simultaneous access to the actual computer file by other means than by the designated software which was used for purchase and subsequent, necessary, download, such as Apple's iTunes software which provides access to the iTunes Store and is simultaneously a music or video player.[350] Being able to exercise control of the computer file means that consumers can use software of their choice, for example, specific music or video players, to play the content, transfer the downloaded *file* to another part of the hard disk, to physical backup storage, cloud storage, a portable device etc. Although the ability to access a computer file or transfer it to a portable device is *not* equivalent to being able to play (consume) the content on that portable device or with other music or video playing software, the common denominator for all these acts is that they can be carried out offline.[351] Streaming, on the other hand, requires consumers to maintain a continuous connection to the servers of the service provider while the content is being consumed because the consumer device needs to be able to continuously access the data, as well as maintain access to the content catalogue. 'Permanent downloads' are instead accessible directly from the device to which they were downloaded following a transaction, and also often from the portable device to which they were subsequently transferred. Hence, in the case of purchases and rentals, while access to the digital marketplace is only necessary to acquire the content (complete the transaction) but not necessarily to consume it, in the case of streaming access to the service is continuously required during the act of consumption. In other words, in the case of streaming, access to (acquisition of), and consumption of, content are virtually equivalent events which do not require an intermediary act.

Admittedly a number of streaming services offer so-called offline use which enables consumers to consume content without having to be connected to the servers

349. *See* Commission, 'Impact Assessment accompanying the document Proposal for a Regulation of the European Parliament and of the Council to ensure the cross-border portability of online content services in the internal market' (Staff Working Document) SWD(2015) 270 final (Commission Impact Assessment), pp. 7–8.
350. A personal media library manager.
351. It is however not a natural characteristic of digital purchases. It is possible, or not possible, because content protection (the DRM system) has been designed in that way or no protection has been introduced. While desirable, DRM systems need not an Internet connection to be effective. *See* generally on DRM in Chapter 8 below.

of the service. Such offline use does involve the downloading of a file, but it differs from 'permanent downloads' because the entire act of consumption occurs within a closed technological environment, such as the Spotify computer software or Spotify mobile app, there is generally no access to such downloaded files otherwise than through that function-limited environment, and the consumer is either expected to reconnect after a specific number of days, for example, until the next billing period so that the validity of rights can be verified, or the downloaded files are *consumable* for a limited number of days such as a week, after which they will be deleted or rendered unconsumable, despite being stored on the device and need to be re-downloaded again. In this way 'offline streaming', while being reminiscent of 'permanent downloads', is technologically comparable to 'rental downloads', although for the latter consumers may exercise similar control as for 'permanent downloads' depending on the digital marketplace in question, whereas for 'offline streaming' such a possibility is not intended to exist at all. From the perspective of consumer experience, 'downloadable rentals' are similar to streaming because the content is available through the supplier's closed environment, the consumer cannot normally exercise any control over the file, and the content can normally only be accessed online. The difference, however, is the one-time fee character of the transaction, usually shorter availability of content (such as twenty-four or forty-eight hours as opposed to one month), and the unavailability of the remaining content catalogue following the completion of the transaction.

[2] Enabling Access to, and Use of, an Online Content Service

The question is therefore whether 'by any means, including streaming, downloading ...' in recital (15), and therefore the Regulation, as a whole, is meant to cover *streaming, permanent downloads*, and *electronic rentals* (rental downloads and downloadable rentals) or merely *streaming* and *offline use of streaming services* which necessitates downloading.

Regrettably, there is an issue with definitions in the Regulation. Key terms such as *access* or *use*, which are used throughout the Regulation and especially in Article 3 and in the definitions of other terms, are left undefined, while others are circular, or even redundant, such as *temporarily present in a Member State*[352] or indeed *portable*. The obscurity of concepts makes it unnecessarily difficult to establish whether the obligation actually covers something more than merely enabling the *ability to browse* the online content catalogue.

Article 3(1) Streaming Regulation obliges service providers to enable a subscriber 'to access and use the online content service' when they are temporarily visiting another Member State. Must such access and use of the service necessitate the immediate ability to consume content? Reasonable as such a requirement may be, it precludes permanent downloads and rental downloads. As noted above, the ability to access and use a streaming service is equivalent to the ability to consume content

352. 'Being present in a Member State other than the Member State of residence for a limited period of time' (Art. 2(4)).

because access to the streaming service necessitates access to the content – access and use of the *service* is equivalent to access and use of the *content*. The same can be said of downloadable rentals. In the case of permanent downloads and rental downloads, on the other hand, access and use of the service (the digital marketplace) involves the conclusion of a transaction that, for the purpose of access and use of the content, first requires a download. Since actual access to, and use of, content will in most cases occur completely offline[353] and certainly not on an accessible website, access to and use of content does not simultaneously involve access to and use of an online content service. This, if it is accepted that an online content service is also one that offers purchasing and e-renting.

The circular definition of 'online content service' in Article 2(5) defines online content services as essentially services provided on agreed terms and online, 'the main feature of which is the provision of access to, and the use of [*content*] (...) whether in *a linear* or *an on-demand manner* [emphasis added]'.[354] While the latter two terms are also not defined in the Regulation, they are usually used as alternatives to each other and are understood to respectively refer to 'live' transmissions and transmissions which can be initiated by a consumer during a time they see fit (i.e., they are non-linear transmissions). The difference between the two terms relates solely to the time of consumption and the ability to select content out of an available catalogue pre-selected by the service provider and not the consumer.[355] In either case, it is the service that controls the availability of content; it is the service that exercises technological control over the content and therefore over the capacity to consume the content. Á la carte content, purchases and rental downloads, is available *on demand* only because the consumer has downloaded a file to their device and exercises (variable) control over that file, without having to maintain a connection to the servers of the service, as opposed to all-you-can eat buffets and downloadable rentals.

Oddly, recital (9) of the Regulation, in explaining that transmission of content protected by copyright requires the authorisation of rightholders, states that 'This is equally true when such transmission takes place for the purpose of allowing a consumer to carry out a download *in order to use an online content service*'.

Hence, on a literal reading the argument could be made that permanently downloaded content is also provided on demand since the consumer may choose when to play such content once they have purchased and subsequently downloaded it. This does not, however, correspond to the established meaning of *on demand*. In the same way it could be argued that an online seller of music CDs or DVD films provides access to content, which is also digital, and would have to be considered an online content service the main feature of which is the provision of access to content in an on-demand manner. Admittedly, access to digital content stored on a tangible medium is delayed

353. A DRM system may require authentication with the supplier's server, but this is the individual choice of the supplier.
354. The quoted sentence refers to Art. 2(5)(ii) and constitutes an alternative to point (i) which defines an online content service as, essentially, a service provided on agreed terms and online 'which is an audiovisual service defined in point (a) of Art. 1 of Directive 2010/13/EU', i.e., a linear or on-demand audiovisual media service.
355. *See* analogously Art. 1(e) and (g) Audiovisual Media Services Directive.

because of the need to post, or pick up, the CD or DVD, but so is á la carte ordering because the file must be downloaded first.

This makes it difficult to conclude that the Regulation includes this kind of content acquisition. The same cannot, however, be held for downloadable rentals which are after all consumed in an on-demand manner in the same way as content which is consumed through a streaming service.

[3] *Exclusive Rights Affected*

An alternative approach to this issue could be to base the assessment on the type of exclusive rights that a service provider would have to license to be able to offer their service, apart from the right of reproduction. Notwithstanding the rental right,[356] on-demand transmissions are encapsulated by the communication to the public right, as opposed to the distribution right, the latter of which requires that the transaction be considered a *sale*.[357] Unfortunately, whether permanent downloads fall under Article 3 or Article 4 InfoSoc Directive is still highly debated and the CJEU has not yet had the opportunity to cast light on this issue. From a transactional perspective, there appears however not to be any overriding reason to consider a purchase transaction for a one-time fee and designated by the word '*Buy*' as something else than a sale within the meaning of Article 4 InfoSoc Directive. Where additionally the content is DRM-protected and is exclusive to the *buyer*, the specific digital file possesses far better properties than tangible goods such as a printed book, a music CD or a DVD film in terms of excluding consumption by others. Accepting this conclusion means that permanent downloads fall outside the scope of the Regulation because products which are distributed, as opposed to communicated, to the public are not provided on demand in a materially different way than a music CD purchased in an online shop.

[4] *Subscribers Who Subscribe*

That access and use of online content services are intended to be provided for *subscribers* may suggest that solely streaming is intended to fall within the scope of the Regulation because it is difficult to consider consumers who complete one-time fee transactions and receive access to one item, permanently or not, as subscribers. Article 2(1) defines however a subscriber as 'any consumer who, on the basis of a contract for the provision of an online content service with a provider whether against payment of money or without such payment, is entitled to access and use such services in the Member State of residence', without there being reference anywhere to the recurring or continuous nature of such access over a period of time, which the word *subscriber* or *subscription* normally implies.

356. Which, it is presumed, could also apply to digital content delivered over the Internet, as is the case of lending. *See* C-174/15 *VOB*. On this case *see* further Chapter 7 (§7.03) below. Arguably an 'online' rental right overlaps in its entirety with the communication to the public right.
357. *See* Chapter 4 (§4.02) above.

Nevertheless, recital (26) provides that the Regulation should 'enable subscribers to enjoy online content services *to which they have subscribed* in their Member State of residence when they are temporarily present in another Member State [emphasis added]', which reasonably suggests that the service in question ought to be a 'subscription service'. This sentence, and especially emphasised wording, was not part of the original proposal but was introduced by the European Parliament.[358] Moreover, the European Economic and Social Committee seems to have had exclusively subscription services in mind, and therefore what is denoted here as 'streaming and offline-streaming', when it explained in its opinion that the proposal 'covers content that is: distributed by broadcasting organisations or information society service providers; linear or on-demand; downloaded, streamed or delivered by other means; provided by large companies or by SMEs; *against payment (subscription) or free of charge* [emphasis added]'.[359]

As noted above, the Commission's Impact Assessment distinguishes between *transactional services* and *subscription services*. Accepting the equivalence of what the Commission called subscription services in its Impact Assessment, and the implication in recital (26) does not only categorically exclude permanent downloads but also e-rentals from the scope of the Regulation, since neither are part of a subscription service.

[5] Looking Beyond Access to an Online Service

It is noteworthy that a binding and directly applicable legal act which contains obligations that are fundamental to the functioning of the digital internal market makes it so difficult to establish the particular object(s) of the obligation. There is surprisingly little guidance in the legislative work preceding the adoption of the Regulation, with very few details on this particular question in the Commission's communication. The Committee of the Regions limited itself to a laconic, yet differentiating, statement that the proposal 'seeks to enable users who have purchased online content or taken out a subscription in their country of origin to access them ...',[360] while the Economic and Social Committee, as noted above, although referring both to downloading and streaming, qualified the form of payment as subscription. The different Committees of the European Parliament, which was the body that proposed to introduce the excerpt recital (26) quoted above, seem to also have slightly different understandings, referring on the one hand either to 'any digital content lawfully purchased' or on the other hand

358. European Parliament, 'Position of the European Parliament with a view to the adoption of Regulation (EU) 2017/ ... of the European Parliament and of the Council on cross-border portability of online content services in the internal market' EP-PE_TC1-COD(2015)0284 adopted at first reading on 18 May 2017, p. 16.
359. European Economic and Social Committee, 'Opinion on the Proposal for a Regulation of the European Parliament and of the Council on ensuring the cross-border portability of online content services in the internal market' INT/781 27 April 2016, p. 6.
360. European Committee of the Regions, 'Modernisation of the EU Copyright Rules' (Opinion) SEDEC-VI-009, 8 April 2016, p. 11 para. 12.

'online content to which [consumers] have lawful access'.[361] It is rather 'temporarily present' and 'Member State of residence' that have occupied centre stage in the legislative work; concepts which are arguably least difficult to define.

The potential exclusion of permanent downloads and e-rentals from the scope of the Regulation is difficult to accept since there is no convincing reason to treat permanent downloads and e-rentals differently from streaming, from the perspective of the desire to prevent the inaccessibility of content during temporary visits in another Member State. The de facto issue that the Regulation attempts to resolve originates from how technology is being used, rather than how it can be used, which is why the adopted provisions require that [content providers] enable *access and use of a service*, the main feature of which is the provision of access to, and the use of, content in a linear or an on-demand manner. Such a construction of the obligation, with a view of resolving the issue of content accessibility, only makes sense if access to the service and consumption of content are virtually equivalent events.

The Commission's Impact Assessment drew the conclusion that cross-border accessibility issues do not occur for transactional services which require a download (permanent downloads, rental downloads)[362] which may suggest that the Regulation does not in fact concern such modes of content acquisition. As for downloadable rentals, although the Assessment concluded that such issues do occur,[363] the only example provided, out of eleven different examples, related to the inconvenience of having to download an already rented film prior to travelling to another Member State instead of being able to rely on the 'streaming feature'.[364] The reason why such issues do not occur for transactional services, at least permanent downloads and rental downloads, may have nothing to do with natural market constraints but the voluntary abstention from the use of technology in this way, compared to denying access to, or offering different content on, subscription services while visiting another Member State. A supplier of digital content, who may simultaneously be a manufacturer of the device on which that content will be consumed, may very well use technology in such a way that the device, as opposed to an online content service, the marketplace from which the content has been acquired, will refuse to play the content when the consumer is present in another Member State, following the establishment of that a fact, for example, on the basis of the mobile network the consumer's mobile phone has connected to in the other Member State or the IP address that that network will assign to the device. In such a situation the consumer will not be able to watch, listen to, read, or play the content, yet will not be accessing, nor using, an online content service

361. *See* European Parliament, 'Report on the proposal for a regulation of the European Parliament and of the Council on ensuring the cross-border portability of online content services in the internal market' Committee on Legal Affairs, A8-0378/2016, 9 December 2016, pp. 43, 70. *See also* p. 102.
362. Commission Impact Assessment, p. 7.
363. Commission Impact Assessment, p. 7, 'The question of portability however arises where the content is accessible via a digital locker or where it is streamed by the service provider, which is typical for rental, as in these cases the access to content is not within the consumer's control'.
364. Commission Impact Assessment, p. 9, 'If a user of the transactional Universciné (Belgium) film service wants to watch an already rented film while staying temporarily in the Netherlands, he has to download it before travelling – he will not be able to rely on the streaming feature'.

because everything is instead localised to the consumer's device. While preventing a consumer from being able to play content which is stored on their device is counter-intuitive, so is the denial of access to services which a consumer is paying for. From a commercial perspective, controlling the behaviour of devices in such a way may, for example, effectively enable a content provider to require an additional payment for such *extraterritorial* access to content stored on their own device.

The obligation to enable access and use of a service is complemented by a number of supplementary obligations which fall within the ambit of data protection law and it is simply desirable for individual content providers to be able to definitely ascertain whether those obligations, as opposed to voluntary measures which may overlap with legal obligations, also apply to them. In this context, it may be useful to refer to the Article 29 Working Party, an advisory body set up under the old data protection framework,[365] which opined, in relation to the question of whether the concept of personal data also incorporates (dynamic) IP addresses, that 'unless [a service provider] is in a position to distinguish with absolute certainty that the data corresponds to users that cannot be identified [and therefore that the framework will not apply], it will have to treat all IP information as personal data, to be on the safe side'.[366] Such a rhetoric would require compliance with the Regulation regardless of which modes of content acquisition fall within the ambit of the Regulation. However, since the supplementary obligations concern *inter alia* the obligation to cease the provision of cross-border access in specific circumstances, the inclusion of transactional services may in fact force such services to act in a way that they are today not acting according to the Commission Impact Assessment; which is another reason for making it difficult to hold that the Regulation is intended to cover such services.

By not incorporating permanent downloads within the ambit of the Regulation, as is suggested here, the European legislator has drawn a line between content acquired in such a way and content that is streamed, making it clear that the latter requires different legal treatment from the former. Such an outcome, a legal intervention on the market which differentiates between forms of content acquisition, can only be reasonably justified if the transactions, as seen from the perspective of an online marketplace offering digital content, are governed by different exclusive rights, because the exclusive rights provide, after all, different types of exclusive control once payment is completed and content becomes available for the consumer. The scope of the Regulation, in light of the issues that it is intended to address, may therefore very well imply indirectly that the making available of permanent downloads for a one-time fee is simply perceived as constituting a form of dissemination falling under Article 4 InfoSoc Directive, i.e. distribution. That is so because that provision, by virtue of requiring that the transaction be a sale, delimits the control that may be exercised after the transaction is completed and cross-border access issues do not therefore arise as a

365. *See* Art. 29 of Directive 95/46/EC on the protection of individuals with regard to the processing of personal data and on the free movement of such data.
366. Article 29 Working Party, Opinion 4/2007 on the concept of personal data, WP 136, adopted 20 June 2007 p. 17.

matter of law, making therefore legal intervention unnecessary.[367] Analogously, the reason why a book seller is not entitled to decide when a book is available, and when it is not available, for reading by the purchaser *after* it has been sold and collected, is attributable to the change of ownership in the product that was purchased, and not because the book seller is unable to exercise that kind of intrusive control.[368] Ultimately, however, it is a matter for the CJEU to decide.

[C] Compliance

In connection with the obligation under Article 3 to enable access to online content services to subscribers who are temporarily present in another Member State, the Streaming Regulation imposes a number of qualitative and administrative requirements that online content service providers must comply with.

[1] Quality of Service

Most importantly, yet not surprisingly, the obligation requires that the service be essentially identical as in the Member State of subscription (residence). That is, subscribers must be able to access the service in the same way as in the Member State of residence, they must have access to the same content and on the same number and type of devices, and the same functionality.[369] Interestingly, the obligation also requires that the same number of users receive access. One question that arises in connection to this is whether it is a prerogative of the service provider, or alternatively the holder of the exclusive rights, to exclusively offer access to the service in one Member State at a time; i.e., when the actual paying subscriber (customer) connects to the service from another Member State, need the service not simultaneously be available to the remaining users who receive access as part of the same subscription when those users connect from the Member State of subscription or a third Member State?

The arguably broad definition of a subscriber in Article 2(1) potentially precludes this,[370] nevertheless, such a situation cannot ever arise because Article 4 localises cross-border access to an online content service to the Member State of residence. Hence, if each member of a family of four resident in Sweden connects to an online content service from different Member States, for example, if the parents connect during their holidays in Portugal, while the daughter and son each connect from France

367. But not necessarily undesirable, at least for reasons of legal certainty.
368. Whether the suggested applicability of Art. 4 InfoSoc Directive means that so-called digital exhaustion applies is an entirely different, albeit related, question. *See* further Chapter 7 below.
369. Streaming Regulation Art. 3(1).
370. '*Any* consumer who, on the basis of *a* contract for the provision of an online content service with a provider (...) is *entitled* to access and use such service in the Member State of residence [emphasis added]'.

and Italy during their summer language courses, each of them will be connecting to the service from Sweden for the purpose of the Regulation.[371]

The identity of the service, and indeed the localised character of access, means that the service provider cannot require an additional fee for the provision of cross-border access and, for example, offer it as a premium service. Such a prohibition is however expressly provided in Article 3(2).

Moreover, while the service provider need not ensure an identical quality of delivery of the service, unless the contrary has been expressly agreed between the service and the subscriber, the service must provide the subscriber with information about the quality of delivery before providing access to the service, and cannot take any action to reduce the quality of delivery of the service,[372] such as configuring the service in such a way that subscribers accessing the service from another Member State will only be able to view the content in low-quality.

[2] Verification of Member State of Residence

As the obligation to enable cross-border access to an online content service is intended to facilitate access from another Member State to services which individuals have subscribed to in their Member State of residence, the Regulation requires under Article 5(1) that the service provider verifies the Member State of residence, 'at the conclusion and upon the renewal of a contract' for the provision of the service. Such verification may be repeated if the provider has reasonable doubts about the subscriber's Member State of residence,[373] which is an issue that may come up if the subscriber has never connected to the service, or only once during initial access, from what the service provider determined to be the Member State of residence. Regrettably, the Regulation does not prescribe any time periods after which such doubts may reasonably arise but mentions only that a re-verification may occur in the course of the duration of the contract. Another question is whether the obligation to verify residence at the 'renewal of a contract' also refers to the use of the service during the subsequent month if the contract has no specific duration, such as most streaming services which provide access on a monthly basis, as opposed to Web TV services which may be part of an IPTV twelve-month contract. In such cases the provider will be entitled (obligated) to conduct verification on a monthly basis since the contract expires at the end of the billing period and is renewed every time the subscriber continues to use the service. In this way it could be argued that the Member State of residence can be verified a number of times during a thirty-day period. Nevertheless, the entitlement to re-verify the Member State of residence must be viewed in the context of the subscriber's *temporary* presence in another Member State, which, as further discussed below, may be longer than merely a two-week holiday.

Verification of the Member State of residence could have been discretionary instead of obligatory because some service providers are present in all EU Member

371. This rule is further discussed below.
372. Streaming Regulation, Art. 3(3)-(4).
373. Streaming Regulation, Art. 5(2).

States and may not be interested in verifying the specific Member State of residence as long as they are satisfied with the fact that the subscriber is resident in any Member State, while others are only present in one or few Member States and may, therefore, wish to verify that the subscriber is indeed a resident of the specific Member State targeted or uses a form of payment allowing the service provider to determine that the payment is originating from the Member State of operation. Concerns that subscribers resident in one Member State will subscribe to the service provided in another Member State can reasonably be justified only because of differences in subscription fees, rather than the availability of other content on the same service in another Member State (problem (C1) identified above in [A]), however such fragmentation intuitively conflicts the very idea of the Geo-Blocking Regulation,[374] which was proposed as part of the same package as the Streaming Regulation. Not surprisingly that Regulation does not apply to copyright and related rights,[375] nor to 'purely internal situations, where all relevant elements of the transaction are confined within one single Member State'.[376]

Instead, the Streaming Regulation entitles rightholders to authorise the provision of the service without verification of the Member State of residence, who may withdraw such authorisation at any time subject to giving reasonable notice.[377]

As the obligation to verify residence requires the processing of personal data, Article 5(1) requires that the means used to verify residence are *reasonable, proportionate* and *effective*. This is grounded in the need to limit the interference with subscribers' privacy, even though, as suggested above, a service provider might be entitled to verify residence a number of times in the course of a month. Consequently, unless the subscriber's Member State of residence can be verified with sufficient certainty on the basis of a *single* means of verification, and depending on the type of online content service,[378] the provision prescribes that not more than *two* means of verification may be used from the following exclusive list:

374. Regulation (EU) 2018/302 on addressing unjustified geo-blocking and other forms of discrimination based on customers' nationality, place of residence or place of establishment within the internal market and amending Regulations (EC) No 2006/2004 and (EU) 2017/2394 and Directive 2009/22/EC (Geo-Blocking Regulation).
375. Geo-Blocking Regulation, Art. 1(5).
376. Geo-Blocking Regulation, Art. 1(6).
377. Streaming Regulation, Art. 5(4).
378. Streaming Regulation, recital (26).

Permissible Means of Verification of Member State of Residence	
(a) an identity card (b) payment details such as the bank account or credit or debit card number of the subscriber (c) the place of installation of a set top box, a decoder or a similar device used for supply of services to the subscriber (d) the payment by the subscriber of a licence fee for other services provided in the Member State, such as public service broadcasting (e) an Internet or telephone service supply contract or any similar type of contract linking the subscriber to the Member State (f) registration on local electoral rolls, if the information concerned is publicly available (g) payment of local taxes, if the information concerned is publicly available (h) a utility bill of the subscriber linking the subscriber to the Member State	(i) the billing address or the postal address of the subscriber (j) a declaration by the subscriber confirming the subscriber's address in the Member State (k) an Internet protocol (IP) address check, to identify the Member State where the subscriber accesses the online content service.

The means of verification in the second column can only be used in combination with one of the means in the first column, unless the postal address (point (i)) is included in a publicly available official register,[379] such as in Sweden.

Although the Regulation does not require the use of a specific means of verification from the list, and does not preclude rightholders from requiring, by way of agreement with the service provider, the use of specific means of verification,[380] the provider is entitled to request the subscriber to provide the information necessary to determine the Member State of residence. Failure to provide information that enables the service provider to verify the Member State of residence will discharge the obligation, and bar the service provider, to provide cross-border access to the subscriber under Article 3.[381]

[3] Retrospective Effect

Although the Regulation applies from 1 April 2018, it has retrospective effect since it also applies to contracts concluded, and rights acquired, before this date to the extent that such contracts and rights are relevant for the provision of online content services.[382]

379. Streaming Regulation, Art. 5(1).
380. Streaming Regulation, recital (26).
381. Streaming Regulation, Art. 5(3).
382. Streaming Regulation, Art. 9(1).

[4] *Service Providers' Obligation and Discretionary Entitlement Not to Provide Cross-Border Access*

The obligation under Article 3(1), and any supplementary obligations applying as a result, to enable a subscriber cross-border access applies to subscribers who are *temporarily* present in another Member State. Hence, if a subscriber is not temporarily present in a Member State, the obligation does not apply. This does not however of itself entitle the service provider to decide whether to continue to provide access or not. Rather, the service provider is obliged not to provide cross-border access. The localisation of events under Article 4, which justifies cross-border access, which is discussed further below in relation to territorial exclusivity, takes place also only when the subscriber is temporarily present in another Member State. Similarly, therefore, when that is not the case, localisation does not occur.

Consequently, it seems that only those service providers who have obtained a licence for the Member States in question and are normally able to provide the service there are able to decide whether to continue to provide cross-border access when the subscriber is no longer merely temporarily present in that Member State.[383]

In any event, the definition of 'temporarily present in another Member State' in Article 2(4) is not helpful in appreciating what this is particularly intended to mean because such presence is laconically defined as being present in another Member State (...) 'for a limited period of time'. Recital (1), on the other hand, provides a non-exhaustive list of purposes for which subscribers may be temporarily present in another Member State, some of which can easily be longer than the billing period of a monthly subscription service or even a one-year contract. That the recital makes reference to the free movement of persons and services, two of the fundamental freedoms underpinning the EU may very well evidence that such periods are in fact meant to fall within the ambit of the definition:

> Since the internal market comprises an area without internal borders relying, *inter alia*, on the free movement of persons and services, it is necessary to ensure that consumers can use portable online content services which offer access to content such as music, games, films, entertainment programmes or sport events, not only in their Member State of residence but also when they are temporarily present in another Member State for purposes such as leisure, travel, business trips or learning mobility.

Consequently, the question of when exactly a subscriber can be taken to no longer temporarily be present in another Member State for the obligation to cease to apply, or alternatively after which point in time the service provider's 'reasonable doubts' as to the Member State of residence may arise to justify a repeated residence verification under Article 5(2), is at the moment a matter for the CJEU.

---

383. The contract between the rightholder and the service provider may however preclude cross-border access in a way mandated by Art. 3 (identical content etc.) in such a situation. Since such a preclusion would operate outside circumstances regulated by the Regulation, it does not appear to fall within the ambit of Art. 7, which is discussed further below in relation to contractual freedom of the parties.

[5] Online Content Services Provided Without the Payment of Money

The obligation to provide cross-border access to subscribers and to verify the Member State of residence is intended to primarily apply to content services provided against the payment of money. Such payments can take the form of indirect payments, for example, through payments to the provider of another service of which the online content service is part.[384] The Regulation contains however special provisions in relation to services which are not provided against the payment of money. In particular, providers of such services are entitled to choose whether they wish to enable cross-border access to their online content service, and if they so choose, they are subject to the same obligations as providers of services provided against the payment of money,[385] and must inform its subscribers and relevant rightholders of their decision to offer such access.[386] Although Article 6(2) specifies that such information shall be provided by means which are 'adequate and proportional', it seems to suffice to publish such information on the service provider's website.[387]

The categorisation of services into *services provided against the payment of money* and *services provided without the payment of money* naturally raises the question of which kind of services fall into the latter. Regrettably, the Regulation does not define the term nor otherwise imply what specific services ought to fall into the latter category.

It is submitted that the latter category relates to any online content services which do not fall into the former category; i.e., services provided against any kind of performance other than the payment of money, e.g., the provision of personal data or the creation of a user account, as well as gratuitous online content services whose use is subject to terms and conditions. Although the Regulation defines a 'subscriber' of a service as a consumer who is entitled to access and use a service 'on the basis of a contract',[388] which raises the question whether a user accessing and using a gratuitous online content service is also a subscriber within the meaning of the Regulation, recital (15) makes clear that the term 'contract' should be regarded as covering 'any agreement between a provider and subscriber, including any arrangement by which the subscriber accepts the provider's terms and conditions for the provision of online content services'.

The introduction of a discretionary rule for services provided without payment of money is intended to address the concern that whereas subjecting such services to the obligations in the Regulation would involve disproportionate costs (especially in connection with the obligation to verify the Member State of residence) and a major change to the way such services are delivered, such services should not be precluded as such from being able to take advantage of the legal mechanism to provide cross-border access.[389] Online content services which are accessible on the basis of the

384. Streaming Regulation, recital (18).
385. Streaming Regulation, Art. 6(1).
386. Streaming Regulation, Art. 6(2).
387. Streaming Regulation, recital (20).
388. Streaming Regulation, Art. 2(1).
389. Streaming Regulation, recital (20).

provision of personal data do not seem to create prohibitive costs compared to other services provided without the payment of money because the same effort does not need to be expended in verifying the Member State of residence. Such services ought to perhaps have been included in the category of services to which the obligation under Articles 3 and 5 always applies; especially that the value of provision of personal data as a form of contractual performance in the context of acquisition of digital content was recognised by the Commission in its proposal for the Supply of Digital Content Directive,[390] which was part of the same reform package as the Streaming Regulation.

[6] Enforcement

Interestingly, while the provisions of the Regulation are mandatory, the Regulation does not prescribe any enforcement measures or competence to specific bodies, such as a court or a consumer protection agency, to ensure compliance with the obligations.

Admittedly data protection issues that may arise in connection with the obligation, and conditional discretion, to verify the Member State of residence will fall under the General Data Protection Regulation[391] and the e-Privacy Directive[392] which prescribe specific measures, rights and competent bodies.

Arguably, an enforcement mechanism may not be necessary since the country-of-origin principle localising cross-border access to the Member State of residence means that service providers are not required to negotiate a licence to be able to provide such cross-border access.[393] Difficulties in obtaining licences to serve specific territories were not, however, the only contemplated barrier to cross-border access but also the fact that 'providers of online content services might choose to service specific markets only'.[394]

[D] Territorial Exclusivity

[1] Challenges Arising out of Territoriality of Rights

Copyright protection within the EU is national, and not pan-European. This means that the rights exist in each EU Member State as independent entitlements and are capable of being infringed in each Member State separately.[395] As such, authorisation to carry out acts which fall within the scope of the exclusive rights must be obtained for each relevant Member State. In this way, the territorial scope of the exclusive rights, while being a natural limitation in copyright law, provides at the same time prerogatives to

390. *See* in particular Art. 3(1) and recital (14) of the proposed Supply of Digital Content Directive COM(2015) 634 final.
391. Regulation (EU) 2016/679 on the protection of natural persons with regard to the processing of personal data and on the free movement of such data, and repealing Directive 95/46/EC.
392. Directive 2002/58/EC concerning the processing of personal data and the protection of privacy in the electronic communications sector.
393. To the extent that such a licence was necessary in the first place.
394. *See* recital (4) Streaming Regulation.
395. *See* further Chapter 10 below.

rightholders. For example, a content service provider that is entitled to provide access to subscribers within one territory only and necessarily communicate works to the public, must obtain a licence to be able to provide the service in another territory, yet may be refused that licence because the rightholder has granted an exclusive licence for that territory to another content service provider. Or the cost may be prohibitively high, discouraging the content service provider from obtaining a licence at all. In the absence of a licence for the given territory, the provision of a service exposes the service provider significant legal risks since, except communicating works, they may be contributing to the subscriber's, effectively, unlawful transient reproduction in the memory of the device that occurs during the consumption of content when the subscriber is streaming or non-transient reproduction in case of downloading content for the purpose of 'offline streaming' while temporarily visiting another Member State in which there is another (or no) provider. The Regulation recognises these challenges in, for example, recital (10), according to which:

> The acquisition of a licence for relevant rights is not always possible, in particular when rights in content are licensed on an exclusive basis. In order to ensure that territorial exclusivity is effectively complied with, providers of online content services often undertake, in their licence contracts with rightholders (...) to prevent their subscribers from accessing and using their services outside the territory for which the providers hold the licence. Such contractual restrictions imposed on providers require them to take measures such as disallowing access to their services from Internet protocol (IP) addresses located outside the territory concerned. Therefore, one of the obstacles to the cross-border portability of online content services is to be found in the contracts concluded between the providers of online content services and their subscribers, which reflect the territorial restriction clauses included in contracts concluded between those providers and the rightholders.

and recital (24):

> Whenever providers have the right to carry out acts of communication to the public or reproduction in their subscribers' Member State of residence on the basis of an authorisation from the rightholders concerned, subscribers who are temporarily present in a Member State other than their Member State of residence should be able to access and use the service and where necessary carry out any relevant acts of reproduction, such as downloading, which they would be entitled to do in their Member State of residence. The provision of an online content service (...) to subscribers temporarily present in [another Member State] (...) and the access to and use of the service by such subscribers in accordance with this Regulation should not constitute a breach of copyright or related rights or any other rights relevant for the provision of, access to and use of the online content service.

[2] Constraining Territorial Exclusivity

The obligation under Article 3 to provide cross-border access to online content services to subscribers temporarily present in another Member State is clearly overlapping with rightholders' exercise of territorial exclusivity. However, the Regulation cleverly resolves these challenges by localising the copyright-relevant events to the Member

State of residence. In particular, Article 4 provides that the provision of an online content service to a subscriber temporarily present in another Member State and access to, and use of, the service by the subscriber 'shall be deemed to occur solely in the subscriber's Member State of residence'. In this way the Regulation ensures that any copyright-relevant act arising out of the provision or use of the service takes place within the territorial confines of the Member State of residence.

Such legal fiction, a country-of-origin rule, is not new to the copyright industry since the SatCab Directive introduced a comparable provision in relation to satellite transmissions by broadcasting organisations.[396] However, whereas the SatCab provision was primarily designed to address legal uncertainty and fragmented approaches in the course of harmonising the broadcasting right,[397] the Streaming Regulation provision is exclusively designed to legitimise the obligation to provide cross-border access under Article 3:

> In *order to ensure* that providers of online content services covered by this Regulation comply with the obligation to provide cross-border portability of their services, *without acquiring the relevant rights in another Member State*, it is *necessary* to stipulate that those providers should *always be entitled* to provide such services to subscribers when they are temporarily present in a Member State other than their Member State of residence. This *should be achieved by* establishing that the provision of, access to and use of such online content services should be deemed to occur in the subscriber's Member State of residence. This legal mechanism should apply for the *sole purpose* of ensuring the cross-border portability of online content services (...).[398]
>
> [emphasis added].

Within the limited type of cross-border access that the Regulation deals with, a service provider operating in Sweden does not, therefore, have to obtain permission to be able to make the service available from the territory of the remaining EU Member States.[399] In this way the country-of-origin rule constrains the scope of rightholders' exclusivity arising out of the territorial character of the (already harmonised) exclusive rights. Put differently, the 'national portion'[400] of the exclusive rights that would normally have applied in the respective territories to the provision of access to the service, and use of it by the subscriber, has been rendered inapplicable to such acts because those acts are legally deemed to occur within the subscriber's Member State of residence.

---

396. *See* Art. 1(2)(b) and (d) SatCab Directive.
397. *See* recital (14) together with (5)-(7) SatCab Directive.
398. Streaming Regulation, recital (23).
399. And the three EEA EFTA States (Iceland, Norway, Lichtenstein) once the Regulation is incorporated into the EEA Agreement. *See* Decision of the EEA Joint Committee No 158/2018 of 6 July 2018.
400. This term is borrowed from patent law as used in the context patents granted within the framework of the European Patent Convention.

[E] Contractual Freedom

The Streaming Regulation contains two important provisions that expressly affect the agreements between rightholders and service providers as well as between subscribers and service providers in the context of cross-border access. With the limited exception of the Computer Programs Directive,[401] such legislative techniques are uncommon in EU copyright law, or even in the copyright laws of many Member States. Provisions, or principles, which are designed to affect contractual arrangements are usually intended to strengthen, or restore, the position of the author, such as the ability to claim additional remuneration in the case of significant inequality between the remuneration paid to the author and the profit that was made from exploitation by a publisher (e.g., the Netherlands),[402] or the interpretation of ambiguous contract provisions in favour of the author as opposed to the other party (e.g., Sweden).[403]

By virtue of Article 7(1) Streaming Regulation any contractual provisions 'which are contrary to this Regulation, including those which prohibit cross-border portability of online content services or limit such portability to a specific time period' are rendered 'unenforceable'. Hence, on the one hand the entire Regulation is made mandatory, including the availability of only two means of residence verification where one is not sufficient as well as the prohibition not to impose any additional charges for cross-border access during temporary presence in another Member State. That service providers, alternatively rightholders, are unable to limit such access to a specific time period may seem like a draconian measure. Limiting access to a specific time period could, for example, either take the form of a direct limitation, such as the continuous provision of the service for a duration of two months while accessing the service from another Member State, or indirectly through an obligation to reconnect to the service from the Member State of residence after a number of months, or even one year. While there naturally is substance to such contract terms, if only to lessen the administrative burden, the provision seems to be a way to force address verification as the only permitted course of action; in lieu of letting service providers and rightholders find alternative solutions to cease providing cross-border access, for example, in cases where rightholders authorise by virtue of Article 5(4) the provision of the service without address verification.

Interestingly, and rather surprisingly, Article 7(1) makes contract terms conflicting the Regulation *unenforceable*. By contrast, the Computer Programs Directive makes contract terms preventing decompilation, making backup copies and the testing of the functionality of the program, *null and void*. The preparatory work does not shed much light on the choice of the former term over the latter term. The former term was already used in the Commission's original proposal and seems to have not been given any particularly relevant attention because it has remained in the text, even though the original provision (Article 5 in the proposal) had undergone significant changes.

---

401. *See* Chapter 5 above.
402. *See* Art. 25d Wet van 23 September 1912, houdende nieuwe regeling van het auteursrecht.
403. *Specifikationsprincipen*; which in the context of consumer agreements may position itself directly opposite Art. 5 Directive 93/13/EEC on unfair terms in consumer contracts.

Terms which are null and void have normally no legal effect and should be considered as if they did not exist in the agreement. Terms which are unenforceable, on the other hand, are simply not enforced by a court. Normally this difference is significant, and would have been here since not enforcing a clause does not of itself imply rectification, however since the Regulation mandates a specific course of action by default, the difference is rather only theoretically relevant in the context of the Regulation. For example, even though it will not matter for the service provider (but may for the rightholder) that a court will not enforce a clause preventing cross-border access in the agreement between the service provider and the subscriber, since the service provider is using technology to prevent that from occurring anyway, the Regulation obliges the service provider to provide such access by default.

Second, the Regulation applies irrespective of the law that governs the contract, whether between the service provider and rightholder, or the service provider and subscriber. This is particularly relevant for the former group, especially where either of them is based outside the EU, such as American rightholders or service providers providing a service in a Member State, and prefers for that reason to let the contract be governed by the laws of that country. It is arguable however whether the contract between the service provider and the subscriber can be governed by a law other than an EU Member State, and therefore that the Regulation might not apply if it has the effect of depriving the subscriber of cross-border access in accordance with the Regulation.[404]

[F] A Consumer Copyright Law Instrument

In theory the Streaming Regulation is an ambitious project because it aims to ensure that EU consumers can travel within the EU and seamlessly access services that they are paying for without affecting the existing copyright status quo:

> This Regulation should ensure cross-border portability of online content services in all sectors concerned and hence provide consumers with an additional means of accessing online content lawfully, without affecting the high level of protection guaranteed by copyright and related rights in the Union, without changing the existing licensing models, such as territorial licensing, and without affecting the existing financing mechanisms.[405]

At the same time, the Regulation recognises that that is the problem:

> There are a number of barriers which hinder the provision of online content services to consumers temporarily present in a Member State other than their Member State of residence (...) The barriers stem from the fact that the rights for the transmission of content protected by copyright or related rights (...) are often

404. *See* Arts 6(1)-(2) Regulation (EC) No 593/2008 of 17 June 2008 on the law applicable to contractual obligations (Rome I). *See* however Art. 6(4)(a) Rome I Regulation in light of Art. 4 Streaming Regulation.
405. Streaming Regulation, recital (12).

licensed on a territorial basis, as well as from the fact that providers of online content services might choose to service specific markets only.[406]

Ensuring cross-border access while keeping territorial fragmentation of the market are mutually exclusive outcomes and cannot be reconciled without making changes to the status quo.

In dealing with cross-border access to online content services, three positive courses of action were considered by the Commission.[407] As a first, and least intrusive, course of action the Commission could simply encourage service providers to provide such access across the EU. Alternatively, more direct legislative action could take place, whereby the provision, access and use of the service to or from another Member State would be deemed to occur in the Member State of residence. This would follow the established trend of letting the industry decide on any course of action following limited intervention, known especially from the SatCab Directive. Lastly, that same rule could be introduced, provision of cross-border access to, and use of, an online service could be made compulsory, and limitations on contractual freedom could be imposed. Eventually, the Commission concluded that only the last alternative 'would effectively ensure that the cross-border portability feature is offered and the demand of consumers is met', for which reason it was 'considered the best policy choice'.[408]

At its core the Streaming Regulation concerns limited cross-border access to *legal* services. On the one hand, the aims of the Regulation ought to be welcomed from the perspective of the single market because the Commission's consultation on the review of copyright rules showed that the issue concerned accessibility *as such* to services and the availability of different content depending on the Member State in question, if the service was available at all; rather than, for example, unreasonably high prices for access to content. Even if a truly DSM would incorporate cross-border access to online services available in any Member State, the Regulation does nevertheless address an important issue. On the other hand, it is lamentable that market actors must be told what to do, or what not to do. Most of the key legal developments of the 1990s and 2000s within the area of copyright law had been driven by piracy concerns, without there really being any, or very few, legal alternatives in a limited number of Member States. Now that legal alternatives have actually been available for some time, and digital markets are thriving, the European legislator feels compelled to act, rather expeditiously, to ensure that consumers are able to access services that they are, after all, paying for. The objectives of this Regulation ought to serve as a fundamental starting point for future copyright policy.

406. Streaming Regulation, recital (4).
407. *See* Commission Impact Assessment, pp. 23-27.
408. COM(2015) 627 final, p. 6.

CHAPTER 7

Copyright Exhaustion

§7.01 INTRODUCTION

Exhaustion is an important doctrine in intellectual property law generally and copyright law specifically.[409] At European level exhaustion is central for the free movement of goods and services. It is present in several EU directives, specifically in Article 4(c) Computer Programs Directive, Articles 1(4), 3 and 9(2) Rental and Lending Right Directive and Article 4(2) InfoSoc Directive.

Exhaustion is considered to be a limitation of the right of distribution, although it is normally not associated with the L&Es to the exclusive rights listed in Article 5 InfoSoc Directive, such as, for example, quotation or temporary reproduction. It serves foremost to define the general scope of the right, rather than to enable exploitation of protected material, even if the latter is a natural consequence of its applicability. In this sense it is similar to the finite duration of copyright protection.

When a rightholder has put copies of their work on the market, they lose their right to control the circulation of these particular copies on the market and cannot, therefore, hinder their further distribution (resale). This only applies to the distribution right and does not as such affect the remaining exclusive rights.

There are two separate legal frameworks for exhaustion in EU copyright law. The applicable framework depends on whether the work in question is categorised as a computer program, in which case it falls under the specialised regime in the Computer Programs Directive. In any other case it will be governed by the provisions of the general InfoSoc Directive.

Before the breakthrough of the Internet and broadband, the traditional point of departure was that exhaustion is attached to tangible, hard copies of works. Exhaustion of hard copies was actually not an (important) issue before copying was becoming easier from the 1950s through to the 1990s with the development of phonograph

409. In the USA it is known as the first-sale doctrine.

records, cassettes, videotapes etc. Therefore, there is no particular guidance regarding exhaustion of copyright-protected works in the Berne Convention, and, perhaps more surprisingly, in the Rome Convention. However, aspects of exhaustion were negotiated in connection with both the TRIPS and the WCT. Both TRIPS and the WCT make an express reference to exhaustion of the distribution right. According to Article 6 TRIPS signatories are free to regulate the question of exhaustion. The issue addressed in the TRIPS is, however, related to parallel importation rather than to the dichotomy between analogue and digital exhaustion. Further, from Article 6 WCT relating to the right of distribution it follows that authors of copyright-protected works 'shall enjoy the exclusive right of authorising the making available to the public of the original and copies of their works through sale or other transfer of ownership'. As such, the Article is technologically neutral and could cover both tangible and intangible copies of a work. However, according to the Agreed Statement to Article 6 it 'refer[s] exclusively to fixed copies that can be put into circulation as tangible objects'. Hence in the mid-1990s when these instruments were formally negotiated, during the early stages of Internet connectivity and the proper pre-digital transition of society, the point of departure was that electronic delivery of software and other copyright-protected works should not be exhausted. At this time Internet connectivity was relatively slow and it would have been *inter alia* too time and resource-consuming to distribute books, music, films, business software and games online, and copyright-protected works were, after all, being delivered on tangible media. On top of that, the development of consumer electronics capable of rendering such media, not to mention providing comparable experiences, were also in the early stages of development. Eventually, technological developments and faster broadband permitted online distribution which became a regular form of delivery during the 2000s. Pure electronic delivery without any reliance on tangible media such as CDs or DVDs was therefore not an aspect that really could properly have been considered when the WCT was negotiated.

It is not an exaggerated statement to say that the development of new (digital) technologies, requiring new legal frames, is among the strongest forces driving the development of copyright industries. The copyright law system is, and must be, transforming in light of these rapid changes.

§7.02 COMPUTER PROGRAMS

The computer industry is a hardware industry on the one hand, and a software industry on the other hand. Computers were first developed and used at the end of the 1930s. The machines were regarded as scientific instruments, primarily useful for research and for military purposes. However, commercial manufacture of computers became practically possible only by the technological advances made during the 1940s and 1950s. Word processing software and games were harder to imagine then. An important step in the technological development was the advent of the transistor, the integrated circuit and the microprocessor, and during the 1960s computers were used in different areas, and it became more regular to use computers for administrative work, besides calculating. During the 1970s the first personal computers were developed.

For a long time, however, the same actors were developing hardware and software, with limited software development. In particular, standardisation of hardware and software and interoperability were rather unknown, arguably uninteresting, concepts in the beginning. It was not before computers were developed to manage different types of programs when the interest of developing software with a user-friendly interface became more common. This resulted in a separation of the software and hardware business during the 1980s.[410] At this time software were delivered on a machine-readable medium, such as on a floppy disc or magnetic tape, and later on CDs.

With time, increasingly more software has come to be delivered over the Internet and the different ways of making software available today have transposed the notion of exhaustion to the legal foreground. Today it is common for consumers to obtain software by downloading a copy to the hard disk and installing it on the device without having to own tangible storage media. Since computer memories have become overwhelmingly large, there is simply no need to acquire and own separate storage media such as CDs or DVDs on which copies of programs have been delivered or on which such copies can be kept for the purpose of conserving storage space on the computer, if only to be able to make a backup. Another method is to offer direct access to software over the Internet requiring the user to remain connected online, and where access is not free requiring the payment of recurring subscription fees, as opposed to a one-time fee. This business model is often referred to as the provision of Software as a Service and, alternatively, IT as a Service which instead focuses on the entire IT infrastructure of an organisation. Yet, where users are not expected to pay recurring fees to be able to use software but instead pay once and download, there exist a tension between the interests of copyright holders in controlling the distribution of software on the one hand, and such users' interests of being eventually able to trade software on a second-hand market once they no longer wish to use it.

The question of exhaustion is strongly rooted in the *sale* or *licence* dichotomy. When online software is considered to be licensed, a potential second-hand market can be fairly easily controlled by software owners. A commercially aware software developer will prefer to license, rather than to sell software. Popular belief has been that licensing as a method of distributing software irrespective of whether the software is delivered on tangible medium or over the Internet, and even for a one-time fee, will allow controlling how a licensee may use the program, and imposing post-acquisition restrictions since the rightholder will be in an ongoing contractual relationship with the licensee of the program or game, and the seemingly absent transfer of ownership to a copy will render the possibility to resell inapplicable. This traditional understanding has now been set aside for software delivered online.

410. From the earlier 2000s, however, we see a trend to connect a user-friendly design for both hardware and software, such as Apple's (i) concept.

[A] Exhaustion under the Computer Programs Directive

Article 4(2) Computer Programs Directive provides that the first sale in the Community of 'a copy of a program' by the rightholder shall exhaust the distribution right within the Community. Since a copy of a computer program is always and only digital, the material difference relating only to the form of storage and delivery, exhaustion is not precluded by the digital character of the work, and the delivery of a computer program on a storage medium will exhaust the distribution right if the transaction can be considered a *sale*. However, when a computer program is stored on a *non-original medium*, such as a new CD or a DVD, the lawful acquirer of the copy of the computer program may not resell the, effectively, reproduced copy to a third party. Hence, a person who has destroyed, damaged or lost their copy of the program and instead wishes to sell the backup copy will not, despite being ordinarily entitled to make such a backup copy, be able to benefit from Article 4(2) Computer Programs Directive and will instead need to obtain the rightholder's consent. Consequently, when a computer program is delivered on a tangible medium, it is only the resale of the computer program as stored on the original tangible medium that the re-seller may rely on the exhaustion of the distribution right.[411] The backup copy may only be used to meet the sole needs of the person having the right to use that program.[412]

Downloadable copies are not as such precluded from the wording of Article 4(2), in fact the contrary may be inferred because the provision simply refers to a 'copy' of the program, so it seems that it instead is a matter of establishing whether such copies fall within the scope of the distribution right contained in Article 4(1)(c), and necessarily whether such copies can be *sold* (as opposed to being licensed) for exhaustion to apply. The wording of Article 4(1)(c) Computer Programs Directive does not appear to limit the distribution right to tangible media because it refers to 'any form' of distribution. This term appeared for the first time in 1991 in the original Directive 91/250/EEC on the legal protection of computer programs.[413] It is unclear if this provision, when the Directive was adopted, was also intended to include distribution, and necessarily exhaustion, of software delivered over the Internet. With the delivery methods of the 1990s it is likely that the wording probably referred to the technology of the time, e.g., floppy disks and CDs. Moreover, in the preparatory works to the 1991 Computer Programs Directive the issue of exhaustion had not really been fully considered. In the Green Paper of 1988 the Commission's view was that computer programs should be protected by copyright and further commented on a number of issues relating to the precise nature and scope of the exclusive rights for software.[414] Nevertheless, exhaustion was not analysed in detail during the period of consultation. In the proposal, in 1989, it was merely pointed out that once 'a product has been sold with the rightholder's consent he should no longer be able to exercise control over the

411. Case C-166/15 *Ranks*, para. 57.
412. Case C-166/15 *Ranks*, para. 43.
413. *See* Art. 4(c) of that Directive.
414. *See* COM(88) 172 final.

subsequent sale, that is sale to third parties of legally acquired programs.'[415] In the Green Paper of 1995, however, the Commission stated that rights other than the distribution right for tangible items that are 'transmitted by electronic means can hardly be made subject to exhaustion.'[416] Subsequently, in the Commission report from 2000 on the implementation of the Computer Programs Directive the wording, 'any form' was pointed out.[417] According to the report it was possible to interpret Article 4(c) widely in relation to the distribution right, which according to the Commission was not in line with Article 6 WCT. In light of this the Commission suggested that the provision should be modified, but this did not eventually occur in the subsequent codifying 2009 Computer Programs Directive.

In so far as the categorisation of a transaction is concerned, i.e., whether the initial transaction can constitute a *sale*, the Directive does not shed light on this, but this was instead resolved by the CJEU in its ruling in *UsedSoft*.

[B] The CJEU's Decision in *UsedSoft*

UsedSoft concerned the resale of user licenses which were no longer used by the initial purchaser. In order to use the software, the new purchaser was asked to download a copy of the computer program from the developer's website (Oracle). Such a download was, needless to say, lawful in the sense that the electronic copy originated directly from the rightholder and the copy of the program would therefore not be reproduced by the re-seller following the transaction. The CJEU concluded that the contractual relationship between the rightholder and the initial purchaser can be regarded as a sale and that the rightholder's right can be exhausted. The Court held that the term 'sale' designates, for the purpose of applying the Computer Programs Directive, an autonomous concept of EU law, which must be interpreted in a uniform manner throughout the territory of the EU,[418] and defined a sale as:

> an agreement by which a person, in return for payment, transfers to another person his rights of ownership in an item of tangible or intangible property belonging to him.[419]

Most interestingly, the Court stated that 'the downloading of a copy of a computer program and the conclusion of a user licence agreement for that copy form an indivisible whole' and in a legal context those 'two operations must therefore be examined as a whole for the purposes of their legal classification'.[420] Since consumers where offered (1) a non-exclusive and non-transferable user right, (2) for an unlimited period and (3) for remuneration (a one-time fee), this constituted according to the Court a first sale of a copy within the meaning of Article 4(2) Computer Programs Directive. The Court's conclusion was essentially that the method of delivery was

415. *See* COM(88) 816 final – SYN 183, p. 25.
416. COM(95) 382 final, p. 48.
417. *See* COM(2000) 1999 final, p. 17.
418. C-128/11 *UsedSoft*, para. 40.
419. C-128/11 *UsedSoft*, para. 42.
420. C-128/11 *UsedSoft*, para. 44.

irrelevant and the distribution right of copies of computer programs under the Directive covered both tangible and intangible copies of software.

The Court's ruling essentially implies that copyright is not a one-way street. The copyright system must adapt to modern ways of using, consuming and distributing copyright-protected works, and the Court reshaped the traditional principle of exhaustion by putting the free movement of goods and services in the centre. For a computer program that has been lawfully distributed, the exhaustion rule will be the same as for copies of computer programs lawfully distributed on tangible media such as DVDs, CDs. In this way, the CJEU has taken a significant step to get the copyright system to work in a modern society while simultaneously recognising the interests of rightholders, consumers and the society.

§7.03 LITERARY AND ARTISTIC WORKS*

Literary and artistic works which are not computer programs are, as mentioned, governed by the InfoSoc Directive. This appears to include original video games.[421] The relevant provision in the InfoSoc Directive is Article 4(2) which provides that:

> The distribution right shall *not be exhausted* within the *Community* in respect of the original or copies of the work, *except where the first sale* or *other transfer of ownership* in the *Community* of that object is made by the rightholder or with his consent [emphasis added].

Rightholders' distribution right to works other than computer programs is also not absolute for the duration of copyright protection. As to the mandatory character of the provision, although this is not made explicitly clear, it seems that (in contrast to Article 5(2) concerning L&Es) the provision must be implemented. As will be seen below the somewhat unusual construction extends the scope of the distribution right and since that right has been harmonised in Article 4(1) and must, therefore, be implemented, so does Article 4(2). Moreover, conversely to the wording of the provision, the distribution right *shall* be exhausted only where the transfer of ownership occurs in the Community. This obligatory character of the provision seems to indicate that the distribution right will indeed be exhausted irrespective of whether attempts are made to contract the provision out. This has also been confirmed by the CJEU in *UsedSoft*, however in relation to the Computer Programs Directive.[422]

As to the wording of Article 4(2) InfoSoc Directive, one question that immediately arises is why the provision has been constructed in the negative and in the form of an exception.[423] Various provisions concerning the exhaustion of the distribution right in

* Parts of this section are based on the author's ongoing research in Szkalej, K., 'Consumption of digital works – an analysis of EU copyright law within the framework of lawful acquisition and use of protected content' (forthcoming 2019).

421. C-355/12 *Nintendo*, para. 23.

422. C-128/11 *UsedSoft*, para. 77.

423. 'The distribution right shall not be exhausted (...) except where...'.

the area of *copyright law* generally do not have a consistent wording.[424] Should exhaustion be viewed as an exception to an otherwise general rule, that rule being the right of distribution, the CJEU's ruling in *Infopaq* dictates that it must be interpreted strictly. The Court has however not indicated such an approach in the few cases that have dealt with exhaustion under the InfoSoc Directive.[425]

[A] Geographical Scope

Once the distribution right is exhausted, the rightholder will no longer be able to exercise their right to authorise or prohibit any kind of distribution *in the Community* of that specific copy. This is significant because if a work has been acquired through sale in the Member States,[426] the rightholder will subsequently not be able to exercise their distribution right with respect to the particular copy of the work within this area. Put in other words, they will not be able to prevent someone from distributing the one specific copy further.

It should be noted that whereas the scope of the exclusive rights remains territorial and national, exhaustion of the distribution right is regional. Hence, from the perspective of Article 4(2) InfoSoc Directive, a rightholder from whom a work is purchased in France is not able to authorise or prohibit the (re-)distribution of the specific copy of the work either in France, Sweden or any other Member State. This will not be the case, however, where the copy is legitimately acquired outside the Community, such as where a printed book is purchased in the USA, and subsequently disposed of in the Community. This is also expressly confirmed by recital 28 InfoSoc Directive which provides that this 'right should not be exhausted in respect of the original or copies thereof sold by the rightholder or with his consent outside the Community'.[427] Consequently, where a work is acquired outside the Community, in the absence of the rightholder's consent anyone wishing to dispose of their copy within the Community will be infringing the author's distribution right, even though, it seems, transfer of ownership (to at least the tangible medium on which the work is stored, recorded or expressed) has occurred.

---

424. Whereas Art. 9(2) Rental and Lending Rights Directive has the same wording as Art. 4(2) of the much later InfoSoc Directive, Art. 4(c) of the earlier Directive 91/250/EEC on the legal protection of computer programs has a noticeably different grammatical construction. Both of these directives have been replaced by Directives 2006/115/EC and 2009/24/EC respectively and the respective grammatical construction of the exhaustion provisions was transferred to the new instruments.
425. *See* C-479/04 *Laserdisken*, Case C-419/13 *Art & Allposters International* v *Stichting Pictoright* ECLI:EU:C:2015:27, Case C-174/15 *Vereniging Openbare Bibliotheken* v *Stichting Leenrecht* ECLI:EU:C:2016:856. *See also* C-456/06 *Peek & Cloppenburg*, para. 35.
426. Or alternatively the European Economic Area (EEA), which is comprised of the Member States of the EU, Iceland, Lichtenstein and Norway. The InfoSoc Directive was not originally adopted with EEA relevance, but was extended to it subsequently by EEA Joint Committee Decision No 110/2005 of 9 July 2004 amending Annex XVII (Intellectual Property) to the EEA Agreement [2004] OJ L 376/45. The question is whether this changed the meaning of the term 'Community' as used in Art. 4, from the perspective of the EU (Member States).
427. *See also* C-479/04 *Laserdisken*, paras 24–26.

Interestingly, in so far as this provision can be regarded as having extraterritorial effect, the rightholder might also be able to exercise their right where the work has been acquired in the Community but disposed of outside the Community. After all, the provision states that the right shall not be exhausted *within the Community* unless sale or other transfer of ownership has occurred *in the Community*. This double qualification implies that re-distribution cannot occur outside the Community, even if the first transaction takes places in the Community. While it is likely that, in such a case, a claim of infringement would have to be brought before a court of a jurisdiction where the InfoSoc Directive is applicable or can be applied, the point to note is that despite the fact that transfer of ownership has occurred, in the Community, the distribution right appears to be still enforceable against a subsequent transaction outside the Community. From the perspective of (EU) private international law, it would seem that such a claim could indeed be brought before a court of a Member State as by virtue of the general rule contained in Article 4(1) Brussels I *bis* Regulation 'persons domiciled in a Member State shall, whatever their nationality, be sued in the courts of that Member State'.[428] Hence, a resident of Sweden who has acquired a book of a Polish author in Belgium and subsequently sells that book in the USA can be sued in Sweden for the infringement of the distribution right provided in the InfoSoc Directive. How the Swedish court would apply Article 8(1) Rome II Regulation (mandating *lex protectionis*) is indeed a very interesting question because the infringing act occurred on the territory of a country outside the EU, the result of which is that the Court would likely have to apply US law, rather than the, arguably, extraterritorial provision in the InfoSoc Directive. Consequently, the seemingly extraterritorial effect might very well be obsolete.

This geographical limit that has been imposed on the exhaustion of the distribution right essentially means that one cannot import, nor potentially export, works to or from the Community without the rightholder's consent, even where such import or export is preceded by a transfer of ownership in the specific object of the transaction. This is an important limitation, or perhaps an *extension*, of the distribution right because even though *sale or transfer of ownership* must occur for exhaustion to be applicable, it does not mean that it has erga omnes effect.

While none of the recitals in the InfoSoc Directive expressly shed light on why specifically regional exhaustion has been introduced, such a measure would be the most optimal option contributing to the establishment of an internal market. Limiting exhaustion to the territory of Member States (national exhaustion) would only further the segregation of markets in an economic sense, and serves therefore in no way the establishment of an internal market. In particular because there could be fewer transactions as the costs of transacting would rise significantly because one would need to obtain consent from the rightholder to sell a work in another Member State, and such consent would likely not be provided for free because the re-seller could become a direct competitor of the rightholder in the Member State in which they would like to resell the copy of the work.

428. *See* further Chapter 10 below.

It would also unduly limit the transnational character of the information society. Article 6(2) WCT leaves Contracting Parties free to 'determine the conditions, if any, under which the exhaustion of the [distribution right] (...) applies after the first sale or other transfer of ownership ...'. Consequently, as no geographical area is expressly stipulated, regional exhaustion as embedded in the EU framework should be viewed as an EU norm introduced on its own initiative, rather than as a result of its international commitments. In light of this, one does indeed wonder why the EU has not opted for global exhaustion. Such exhaustion would likely not affect the establishment of an internal market in so far as the free movement of goods is concerned from the perspective of trade between Member States. It is sometimes argued that this might, however, open the gates for (parallel) import from outside the EU. The question of whether this would have a negative impact on the establishment of an internal market falls outside the scope of this book, but global exhaustion (and potential importation following from it) does not of itself mean that goods can be imported free from customs fees and that this, therefore, would likely have come at a cost anyway. Most importantly, however, even if exhaustion could occur against the whole world, it would not preclude trade from occurring in the Community as such because global exhaustion does not require that the first transaction that triggers it also be global. In other words, although one would in such a case be allowed to export without the rightholder's consent, they would still need to acquire the work in the Community with the rightholder's consent. This would also partly eliminate the incoherency resulting from the fact that even though it is a transfer of *ownership* that triggers exhaustion of the distribution right, the rightholder can still, at least in theory, invoke the distribution right against a subsequent transaction occurring outside the Community.

As a result of the exhaustion rule not being global the exclusive right of distribution is essentially extended to cover extraterritorial areas and therefore seems to extend copyright protection, even though copyright remains a national right. This extension of the distribution right creates a very interesting difference in comparison to the remaining exclusive rights – while, because of territoriality, one may essentially engage in activities which would otherwise be perceived as infringing if they were done on the territory of the Statewhere protection has been granted, alternatively because an exception or limitation exists in that state, one cannot do so with the distribution right because it is not exhausted:

The Commission was however clear in its proposal that:

> the Directives dealing with computer programs and database works as well as topographies of semiconductor products set precedents in this area (...) they must be interpreted as not permitting exhaustion of the distribution right on an international basis. It is therefore logical to continue on the basis of, and to complement, the existing *acquis communautaire*.[429]

429. Commission, 'Proposal for a European Parliament and Council Directive on the harmonization of certain aspects of copyright and related rights in the Information Society' COM(97) 628 final, 10 December 1997, p. 22 (para. 7).

The reason why specifically regional exhaustion has been chosen in the InfoSoc Directive is therefore attributable to earlier legislation and case law and in an effort to create a homogeneous framework it has also therefore been introduced in the InfoSoc Directive.

[B] Sale or Other Transfer of Ownership

Surprisingly, the InfoSoc Directive does not define the type of transaction that triggers exhaustion, but refers simply to 'sale or other transfer of ownership'. The question that transpires is therefore whether *sale* should be understood as the *transfer of ownership* or whether it may be something else. In relation to Article 4(1), the distribution right, the CJEU has stated that the right exclusively relates to transfer of ownership,[430] without however defining what a sale actually is or what it may have as its object. This was instead done in *UsedSoft* in which the Court pointed out that:

> The wording of *Directive 2009/24* does not make any reference to national laws as regards the meaning to be given to the term 'sale' in Article 4(2). It follows that that term *must* be regarded, for the purposes of *applying the directive*, as designating an *autonomous concept* of European Union law, which *must be interpreted in a uniform manner* throughout the territory of the European Union ... [emphasis added].[431]

On the one hand it seems that this statement should be limited to the specific context in which it is given. After all the CJEU makes it clear that they refer to the word *sale* as used in the Computer Programs Directive, and it should be regarded as an autonomous concept of EU law *for the purposes of applying* [that] *directive*. This may, therefore, have little value for interpreting the InfoSoc Directive, especially that, as the CJEU further underlines, the Computer Programs Directive constitutes *lex specialis*. However, the word *sale* is used in exactly the same legal context in the InfoSoc Directive, namely that of exhaustion of the distribution right. Moreover, exactly like in the Computer Programs Directive, the wording of the InfoSoc Directive does not make any reference to national laws as regards the meaning to be given to the term *sale*. Consequently, this should also be understood as an autonomous concept of EU law. Furthermore, there appears not to be any compelling reason to treat the word *sale* as used in the general InfoSoc Directive differently from the word *sale* as used in the narrow and specific Computer Programs Directive for it would result in the existence of two autonomous concepts of EU law designated by an identical word and used in the same IP-relevant context. Following therefore the reasoning of the CJEU in *UsedSoft*, as quoted above '... a 'sale' is an agreement by which a person, in return for payment, *transfers to another person his rights of ownership* in an item of *tangible or intangible* property belonging to him [emphasis added]'.[432]

430. C-456/06 *Peek & Cloppenburg*, paras 35–36.
431. C-128/11 *UsedSoft*, para. 40.
432. C-128/11 *UsedSoft*, para. 42.

In general, therefore, once a work has been *purchased*, the rightholder's right to control further distribution of that specific copy of the work will be exhausted. This is fairly straightforward for works which are tangible in their entirety, such as a work of art fixed to a canvass, text printed on paper or a designer chair, but it also forces the question of whether Article 4(2) InfoSoc Directive encapsulates the exhaustion of downloadable digital works.

[C] Digital Exhaustion

Ever since the CJEU's ruling in *UsedSoft*, exhaustion of downloadable works other than computer programs has seriously been debated. The Court has however not yet had the opportunity to finally settle this question for the InfoSoc Directive, and whether *UsedSoft* will have any further implications for other types of copyright-protected works. Both sides of the discourse provide strong arguments.

[1] Existing CJEU Case Law

The Court's reasoning in *Allposters* might be understood as implying that Article 4(2) InfoSoc Directive exclusively concerns tangible objects and that it, therefore, cannot apply to downloadable copies, however in that case, which concerned the transfer of works originally printed on a poster to a canvass by using a special chemical process and the subsequent distribution of such canvass-transferred products, the Court merely confirmed that the distribution right concerns all tangible products (objects) put on the market and that, because, in the opinion of the Court, a reproduction has taken place, which renders the copy of the work a different product, exhaustion cannot apply.[433]

In the subsequent *VOB* case, the CJEU was much closer to the question of digital exhaustion. Essentially the case concerned the question of whether the concept of *lending* under the Rental and Lending Rights Directive, specifically in Article 6(1) permitting public lending despite the exclusive lending right in Article 1 on condition that authors obtain remuneration for such lending, includes *e-lending*, i.e., 'making available of e-books by placing digital copies on a server and enabling a user to download the copy in such a way that the copy is not usable after a specified time period and that other users cannot download that same title during this period'. If that is the case, then whether a Member State may require that the copy of the work which is being made available for e-lending must have been brought into circulation by an initial sale or other transfer of ownership of that copy within the meaning of Article 4(2) InfoSoc Directive. In other words, whether in order be able to publicly lend a (digital) copy without prior authorisation from the rightholder a Member State may require that the copy must have been put, essentially, for sale by the rightholder, and therefore (in

433. C-419/13 *Allposters*, paras 34, 35, and 37 read together with 40 and 46. *See also* C-174/15 *VOB*, Opinion of AG Maciej Szpunar, para. 54 stating that *Allposters* 'neither calls into question nor limits in any way the conclusions which follow from the *UsedSoft* judgement'.

light of the answer to question three relating to the lawfulness of the source) must necessarily have been purchased by the establishment prior to such e-lending.

While the Court confirmed that the concept of lending includes such e-lending, in relation to the second question it first stated that Article 4(2) InfoSoc Directive is not relevant for the interpretation of Article 6(1) Rental and Lending Rights Directive,[434] but stated subsequently that such a condition, by virtue of being capable of *reducing the harm on the legitimate interests of authors* that Article 6(1) might otherwise cause some works, *improves the protection of authors' rights* in the implementation of Article 6(1), and therefore held that such a condition must be considered to be compatible with Article 6(1).[435]

Hence, given the circumstances of the case, before a copy of a work is made available for e-lending under Article 6(1) by an establishment that may benefit from that provision, that copy must first have been put on the market for sale or other transfer of ownership by the rightholder (distributed). But following the completion of such a transaction, the distribution right will invariably be exhausted. Regrettably, the Court does not characterise the transaction, in particular whether it must be the sale (purchase) of a tangible copy or whether it instead can be a downloadable copy, therefore rendering the question of digital exhaustion inconclusive.

Yet, if the relevant transaction must be limited to tangible copies, then an establishment being entitled to make a copy available for e-lending will necessarily have to digitise such a copy and alter the properties of such a new, digitised, copy in order to achieve the functionality necessary to be able to make it available for e-lending, and this will involve materially relevant reproductions, which in the absence of an exception or limitation permitting such reproductions will make the applicability of Article 6(1) contingent upon the rightholder's consent, therefore rendering Article 6(1) useless for e-lending. Of the available alternatives it, therefore, seems that accepting digital exhaustion not only upholds the effective application of the law but also causes the least harm, if any.

Nonetheless, in a case involving the resale of e-books, the CJEU has now finally been asked to rule on digital exhaustion. In *NU and GAU* v *Tom Kabinet*[436] the Dutch national court has requested a preliminary ruling for the following questions:

(1) Is Article. 4(1) InfoSoc Directive to be construed as meaning that 'any form of distribution to the public by sale or otherwise of the original of their works or copies thereof' as referred to therein includes making available remotely by downloading, for use for an unlimited period, e-books (being digital copies of books protected by copyright) at a price by means of which the copyright holder receives remuneration equivalent to the economic value of the work belonging to him?

434. C-174/15 *VOB*, para. 57.
435. C-174/15 *VOB*, paras 63–64.
436. Case C-263/18 *Nederlands Uitgeversverbond and Groep Algemeine Uitgevers* v *Tom Kabinet Internet and Others*.

(2) If question 1 is to be answered in the affirmative, is the distribution right with regard to the original or copies of a work as referred to in Article 4(2) InfoSoc Directive exhausted in the Union, when the first sale or other transfer of that material, which includes making available remotely by downloading, for use for an unlimited period, e-books (being digital copies of books protected by copyright) at a price by means of which the copyright holder receives remuneration equivalent to the economic value of the work belonging to him, takes place in the Union through the rightholder or with his consent?
(3) Is Article 2 InfoSoc Directive to be construed as meaning that a transfer between successive acquirers of a lawfully acquired copy in respect of which the distribution right has been exhausted, constitutes consent to the acts of reproduction referred to therein, in so far as those acts of reproduction are necessary for the lawful use of that copy and, if so, which conditions apply?
(4) Is Article 5 InfoSoc Directive to be construed as meaning that the copyright holder may no longer oppose the acts of reproduction necessary for a transfer between successive acquirers of the lawfully acquired copy in respect of which the distribution right has been exhausted and, if so, which conditions apply?

[2] Realistic Policy Considerations

The question of whether the acquisition of downloadable works other than computer programs for a one-time fee is also subject to exhaustion is extremely important for the functioning of the digital market and its innovation potential, and in particular for the use of DRM (TPM) systems that often protect such kinds of works. This particular issue is however much more complex than it may initially appear. Exhaustion is part of the legal framework which means that if indeed applicable, courts will simply refuse to enforce rightholders' distribution right upon exhaustion; in infringement proceedings. The question is whether this also implies that courts will as a result positively enforce exhaustion by regarding invasive DRM systems, which may technologically prevent a resale, as incompatible with Article 4(2) InfoSoc Directive. In the event that no such positive enforcement might ensue, a purchaser and subsequent re-seller of content may have no choice but to subject themselves to the lock-in effect created by such a DRM system, despite the fact that they will in such instance be regarded as the owner of the specific digital copy. The resolution of whether exhaustion applies to such downloadable works must therefore also be viewed in the context of the current and future state of DRM technology, and in particular what it may enable and what it may prevent, as well as how it may affect future market developments.

A ruling which categorically precludes digital exhaustion as a matter of law will not as such preclude the introduction of a technological system by rightholders (should they ever wish to do so)[437] that will enable the transfer of purchased content to another person for a fee and the simultaneous removal of that content from the device of the original purchaser, effectively therefore creating a secondary market *but* in an ecosystem technologically and economically controlled by the rightholders and which will be free from legislative constraints normally regulating market relationships. The impossibility of being able to qualify transactions in such a para-secondary market as *sales* and making them instead subject to limited, revocable licenses, despite the seemingly opposite effect, risks leading to high legal uncertainty and unreliability of the law, be it, for example, if the technology is ever abandoned, the licence revoked or the company becoming insolvent; not to mention the asymmetry of information between what consumers might think they receive, and what they actually will receive.

Having different rules on exhaustion depending on the category of work is an undesirable development, especially in the context of converging, multimedia content. The specific categories for copyright-protected works are nowadays mostly of theoretical relevance. However, in light of the *UsedSoft* decision categorisation of games remains important, should the rules on exhaustion be different under the InfoSoc Directive. Such creations can fall either within the framework established by the Computer Programs Directive, or the InfoSoc Directive,[438] rendering it already uncertain whether the existing exhaustion rule in the former directive should apply or whether instead the, still uncertain, exhaustion rule in the latter directive should apply. Attaining a fragmented approach (the so-called distributive approach[439]) to games by disassembling the game into audiovisual components and software components which fall under the InfoSoc Directive and the Computer Programs Directive respectively for the purpose of determining the applicable rule of exhaustion seems also unrealistic from the perspective of distribution as the game is marketed and delivered as a whole.

From a much broader copyright perspective, the non-applicability of exhaustion to digital sales seriously risks impeding the dissemination of knowledge, ideas and culture. If a rightholder decides to remove content from legal services, it will be unavailable until such time that it is made available on the service again, if ever; a decision that is exclusive to the rightholder. The effects of such removal are far more serious in the digital world than in the tangible world because with the aid of DRM systems purchased content can also be rendered inaccessible or even vanish from consumer devices overnight. Circulation of works, because of exhaustion but also because of the possibility to privately lend a book, a music CD, a DVD film etc., can still occur in the tangible world even after the rightholder decides to withdraw from the market by no longer communicating or distributing their works; such a state of affairs enhances access to knowledge. Presently, older versions of computer programs cannot be obtained (neither digitally nor on tangible media) from developers because they are no longer offering them, either in favour of promoting newer versions or because

437. For example, once patent protection of such a system lapses. *See*, for example, Ringewald, E, 'Secondary Market for Digital Objects', US Patent US8364595, granted 29 January 2013 (assigned to Amazon). *See also* Block, E.C. and van Os, M., 'Managing Access to Digital Content Items', US Patent Application US20130060616, filed 12 June 2012 (assigned to Apple).
438. *See* C-355/12 *Nintendo*, para. 23. *See* above on the protection of computer programs.
439. Cf. unitary approach.

support is no longer offered, therefore making the second-hand market the only source of supply.

As more and more content is being made available exclusively digitally, without there being a tangible substitute, rightholders may receive, in the absence of exhaustion, an indirect right to control the dissemination of knowledge and culture in a way that copyright has never entitled them to do. It is not merely a matter of new technology and new opportunities for rightholders which copyright law ought to automatically embrace; if it were, copyright law, and especially EU copyright law, might very well not have expressly required exhaustion of the distribution right when the rightholder has parted with a copy of the work.

CHAPTER 8

Technological Protection Measures*

§8.01 INTRODUCTION

While technology is often said to have enabled new forms of exploitation and consumption of digital content, it is sometimes overlooked that it has also provided new opportunities for rightholders in the digital environment. In particular, technology has enabled rightholders to protect their rights proactively and within the private sphere - an area that has long been considered to be located outside the reach of effective enforcement.

Once an infringement is discovered, in order to enforce the exclusive rights a typical scenario will involve the institution of infringement proceedings in a court of law (sometimes also preceded by a cease & desist letter). Such proceedings will normally require that rightholders identify the infringer, prove their claims and ask the Court for a suitable remedy, which will often include an injunction to cease further infringement and damages for the harm that was caused as a result of the infringement. This process consumes time, costs money,[440] and might expose the rightholder to a legal risk, for example, where the potential infringer successfully claims that an exception or limitation to the infringement is applicable, or indeed that the rightholder has no claim as the object of the potential infringement is not protected by copyright.[441] The simplicity with which digital works can be reproduced combined with the amount and cross-border character of infringements occurring over the Internet can make the

* Parts of this chapter are based on the author's ongoing research in Szkalej, K., 'Consumption of digital works - an analysis of EU copyright law within the framework of lawful acquisition and use of protected content' (forthcoming 2019).

440. For example, costs associated with the administration of the proceedings (court fees, legal fees) and also with identification of infringement and the infringer.

441. Because it either does not satisfy the requirements of protection, or because protection has lapsed. The former is perhaps more probable compared to proceedings relating to other (registrable) intellectual property rights, such as patents and trademarks, although so-called counter-claims for revocation are also common.

overall costs of such proceedings outweigh the benefit that is gained from the potential success of enforcement. However, so-called digital rights management (DRM) systems redesign the copyright enforcement framework, rather significantly. Such systems permit the enforcement of rights *ex ante* or at the time that the infringement is to occur, rather than *ex post.* In other words, infringement of the exclusive rights can be prevented from occurring in the first place. Technology has thus given rightholders the possibility to *effectively* decide what is permitted and what is prohibited. Such a possibility has naturally always existed with rightholders in so far as it concerned the definition and assignment of rights for specific uses (e.g., in a licence), but technology can ensure that rights are honoured, without the rightholder having to resort to the court system and rely on the enforcement of rights by the Statein the absence of compliance by the infringer.

There are ample reasons for rightholders to use DRM systems. Most importantly, this opens up a variety of possibilities to make digital works available in ways that were not possible before. For example, once a printed book is sold, there is little a rightholder can do to prevent a buyer from using the book as they please. As the copyrighted literary work expressed on paper is part of a tangible object, once this object leaves the shelf of the bookstore, the buyer can use that object as decoration, read its contents as many times as they please, destroy it and indeed photocopy it or resell it, without the rightholder having to know or having any possibility to discover this. Technology has changed this paradigm, as it permits the rightholder to prevent all these acts and this has permitted them to introduce new business models, apart from encouraging them to offer content online.

At the same time, the use of DRM systems may extend above and beyond strict enforcement of copyright, for example, to protect content which has fallen into the public domain, or which as such does not satisfy the requirements for obtaining copyright protection, or to fragment different markets by introducing regional coding for consumer electronic devices, such as DVD films and DVD players, or making access to online marketplaces contingent upon the possession of a specific device of a specific manufacturer. But perhaps most importantly, and in contrast to when infringement proceedings are initiated before a court, DRM systems can prevent uses that beneficiaries of certain exceptions and limitations may be entitled to without the consent of the rightholder.

These tensions are exacerbated by an absolute prohibition to circumvent technological solutions which constitute so-called *technological protection measures*. In practice, this means that except controlling the exclusive rights, rightholders are able to carefully define the borders of consumption through licensing and control it through tools that enforce the licence provisions. In such a framework one does not really need copyright law, or even a licence, as an end user can discover by trial and error what they are allowed to do, and what they are not allowed to do. The degree to which this is desirable is, however, an entirely different matter.

§8.02 PROHIBITION ON CIRCUMVENTION OF TPMs

Articles 11 and 18 WCT and WPPT respectively require that Contracting Parties put in place adequate legal protection and effective legal remedies against the circumvention of effective technological protection measures (TPMs). This requirement has resulted in the introduction of a prohibition on the circumvention of TPMs in Article 6 InfoSoc Directive. Paragraph 1 of this Article requires, similarly to WCT and WPPT, that Member States provide legal protection against circumvention of *effective TPMs*, but 'which the person concerned carries out in the knowledge, or with reasonable grounds to know, that he or she is pursuing that objective'.

In contrast to the international framework established by the two treaties, in the EU legal framework the term effective TPM has received its specific definition. By virtue of Article 6(3) InfoSoc Directive, the expression *technological measures* means:

> any technology, device or component that, in the *normal course* of its operation, is *designed to prevent or restrict acts*, in respect of works or other subject-matter, which are *not authorised by the rightholder* of any copyright or any right related to copyright as provided for by law (...). Technological measures shall be deemed *'effective'* where the use of a protected work or other subject-matter is controlled by the rightholders through application of an *access control or protection process*, such as *encryption, scrambling or other transformation of the work* or other subject-matter or a *copy control mechanism*, which achieves the protection objective [emphasis added].

Hence, for a technological solution to benefit from the circumvention provision, it must first be designed to prevent or restrict certain acts in the *normal course of its operation*, and subsequently be *effective*, such effectivity subsisting in the technological solution if use of the content is controlled by access control or copy control mechanisms *that achieve the protection objective*. This definition is problematic for several reasons. First, it implies that there are TPMs which are not effective, and which therefore cannot benefit from the circumvention provision, despite such measures being designed to prevent or restrict certain acts and, needless to say, such measures being *technological* in nature (as opposed to e.g., a legal restriction in the licence). Second, for TPMs to be deemed effective and therefore benefit from protection, the access control and/or copy control mechanism must achieve the protection objective, such objective necessarily consisting in the successful prevention or restriction of undesired acts, which puts in question the degree to which such a system may be imperfect. Last, but not least, it appears not to define the specific acts which the technological solution must be designed to prevent, but refers instead to acts 'not authorised by the rightholder' leaving it inconclusive as to whether this refers to acts that rightholders are entitled to control by virtue of copyright law, specifically reproduction, communication to the public and distribution, or whether it instead refers to acts which rightholders can be capable of controlling by virtue of technology, whether or not copyright provides such entitlements. That access control, which is not an exclusive right granted by copyright law, is either of two components of a TPM which must be present for the technology to enjoy protection might very well be evidence of the latter. Regrettably, the recitals to the InfoSoc Directive use similar wording.[442] It is worth mentioning that the Commission's original intention in its proposal for the InfoSoc Directive had been that the provision only covers acts which constitute an infringement of copyright,[443] and this was made clear in the original wording of what was at the time Article 6(2) which referred to measures 'designed to prevent or inhibit the infringement of any copyright or any rights related to copyright as provided by law or [the database right]'.[444] The current wording implies, however, a different, broader, interpretation.

In *Nintendo*, the only case interpreting the substance of Article 6, the CJEU, while not explicitly stating that the wording in Article 6(3) may give rise to a broad definition of TPMs, nevertheless held that the acts that Article 6(3) refers to constitute the exclusive rights provided in Articles 2–4 InfoSoc Directive, and that 'legal protection referred to in Article 6 (...) applies only in light of protecting that rightholder against acts which require his authorisation',[445] which seems to imply, in line with the Commission's original proposal, that for a technological solution to be protected, a successful act of circumvention would have to result in an infringement of copyright (i.e., when consent has not been obtained for the exclusive use or when an exception or limitation does not apply). The Court continued however that 'legal protection is granted only with regards to [TPMs] which pursue the objective of preventing or eliminating, as regards works, acts not authorised by the rightholder of copyright ...',[446] which instead seems to imply, in light of the previous sentence, that a technological solution will be protected from circumvention as long as the rightholder has not authorised the subsequent (copyright-relevant) use, even if such authorisation is not required by virtue of the applicability of an exception or limitation; but arguably excluding use which falls outside copyright protection entirely.

With regards to the degree of effectiveness that TPMs must possess, the Court held that while it is relevant to consider the relative costs of different types of technological measures, technological and practical aspects of implementation, and a comparison of the effectiveness of different types of measures as regards the protection of rights, the effectiveness need not be absolute.[447]

In comparison to the international framework established by the WCT and WPPT, EU copyright law extends the legal protection of TPMs to acts which directly or indirectly facilitate the circumvention of such measures, recognising that there exists a danger that 'illegal activities might be carried out in order to enable or facilitate the circumvention of the technical protection provided by these measures'.[448] In particular, Article 6(2) InfoSoc Directive requires of Member States to:

> provide adequate legal protection against the manufacture, import, distribution, sale, rental, advertisement for sale or rental, or possession for commercial purposes of devices, products or components or the provision of services which:

442. *See* in particular recitals (47) and (48).
443. COM(97) 628 final, p. 33.
444. COM(97) 628 final, p. 46.
445. C-355/12 *Nintendo*, para. 25.
446. C-355/12 *Nintendo*, para. 31.
447. C-355/12 *Nintendo*, para. [33].
448. InfoSoc Directive, recital (47).

(a) are promoted, advertised or marketed for the purpose of circumvention of, or
(b) have only a limited commercially significant purpose or use other than to circumvent, or
(c) are primarily designed, produced, adapted or performed for the purpose of enabling or facilitating the circumvention of, any effective technological measures.

This makes the protection of TPMs potentially very broad and may inhibit or disincentivise the making of interoperable products or offering services to bona fide purchasers of content who encounter difficulties in consuming purchased content because of the operation of TPMs. At the same time, it follows from recital (48) to the InfoSoc Directive that legal protection of TPMs should respect the principle of proportionality. This was echoed in Advocate General Eleanor Sharpston's opinion in *Nintendo* and subsequently confirmed by the CJEU which stated that any technological measures which are implemented must be suitable for achieving the objective of preventing or eliminating acts not authorised by the rightholder and must not go beyond what is necessary for this purpose.[449] The line between commercially significant purpose on the one hand, and limited commercially significant purpose on the other hand (Article 6(2)(b)), as well as between primary and non-primary purpose (Article 6(2)(c)) can be very difficult to draw, rendering almost as a matter of principle potentially any kind of product or service which results in circumvention of a TPM as falling within the ambit of Article 6(2). In this respect the Court held in *Nintendo* that evidence of *actual use* which is made by the devices by *third parties* will be particularly relevant for determining whether Article 6(2) will apply, exemplifying on the facts of the case to the referring court that:

> the referring court may, in particular, examine how often PC Box's devices are in fact used in order to allow unauthorised copies of Nintendo and Nintendo-licensed games to be used on Nintendo consoles and how often that equipment is used for purposes which do not infringe copyright in Nintendo and Nintendo-licensed games.[450]

The designer's actual intention appears, therefore, to be irrelevant. What proportion of non-infringing use will be sufficient for a device or component to fall outside any of the provisions in Article 6(2) is left unanswered by the Court, such assessment being instead left for the national courts of the Member States.

§8.03 TPMs, LIMITATIONS AND EXCEPTIONS, AND CONTRACTS

The use of technological measures to control access to copyright content combined with the legal protection of TPMs creates obvious tensions with limitations and exceptions to copyright protection. Limitations and exceptions which require that the copy be obtained legally before it can be applied, such as temporary reproduction

---

449. C-355/12 *Nintendo*, para. 31. *See also* Opinion of Advocate General Eleanor Sharpston, paras 53–56.
450. C-355/12 *Nintendo*, para. 36.

under Article 5(1)[451] and reproductions for private purposes under Article 5(2)(b),[452] further these tensions because the legality of the copy will often originate from the legal relationship between the user and the rightholder, such as a licence exclusively drawn up by the rightholder, which may attempt to limit or exclude uses which a user may be entitled to.

These tensions are to some extent addressed in Article 6(4) InfoSoc Directive, which oddly introduces a two-tier approach that first delegates the resolution of such tensions to rightholders by expecting the introduction of voluntary measures, and only subsequently requires of Member States to act, depending on the limitation or exception in question. In particular, if beneficiaries of specifically Articles 5(2)(a) (reprography), 5(2)(c) (reproductions by libraries, educational establishments, museums and archives), 5(2)(d) (ephemeral recordings), 5(2)(e) (reproductions of broadcasts by social institutions such as hospitals or prisons), 5(3)(a) (illustration for teaching or scientific research), 5(3)(b) (use for the benefit of people with a disability) and 5(3)(e) (use for purpose of public security or ensure proper performance or reporting of administrative, parliamentary or judicial proceedings), in the absence of voluntary measures taken by rightholders within a 'reasonable time',[453] are unable to benefit from their respective limitation or exception, Member States *must* ensure, that 'rightholders make available to [any of these beneficiaries] (...) the means of benefiting from the exception or limitation' to the extent necessary to benefit from the exception and limitation, on condition that the beneficiary has legal access to the content in question.

On the other hand, with regards to beneficiaries of Article 5(2)(b) (reproductions for private use), Member States *may* take such measures, without preventing rightholders from limiting the number of reproductions 'in accordance with [Article 5(2)(b) and Article 5(5) (three-step test)]'. Interestingly, neither Article 5(2)(b) nor Article 5(5) prescribes a cap on the permitted number of reproductions that may be made for Article 5(2)(b) to continue to apply.

The large margin of discretion that Article 6(4) provides is noticeable and Member States have fully used this discretion to introduce a variety of different solutions.[454]

Nevertheless, by virtue of paragraph 4 of Article 6(4) neither the obligation nor discretion of the Member States to introduce such measures will apply where the protected content has been 'made available to the public on agreed contractual terms in such a way that members of the public may access them from a place and at a time individually chosen by them'. This appears to be a reference to the communication to the public right in Article 3 and seems therefore to foremost concern activities commonly referred to as streaming, although the provision is aimed to only cover

451. C-527/15 *Stichting Brein*.
452. C-435/12 *ACI Adam*.
453. InfoSoc Directive, recital (51).
454. *See* Commission, 'Report to the Council, the European Parliament and the Economic and Social Committee on the application of Directive 2001/29/EC on the harmonisation of certain aspects of copyright and related rights in the information society' (Staff Working Document) SEC(2007) 1556, 30 November 2011, p. 9.

'interactive on-demand services' but not 'non-interactive forms of online use'.[455] It is difficult to comprehend the difference between these two forms, especially in light of the fact that the InfoSoc Directive was passed as early as 2001. Should the permanent download of a digital work, for a one-time fee, be considered as falling within the communication to the public right instead of the distribution right, as some commentators suggest, paragraph 4 of Article 6(4) may potentially become applicable to such transactions, effectively rendering Member States' discretion to introduce measures in favour of reproductions for private use inapplicable and therefore dangerously impairing the relevance of Article 5(2)(b) whenever TPMs are used; despite that fair compensation will have been paid, be it directly through the one-time fee, or indirectly through the private copying levy that most Member States have introduced. This, rather absurd, effect may be another reason why permanent downloads for a one-time fee ought to be instead considered to be a form of distribution (Article 4) and not communication to the public (Article 3).[456]

455. InfoSoc Directive, recital (53).
456. For the other reasons *see* Chapter 6 (§6.02 [B][5]) and Chapter 7 (§7.03 [C][2]).

CHAPTER 9

Copyright Infringement and Enforcement of Rights

§9.01 INTRODUCTION

Copyright grants authors and other creators exclusive right in their works and other protected subject matter. Making copies of a work or making it available to the public without permission, or without it being allowed according to a limitation or exception, constitutes an infringement of economic rights. On a national level the same is generally true if the name of the author is not stated to the extent and in the manner required by proper usage or if the work is changed in a manner which is derogatory.

Infringement of copyright can also occur where someone engages in copyright-relevant acts in relation to a subject matter which *resembles* the original work, without being identical to it. To put it in another way, copyright law also protects adaptations and derivative works and will therefore also apply to the making of a film based on a novel, translation of a book into another language, dramatisation of a novel, or making a piece of furniture which resembles another one without being identical to it. Moreover, it may also be an infringing act to use a small part of the work, for example, if one without permission re-uses, say, three pages from a book or eight bars of a musical work.

The adaptation right is not harmonised by EU copyright law.[457] In some Member States adaptation may be a form of exploitation falling under the exclusive rights, such as in the Scandinavian Member States, while in others it is a separate right that exclusively concerns the adaptation of the work to another form of expression, e.g., the dramatisation of a novel, such as in the UK.[458] The term *derivative work* (creation) is somewhat ambiguous since it may both refer to adaptations of a work to another form

457. C-419/13 *Art & Allposters International*, para. 26.
458. *See*, for example, 2 § 1st. Lag (1960:729) om upphovsrätt till litterära och konstnärliga verk for Sweden and s. 21 Copyright, Designs and Patents Act 1988 for the UK.

of expression, as well as to the inclusion of an existing work of another author in one's own creation, e.g., a collage, a meme, or where a previous work has clearly been used as inspiration, such as a caricature based on a portrait.

The conditions under which such acts infringe copyright or related rights protection – or, to put it in another way, the scope of protection – are harmonised only to a very limited extent by EU law.

An infringement will usually trigger various remedies and sanctions. Although EU copyright law does not prescribe when a specific remedy or sanction must apply, some harmonisation has also taken place in this area. This is further discussed below.

§9.02 INFRINGEMENT BY DIRECT EXPLOITATION OF PARTS OF WORKS AND OTHER SUBJECT MATTER

[A] Copyright-protected Works

The CJEU has made it clear that the unauthorised use of a part of a protected work can only be considered a copyright infringement if the part is in itself original in a copyright sense, i.e., it constitutes the intellectual creation of the author and reflects free and creative choices. On the other hand, it is not an infringement to copy for instance a non-original, trivial sentence from a book or three non-original chords from a song.[459]

The original part does not have to be an easily identifiable block such as the first 3 pages of a book or eight bars in a musical work. It can also be an original *structure*, i.e., an original way in which a number of elements are selected and/or arranged in a work. For example, it can be a copyright infringement to use the original structure of a non-fictional work, including the order of the arguments and examples, even though the actual wording of the work is not copied. In the same way it can be a copyright infringement to use, say, the plot of a book in a silent movie. However, in such cases it is a requirement that the structure borrowed reflects originality and creativity. It follows from the Database Directive that original databases which reflect creative choices must be granted copyright protection. The creativity can both lie in the selection of the objects going into the database, in the arrangement, or in both. The taking of a part of a copyright-protected database can only be considered infringing if the part taken reflects the original selection and/or arrangement. However, it does not infringe the copyright in an original database to borrow isolated elements which do not reflect the originality of the database. Sometimes the elements will be protected in themselves as works, the contents making up the database, and in such situations any relevant use will infringe the copyright of the respective authors in those works. This is the case, for example, in connection with a database containing protected photographs. But it will not infringe the copyright in the database as such.

459. *See* C-5/08 *Infopaq*, paras 38 et seq. and 47 et seq., C-403/08 and C-429/08 *FAPL*, para. 159, and C-355/12 *Nintendo*, para. 22.

[B] Related Rights and Sui Generis Databases

First of all, the object of protection in Articles 2 and 3 InfoSoc Directive in relation to related rights subject matter is *fixation* and not the content. The difficulty in establishing the degree to which parts of subject matter protected by related rights may be reproduced is attached to the fact that subject matter protected by related rights need not satisfy any qualitative criteria to enjoy protection, such as originality. Hence, there may not be any distinguishing feature, as opposed to copyright-protected works, parts of which must also be original for infringement to ensue. This may suggest that it is a matter for the Member States to decide.

Nevertheless, the breadth of the reproduction right in the InfoSoc Directive implies that it is a matter for the CJEU to determine the scope of such protection, since Article 2 requires that performers, phonogram producers, producers of the first fixation of films and broadcasting organisations are provided with the exclusive right to authorise reproduction 'in whole or in part' of the fixations of performances, phonograms, fixations of films, and of broadcasts, respectively; and it is a question that should soon be resolved by the CJEU in *Pelham*.[460] With regards to making available, Article 3(2) InfoSoc Directive does not use the same wording, 'in whole or in part'. Consequently, it may be for the Member States to decide.[461]

In relation to sui generis databases the question when it is an infringement to use a small part of a database is dealt with by Article 7 Database Directive and has to some extent been addressed by the CJEU.[462]

§9.03 INFRINGEMENT BY INDIRECT EXPLOITATION OF THE WORK OR OTHER SUBJECT MATTER: THE REQUIRED DEGREE OF SIMILARITY

Copyright infringement may also occur when there has been an indirect exploitation of a work, in the sense that the new creation resembles the existing work because it has, for example, been used as inspiration for the new creation, as opposed to having been included by directly being copied into the new creation. This forces the question of the degree to which the new creation must resemble the existing work for copyright infringement to ensue.

[A] Copyright-protected Works

As mentioned earlier, copyright protection extends to expressions and not to ideas. This *idea-expression dichotomy* means that abstract parts of a work are not protected

460. C-476/17 *Pelham and Others* v *Hütter and Schneider-Esleben*.
461. *See* to this extent C-279/13 *C More Entertainment*. *See* also Agreed Statement to Art. 1(2) WPPT, making clear that Contracting Parties are not precluded from providing rights to performers and producers of phonograms going beyond those required under the Treaty. Cf. C-466/12 *Svensson*, paras 40–41.
462. *See* above, in relation to the scope of the sui generis right.

and that there is no copyright in, for example, the morale of a novel or the atmosphere of a song. Consequently, writing a Nordic noir novel with the same plot as an existing whodunit, or painting the same landscape as a previous artist, will not amount to copyright infringement since it is the idea that has been taken, not the expression of that idea.

It is a basic copyright principle in a number of Member States that the scope of protection of a work depends on its originality. Thus, works which only show little originality are only infringed by other works which resemble them to a large extent. On the other hand, very original works can be infringed when there is some resemblance. The more original a work, the broader the scope of protection, but the principle serves as a copyright safety valve, which makes sure that protection does not go too far.

Arguably, the principle was abolished by the CJEU in *Painer*. The Court rejected the idea that a simple portrait photograph had a narrow scope of protection. The Court stated that protection conferred by Article 2 InfoSoc Directive (reproduction right) must be given 'a broad interpretation',[463] and that 'nothing in [the InfoSoc Directive] or in any other directive applicable in this field supports the view that the extent of such protection should depend on possible differences in the degree of creative freedom in the production of various categories of works'.[464] The Court held that original photographs, although perhaps simple, must be given a protection which is 'not inferior to that enjoyed by any other work'.[465]

[B] Related Rights

This matter is not expressly harmonised by EU law. However, because of the character of related rights protection (fixation, not content), derivative and transformative works may fall outside related rights.

§9.04 ENFORCEMENT OF RIGHTS

Once infringement of copyright is established different sanctions may become available, such as injunctions, economic compensation and other damages, seizure of infringing goods, fines and even imprisonment. Certain sanctions, especially injunctions, may also become available during proceedings. For example, a rightholder may apply for a preliminary (interlocutory) injunction requesting the Court to order the other party to refrain from engaging in the contested activity, pending the final outcome of the case. This particular form of injunction works however as a double-edged sword – should the rightholder lose the case, the defendant may be entitled to recover the loss following from the issuing of such an injunction.

463. Be that as it may, the literal scope of the reproduction right is already very broad.
464. C-145/10 *Painer*, paras 96–97.
465. C-145/10 *Painer*, paras 96–97 and 99.

[A] Knowledge and the Changing Nature of Copyright Infringement

Copyright infringement is regarded as a *strict liability* offence. Hence, once a copyright-relevant act has taken place without permission or in the absence of the applicability of a limitation or exception, infringement of the relevant rights will deem to have occurred, regardless of the intention of the person involved in the relevant act. Intention, awareness, negligence, or lack thereof, has normally only been relevant for the availability, and scope, of specific remedies and sanctions. For example, the lack of intention or gross negligence to commit copyright infringement may make imprisonment unavailable, or it may affect the level of compensation.

Regrettably, the CJEU's recent judgements in cases such as *GS Media*, *Stichting Brein and Stichting Brein II*, change the strict liability character of copyright infringement since they make the determination of whether infringement has occurred contingent upon the existence of knowledge (or negligence), and for that reason also automatically increase the severity of the infringement, and therefore the severity of the sanction that may be prescribed. This has profound consequences where the *GS Media* presumption applies since if a party fails to rebut it, it will have committed copyright infringement, knowingly or at least negligently, for a profit-making purpose. A circumstance that is arguably highest on the penalty scale.

[B] EU Harmonisation and Enforcement Strategies

EU copyright law approaches enforcement in the following way. It prescribes certain standards for the scope of measures and requires that certain measures are available in the Member States, without however prescribing rules governing the issuing of specific measures. This latter aspect is a matter for national law. Most importantly, the degree of harmonisation that has occurred only relates to *civil* enforcement (i.e., not including criminal sanctions).

In particular, Article 3 Enforcement Directive requires that measures, procedures and remedies which are provided by Member States must be 'fair and equitable and shall not be unnecessarily complicated or costly, or entail unreasonable time-limited or unwarranted delays'. With this, the directive seeks to ensure an operative framework for the efficient enforcement of the different rights. Heavy procedural, administrative or financial burdens discourage the institution of proceedings and may, in turn, affect the effectivity of the rights which EU copyright law harmonises.

Simultaneously, the measures, procedures and remedies must be *effective*, *proportionate*, and *dissuasive* and must be applied in a way 'to avoid the creation of barriers to legitimate trade and to provide for safeguards against their abuse'. Consequently, while the different measures must be suitable and actually 'work', they may not be absolute in time or scope by default.

The Enforcement Directive requires the availability of the following measures relating to infringement of rights:

- *injunctions* intended to prohibit the continuation of an infringement, including injunctions against intermediaries whose services are used to infringe copyright,[466] and *preliminary (interlocutory) injunctions*, intended to prevent 'imminent infringement' or provisionally prohibit the continuation of the alleged infringement;[467]

- *recall or removal of infringing goods* from the market, or their destruction,[468] and *seizure of goods suspected of infringing copyright* 'to prevent their entry into or movement within' commerce;[469]
- *preservation of evidence* of the alleged infringement;[470]
- *damages* (monetary award) appropriate to the actual prejudice suffered by the rightholder resulting from the infringement, including economic and non-economic compensation.[471] The directive permits the calculation of damages as a lump sum based on, for example, the amount of fees that would have been payable if the infringer licensed the rights,[472] or indeed twice that amount;[473]
- *provision of information* on origin and distribution networks of goods or services that infringe copyright. The entitlement is directed towards the infringer or any other person who was found in possession of, or was using, the infringing goods or services, was found to be providing services on a commercial scale used to infringe the rights, or was indicated by any of the persons above as being involved in the infringements.[474]

The number of measures that the Member States must introduce means that rightholders have a variety of different ways to secure their rights, including in the digital world. This makes it possible to employ a variety of strategies, depending on the circumstances of the case, especially that acts of contributory (secondary) infringement, i.e., contributing to the infringement by, for example, making it possible, are usually also encapsulated by these measures. Contributory infringement is, however, a matter exclusively regulated by the national laws of the Member States.[475]

For example, instead of using resources to discover the identity or location of the infringer for the purpose of instituting proceedings against the infringer, it may be more feasible to direct attention towards an intermediary who may be better placed to put an end to the infringement;[476] and who may be obliged to comply under the E-Commerce

466. Enforcement Directive, Art. 11. *See also* Art. 8(3) InfoSoc Directive and C-314/12 *UPC Telekabel Wien*.
467. Enforcement Directive, Art. 9(1)(a).
468. Enforcement Directive, Art. 10(1).
469. Enforcement Directive, Art. 9(1)(b).
470. Enforcement Directive, Art. 7(1).
471. Enforcement Directive, Art. 13(1).
472. Enforcement Directive, Art. 13(1)(b).
473. Case C-367/15 *Stowarzyszenie OTK* v *Stowarzyszenie Filmowców Polskich* ECLI:EU:C:2017:36.
474. Enforcement Directive, Art. 8(1).
475. Although in C-610/15 *Stichting Brein II* the CJEU expanded the concept of communication to the public (i.e., primary infringement) to the operation of a website making it easier to find, and share, infringing content but which did not host copies (The Pirate Bay), and therefore constituting an act(s) which would normally have been regarded as contributory infringement. Similarly in C-527/15 *Stichting Brein*, the sale of a device containing links to unlawful content was considered to a communication to the public right, and therefore constituted primary infringement.
476. *See* recital 59 InfoSoc Directive.

Directive in order to continue being absolved from liability. It may therefore very well suffice to, for instance, directly request from an online content sharing platform to simply remove infringing content, and in the absence of compliance, only then apply for an injunction against that intermediary.

Where instead an entire website contains infringing content and the service is located outside the jurisdiction of the Court, making, therefore, such injunctions ineffective, it may nevertheless be possible to end infringements enabled by such a website by applying for a so-called website blocking order, i.e., applying for an injunction against an ISP ordering that ISP to block its customers' access to the website.[477] It is however not possible to require from ISPs, or any other intermediary, the active monitoring, discovery and prevention of infringements by its customers or users.[478]

The enforcement landscape is not however without tensions on a national level. For example, the last measure mentioned on the list above (the right to information) is intended to apply 'in the context of proceedings concerning an infringement', which may imply *judicial court proceedings*. This is not however made clear in Article 8 Enforcement Directive, nor can it be inferred from recital 21 which refers to this right. Member States such as Sweden have implemented the right to information in such a way as to create a free-standing sanction, a final *information injunction*, in the sense that its applicability is not contingent upon the institution of court proceedings (pending or contemplated) for infringement of copyright. In other words, rightholders are entitled to information, including about the identity of the infringer, regardless of whether they plan to sue the infringer or not.[479] The degree to which such a solution is compatible with *inter alia* the Enforcement Directive can be discussed, however, Article 16 Enforcement Directive permits Member States to introduce 'other appropriate sanctions in cases where intellectual property rights have been infringed'. While the existence of infringement must still be evidenced before a court, the receipt of information about the infringer without having to subsequently institute proceedings means that rightholders are free to decide on any course of action. For example, rightholders may (easily) identify and gather an exorbitant amount of IP addresses on peer-to-peer networks from which infringements are originating, apply for an information injunction compelling the ISP to identify the *customers* who had the specific IP address assigned to them at the relevant time, and subsequently contact each relevant customer (as opposed to *infringer*) individually with an offer to settle the infringement, for an amount that the rightholder considers adequate, and threaten with litigation in the absence of payment.

---

477. *See*, for example, C-314/12 *UPC Telekabel Wien*.
478. C-70/10 *Scarlett Extended* and Art. 15 E-Commerce Directive.
479. *See* 53e § Law on copyright to literary and artistic works (1960:729).

CHAPTER 10

Jurisdiction and Applicable Law

§10.01 INTRODUCTION

Cross-border conflicts are not uncommon in copyright law. The EU copyright framework does not, however, contain any special rules governing applicable law and jurisdiction, unlike certain forms of industrial property.[480] Instead, cross-border litigation is governed by the general EU instruments on private international law, in particular Brussels I *bis* Regulation, Rome I Regulation, and Rome II Regulation.

The private international law framework prescribes specific rules depending on the type of claim and in particular whether it is a non-contractual type of claim or whether it originates from contract. This section focuses only on non-contractual types of claims.

Before the law applicable to the case can be determined, it is common to first establish the competency of the Court to hear the case. This section will, therefore, proceed in the same order.

§10.02 JURISDICTION

Questions relating to applicable jurisdiction are governed by Regulation No 1215/2012 of 12 December 2012 on jurisdiction and the recognition and enforcement of judgements in civil and commercial matters (Recast)[481] (Brussels I *bis* Regulation), which applies from 10 January 2015.[482] The instrument replaced Regulation (EC) No 44/2001

480. *See* in particular Arts 122–135 EU Trademark Regulation, Arts 79–92 Community Design Regulation, and, although not an EU piece of legislation but available for signature to Member States of the EU, generally the UPC Agreement. Regarding the latter, *see* further Council Notice on the Agreement on a Unified Patent Court [2013] OJ C 175/1, 20 June 2013.
481. Replacing Regulation (EC) No 44/2001 and further amended by Regulation (EU) No 542/2014 amending Regulation (EU) No 1215/2012 as regards the rules to be applied with respect to the Unified Patent Court (UPC) and the Benelux Court of Justice.
482. Brussels I *bis* Regulation, Art. 81.

that succeeded the Brussels Convention 1968[483] and applies in all EU Member States except Denmark[484] which is instead part of the Lugano Convention 2007.[485] The latter Convention succeeded the Lugano Convention of 1988[486] that established a virtually identical framework as the Brussels Convention for EFTA Members.[487]

Like its predecessor the Brussels I *bis* Regulation does not apply to arbitration and it is expressly recognised that the New York Convention 1958[488] takes precedence over the Regulation.[489]

It is settled case law that the provisions of the framework established by the Regulation must be interpreted independently, by reference to its scheme and purpose, including the foreseeability of conferring jurisdiction, ensuring sound administration of justice and efficacious conduct of proceedings.[490]

Under the general rule in the Brussels I *bis* Regulation, which is often referred to as the fundamental principle,[491] proceedings against a person domiciled in a Member State shall be initiated in that Member State.[492] Where the defendant is not domiciled in a Member State, the national rules of each Member State govern the question of applicable jurisdiction.[493] The basis for conferring jurisdiction is predominantly predictability viewed from the perspective of the defendant but also the connection between the proceedings and the territory of the Member States. For this reason, the Regulation envisages situations that may warrant a different, sometimes stronger, connecting factor than the mere domicile of the defendant.[494] This particular set of situations is contained in Chapter 2 section 2 of the Regulation. The CJEU has made it clear on numerous

483. Convention of 27 September 1968 on Jurisdiction and the Enforcement of Judgments in Civil and Commercial Matters (Brussels Convention). The Brussels Regulation is almost identical in contents. *See* to this effect for instance Case C-98/06 *Freeport* v *Arnoldsson* ECLI-:EU:C:2007:595, para. 23 and case-law quoted therein.
484. Brussels I *bis* Regulation, recital (41).
485. Convention on Jurisdiction and the Enforcement of Judgments in Civil and Commercial Matters, adopted in Lugano on 30 October 2007. *See* [2010] OJ L 140/1.
486. Convention on Jurisdiction and the Enforcement of Judgments in Civil and Commercial Matters, adopted in Lugano on 16 September 1988.
487. *See* Brussels I *bis* Regulation, recitals (7)-(9).
488. Convention on the Recognition and Enforcement of Foreign Arbitral Awards done at New York on 10 June 1958.
489. Brussels I *bis* Regulation, recital (12).
490. *See* Case C-372/07 *Hassett* v *South Eastern Health Board and North Western Health Board* ECLI:EU:C:2008:534, para. 17, and Case C-167/08 *Draka and Others* v *Omnipol* ECLI: EU:C:2009:263, para. 19, Case C-189/08 *Zuid-Chemie* v *Philippo's Mineralenfabriek* ECLI: EU:C:2009:475, para. 17, Joined Cases C-509/09 and C-161/10 *eDate Advertising and Others* v *X and Société MGN* ECLI:EU:C:2011:685, para. 38, Case C-523/10 *Wintersteiger* v *Products 4U Sondermaschinenbau* ECLI:EU:C:2012:220, para. 31, and Case C-228/11 *Melzer* v *MF Global* ECLI:EU:C:2013:305, para. 22.
491. Case C-441/13 *Hejduk* v *EnergieAgentur.NRW* ECLI:EU:C:2015:28, para. 17, Case C-360/12 *Coty Germany* v *First Note Perfumes* ECLI:EU:C:2014:1318, para. 44, and C-228/11 *Melzer*, para. 23.
492. Brussels I *bis* Regulation, Art. 4(1).
493. Brussels I *bis* Regulation, Art. 6(1). This provision contains a number of limitations, none of which are however applicable to non-contractual copyright claims such as infringement. This includes Art. 24(4) concerning exclusive jurisdiction for proceedings concerning certain intellectual property rights.
494. *See* to this effect recitals (14)-(16) Brussels I *bis* Regulation.

occasions that the special rules on jurisdiction must be interpreted strictly and cannot be given an interpretation going beyond the cases *expressly* envisaged.[495] In other words, not only are the enumerated grounds for jurisdiction or types of claims determining jurisdiction exhaustive, but the provisions cannot be interpreted in a way that would extend the scope of the provision. Of particular interest for copyright infringement proceedings are Articles 7(2) and 8(1).

[A] Place Where the Harmful Event Occurred

By virtue of Article 7(2) Brussels I *bis* Regulation, a person domiciled in a Member State may alternatively be sued in the Member State where the harmful event occurred or may occur, such as the place of actual or expected infringement of copyright. This provision ought to be interpreted autonomously and strictly.[496]

This may become particularly challenging where the infringement has been carried out over the Internet as proceedings may have to be brought in each relevant Member State owing to the territorial character of copyright protection. The Court has however interpreted Article 5(3) of the old Brussels Regulation (now Article 7(2)) to include the place where the *event giving rise to* the alleged infringement occurred.[497] In particular, the CJEU has stated that '[Article 5(3)] is intended to cover both the place where the damage occurred and the place of the event giving rise to it, so that the defendant may be sued, at the option of the applicant, in the courts for either of those places'[498] noting that this rule 'is based on the existence of a particularly close linking factor between the dispute and the courts of the place where the harmful event occurred or may occur, which justifies the attribution of jurisdiction to those courts for reasons relating to the sound administration of justice and the efficacious conduct of proceedings'.[499]

While in relation to the infringement of the communication to the public right the harm might be caused in every Member State since it is sufficient for a work to be accessible to a public, rather than actually having been accessed, for the right to be infringed, the degree to which national copyright law could penalise activities (infringements) in another Member State is questionable.[500] In any event, a court of a Member State has jurisdiction, on the basis of the place where the damage occurred, only to rule on the damage caused in the Member State within which the court is situated.[501]

---

495. *See*, for example, C-98/06 *Freeport*, para. 35, Case C-103/05 *Reisch Montage* v *Kiesel Baumaschinen* ECLI:EU:C:2006:471, para. 23.
496. C-441/13 *Hejduk*, para. 16. *See also* C-360/12 *Coty Germany*, para. 45 and C-228/11 *Melzer*, para. 24 noting instead that a 'restrictive' interpretation is necessary.
497. C-523/10 *Wintersteiger*, paras 32–37.
498. C-441/13 *Hejduk*, para. 18 referring to C-360/12 *Coty Germany*, para. 46.
499. C-441/13 *Hejduk*, para. 19. *See also* C-360/12 *Coty Germany*, para. 47, Case C-170/12 *Pinckney* v *KDG Mediatech* ECLI:EU:C:2013:635, C-228/11 *Melzer* and case law quoted therein.
500. *See* Case C-192/04 *Lagardère Active Broadcast*, para. 46. Although the case concerned the SatCab Directive, the Court noted that national law can only penalise conduct engaged in within national territory.
501. C-441/13 *Hejduk*. *See* however C-170/12 *Pinckney* where the Court stated at para. 45 that 'if the protection granted by the Member State of the place of the court seized is applicable only in that

[B] Spider in the Web Doctrine

Another potentially relevant alternative for establishing jurisdiction in infringement proceedings follows from Article 8(1) Brussels I *bis* Regulation, corresponding to the former Article 6(1). Under this provision proceedings may be brought against a person domiciled in a Member State where that person is one of a number of defendants, in the courts for the place where any one of the defendants is domiciled, provided that the claims 'are so closely connected that it is expedient to hear and determine them together to avoid the risk of irreconcilable judgements resulting from separate proceedings'. The provision does not of itself mean that the court seised is entitled to apply the law of one jurisdiction to the different defendants, as this is a question of applicable law, but simply that where the circumstances are essentially identical for the different defendants, a court where either of the defendants is domiciled is entitled to hear the case as it relates to all of the different defendants.[502] The provision does not require that that the action brought against the different defendants have identical legal bases,[503] however it must be shown that there exists a connection of such kind that it is expedient to determine the actions together in order to avoid the risk of irreconcilable judgements resulting from separate proceedings.[504] The Court has made it clear that it is not sufficient that there be a divergence in the outcome of the different disputes, but that divergence must also arise in the context of the same situation of law and fact,[505] which is a matter for the national court to assess. Interestingly, alleged patent infringement conducted by companies belonging to the same group acting in an identical or similar manner (in accordance with a common policy elaborated by one of them) respectively in the territory of the Member State in which each of them was operating, will not qualify as such a situation.[506] By contrast, in proceedings concerning alleged copyright infringement taking the form of publication of photographs in newspapers the majority of which operated in another Member State in which the

---

Member State, the court seized only has jurisdiction to determine the damage caused within the Member State in which it is situated emphasis added', implying that extraterritorial copyright protection is not as such precluded. *See also* Case C-618/15 *Concurrence* v *Samsung Electronic France and Amazon Service Europe* ECLI:EU:C:2016:976, para. 31 where the Court essentially made the same ambiguous point.

502. The CJEU appears, however, to favour an interpretation that at least the factual (as opposed to legal) circumstances, including the location, be the same, effectively therefore making the provision applicable when infringement has been carried out in the same Member State, and therefore entitling the court seised to apply its domestic legislation.
503. C-145/10 *Painer*, para. 80, C-98/06 *Freeport*, paras 38 and 41. The Court also points out the potential existence of a connection between the claims is not as such removed where the claim is based on contractual liability for one defendant and based in tort or delict for the other. *See* para. 42 together with Case C-51/97 *Réunion Européenne and Others* v *Spliethoff's Bevrachtingskantoor* ECLI:EU:C:1998:509, para. 50.
504. C-98/06 *Freeport*, para. 39.
505. C-98/06 *Freeport*, para. 40, Case C-539/03 *Roche Nederland and Others* v *Primus and Goldenberg* ECLI:EU:C:2006:458, para. 26.
506. C-539/03 *Roche Nederland*. However *see* Case C-616/10 *Solvay* v *Honeywell Fluorine Products and Others* ECLI:EU:C:2012:445 in which the defendants were separately accused of having committed the same infringement in relation to same product, in the same Member State, essentially affecting the same national parts of a patent granted under the EPC framework.

claim was initiated, while only one operated in the same Member State, the CJEU stated that 'a difference in legal basis between the actions brought against the various defendants does not, in itself, preclude the application of Article 6(1) [of the old Regulation], provided however that it was foreseeable by the defendants that they might be sued in the Member State where at least one of them is domiciled'.[507] The fact that some of the newspapers were available in the Member State of the court seised may be a factor creating such foreseeability, although the Court did not shed any light on this. The Court continued however that:

> That reasoning is stronger if, as in the main proceedings, the national laws on which the actions against the various defendants are based are, in the referring court's view, *substantially identical*.
>
> It is, in addition, for the referring court to assess, in light of all the elements of the case, whether there is a connection between the different claims brought before it, that is to say a risk of irreconcilable judgements if those claims were determined separately. For that purpose, the fact that defendants against whom a copyright holder alleges *substantially identical* infringement of his copyright did or did not act independently may be relevant [emphasis added].[508]

and concluded that:

> [Article 6(1)] must be interpreted as not precluding its application solely because actions against several defendants for *substantially identical* copyright infringements are brought on national legal grounds *which vary according to the Member States concerned*. It is for the referring court to assess, in the light of all the elements of the case, whether there is a risk of irreconcilable judgements if those actions were determined separately.[509]

Consequently, although the substantive circumstances are for the court seised to determine, the possibility for a copyright holder to institute proceedings against a number of different defendants located in other Member States is not as such precluded. Regrettably, the Court did not make a consequential analysis of the legal and factual circumstances as it subsequently did in *Solvay*,[510] leaving unanswered the question of whether a copyright holder is indeed entitled to institute proceedings against a number of defendants that have allegedly committed copyright infringement in Member States other than the one seised.[511]

[C] Exclusive Jurisdiction

The Brussels framework also lists in Article 24 types of claims which fall under exclusive jurisdiction, meaning that it is only the listed courts that are entitled to hear

507. C-145/10 *Painer*, para. 81.
508. C-145/10 *Painer*, paras 82–83.
509. C-145/10 *Painer*, para. 84.
510. C-616/10 *Solvay*, paras 28–29.
511. On the facts of the case this would relate to Express and the German edition of Bild as these were not distributed in the Member State of the court seised – Austria. *See* C-145/10 *Painer*, para. 32.

the claim, irrespective of the existence of any other rules. However, none of the provisions on exclusive jurisdiction concern copyright. This includes Article 24(4) (ex-Article 22(4)) as it exclusively concerns *registrable* intellectual property rights.

§10.03 APPLICABLE LAW

The question of applicable law for proceedings concerned with infringement of copyright is governed by Regulation (EC) No 864/2007 of 11 July 2007 on the law applicable to non-contractual obligations (Rome II Regulation). This instrument applies to all Member States except Denmark.[512] To date, there appears not to be any special agreement between the EU and Denmark, or a convention analogue to the Lugano Convention 2007, regulating applicable law to non-contractual obligations.[513] Having regard to the universality of the Regulation,[514] this means that in proceedings before a court in a Member State other than Denmark, Danish law may become applicable law; however where proceedings are initiated before a Danish court, that court will be entitled, by virtue of the non-applicability of the Regulation, to apply Danish private international law to determine the law applicable to the proceedings.

Under the Regulation the law applicable to a non-contractual obligation arising from an infringement of an intellectual property right shall be the law of the country *for which* protection is claimed, i.e., *lex loci protectionis*.[515] The wording used in the provision can be compared to Article 5(2) Berne Convention which instead refers to the laws of the country *where protection is claimed*. This provision cannot be contracted out by virtue of Article 14 of the Regulation, which otherwise provides a possibility for the parties to submit non-contractual obligations to the law of their choice by an agreement entered into after the event giving rise to the damage.[516] In so far as a claim concerns unjust enrichment or *negotiorum gestio* that arises from the infringement of an intellectual property right, it is also Article 8 that determines applicable law, rather than the special provisions in Articles 10 and 11, respectively.[517]

However, where the law of the forum prescribes mandatory provisions, the court seised is entitled to override Article 8(1) by applying such provisions, irrespective of the law otherwise applicable to the infringement.[518] What precisely is meant by mandatory provisions in the specific context of non-contractual obligations is left outside the wording of the Regulation. From the perspective of freedom of contract

512. Rome II Regulation, recital (40).
513. For contractual obligations, *see* Convention on the Law Applicable to Contractual Obligations 1980 (Rome Convention).
514. Rome II Regulation, Art. 3.
515. Rome II Regulation, Art. 8(1).
516. Rome II Regulation, Art. 8(3).
517. Rome II Regulation, Art. 13.
518. Rome II Regulation, Art. 16.

such rules encompass indispositive provisions of law. Arguably this may entail the applicability of an exception or limitation existing in the copyright law of the forum state, whether or not that exception or limitation is dispositive in nature.[519] While the exclusive rights provided in the InfoSoc Directive are to a large extent harmonised, and the list of exceptions and limitations in Article 5(2)-(3) is exhaustive, therefore suggesting the existence of a unified copyright framework, all of the exceptions and limitations are discretionary in terms of implementation, therefore effectively diversifying the actual scope of the different exclusive rights as they exist in the Member States. One such notable example is the inexistence of a parody exception in the Scandinavian Member States. To the extent that Article 5(3)(k) InfoSoc Directive is an embodiment of the freedom of expression protected under Article 11 EU Charter,[520] would a Belgian court be entitled to apply the Belgian parody exception[521] in a case before it involving an infringement conducted in the territory of Sweden? The Court has noted, although referring to the Rome Convention 1980 applicable to contractual obligations, that the law of a Member State which meets the minimum protection requirements laid down in a directive may be rejected by the forum court in favour of the law of the forum, owing to the mandatory nature, in the legal order of the forum state, only if the Court before which the case has been brought finds on the basis of a detailed assessment that in the course of transposition the legislature of the State of the forum held it to be crucial, in the legal order concerned, to grant protection going beyond the minimum required by the directive, taking account of the nature and of the objective of the mandatory provisions.[522] It would, therefore, appear that it is a question the answer to which entirely depends on the legislative attention that the parody exception has received in Belgium and the degree to which that exception performs an important function within the Belgian copyright legal order. But since Belgium has decided to implement Article 5(3)(k), and Sweden has not, it may very well be evidence of going beyond the minimum required by the InfoSoc Directive, which, in light of the nature and objective of the parody exception within the EU legal framework, may entitle the Belgian court to apply that exception nevertheless.

---

519. Since in infringement proceedings there is no contract in existence, which would have given the rightholder an opportunity to attempt to contract the relevant provision out had there been a contract, a court ought to apply an exception or limitation where it finds it applicability.
520. *See* to this effect C-201/13 *Deckmyn*, para. 25.
521. Article 22(1) point 6 of the Law of 30 June 1994 on copyright and related rights. *See* C-201/13 *Deckmyn*.
522. Case C-184/12 *Unamar* v *Navigation Maritime Bulgare* ECLI:EU:C:2013:663, para. 52.

APPENDIX I

The InfoSoc Directive

Directive 2001/29/EC of the European Parliament and of the Council of 22 May 2001 on the harmonisation of certain aspects of copyright and related rights in the information society

THE EUROPEAN PARLIAMENT AND THE COUNCIL OF THE EUROPEAN UNION,

Having regard to the Treaty establishing the European Community, and in particular Articles 47(2), 55 and 95 thereof,

Having regard to the proposal from the Commission(1),

Having regard to the opinion of the Economic and Social Committee(2),

Acting in accordance with the procedure laid down in Article 251 of the Treaty(3),

Whereas:

(1) The Treaty provides for the establishment of an internal market and the institution of a system ensuring that competition in the internal market is not distorted. Harmonisation of the laws of the Member States on copyright and related rights contributes to the achievement of these objectives.

(2) The European Council, meeting at Corfu on 24 and 25 June 1994, stressed the need to create a general and flexible legal framework at Community level in order to foster the development of the information society in Europe. This requires, *inter alia*, the existence of an internal market for new products and services. Important Community legislation to ensure such a regulatory framework is already in place or its adoption is well under way. Copyright and related rights play an important role in this context as they protect and stimulate the development and marketing of new products and services and the creation and exploitation of their creative content.

(3) The proposed harmonisation will help to implement the four freedoms of the internal market and relates to compliance with the fundamental principles of law and especially of property, including intellectual property, and freedom of expression and the public interest.

(4) A harmonised legal framework on copyright and related rights, through increased legal certainty and while providing for a high level of protection of intellectual property, will foster substantial investment in creativity and innovation, including network infrastructure, and lead in turn to growth and increased competitiveness of European industry, both in the area of content provision and information technology and more generally across a wide range of industrial and cultural sectors. This will safeguard employment and encourage new job creation.

(5) Technological development has multiplied and diversified the vectors for creation, production and exploitation. While no new concepts for the protection of intellectual property are needed, the current law on copyright and related rights should be adapted and supplemented to respond adequately to economic realities such as new forms of exploitation.

(6) Without harmonisation at Community level, legislative activities at national level which have already been initiated in a number of Member States in order to respond to the technological challenges might result in significant differences in protection and thereby in restrictions on the free movement of services and products incorporating, or based on, intellectual property, leading to a refragmentation of the internal market and legislative inconsistency. The impact of such legislative differences and uncertainties will become more significant with the further development of the information society, which has already greatly increased transborder exploitation of intellectual property. This development will and should further increase. Significant legal differences and uncertainties in protection may hinder economies of scale for new products and services containing copyright and related rights.

(7) The Community legal framework for the protection of copyright and related rights must, therefore, also be adapted and supplemented as far as is necessary for the smooth functioning of the internal market. To that end, those national provisions on copyright and related rights which vary considerably from one Member State to another or which cause legal uncertainties hindering the smooth functioning of the internal market and the proper development of the information society in Europe should be adjusted, and inconsistent national responses to the technological developments should be avoided, whilst differences not adversely affecting the functioning of the internal market need not be removed or prevented.

(8) The various social, societal and cultural implications of the information society require that account be taken of the specific features of the content of products and services.

(9) Any harmonisation of copyright and related rights must take as a basis a high level of protection, since such rights are crucial to intellectual creation. Their protection helps to ensure the maintenance and development of creativity in the interests of authors, performers, producers, consumers, culture, industry and the public at large. Intellectual property has therefore been recognised as an integral part of property.

(10) If authors or performers are to continue their creative and artistic work, they have to receive an appropriate reward for the use of their work, as must producers in order to be able to finance this work. The investment required to produce products such as phonograms, films or multimedia products, and services such as 'on-demand' services, is considerable. Adequate legal protection of intellectual property rights is necessary in order to guarantee the availability of such a reward and provide the opportunity for satisfactory returns on this investment.

(11) A rigorous, effective system for the protection of copyright and related rights is one of the main ways of ensuring that European cultural creativity and production receive the necessary resources and of safeguarding the independence and dignity of artistic creators and performers.

(12) Adequate protection of copyright works and subject-matter of related rights is also of great importance from a cultural standpoint. Article 151 of the Treaty requires the Community to take cultural aspects into account in its action.

(13) A common search for, and consistent application at European level of, technical measures to protect works and other subject-matter and to provide the necessary information on rights are essential insofar as the ultimate aim of these measures is to give effect to the principles and guarantees laid down in law.

(14) This Directive should seek to promote learning and culture by protecting works and other subject-matter while permitting exceptions or limitations in the public interest for the purpose of education and teaching.

(15) The Diplomatic Conference held under the auspices of the World Intellectual Property Organisation (WIPO) in December 1996 led to the adoption of two new treaties, the 'WIPO Copyright Treaty' and the 'WIPO Performances and Phonograms Treaty', dealing respectively with the protection of authors and the protection of performers and phonogram producers. Those Treaties update the international protection for copyright and related rights significantly, not least with regard to the so-called digital agenda, and improve the means to fight piracy world-wide. The Community and a majority of Member States have already signed the Treaties and the process of making arrangements for the ratification of the Treaties by the Community and the Member States is under way. This Directive also serves to implement a number of the new international obligations.

(16) Liability for activities in the network environment concerns not only copyright and related rights but also other areas, such as defamation, misleading advertising, or

infringement of trademarks, and is addressed horizontally in Directive 2000/31/EC of the European Parliament and of the Council of 8 June 2000 on certain legal aspects of information society services, in particular electronic commerce, in the internal market ('Directive on electronic commerce')(4), which clarifies and harmonises various legal issues relating to information society services including electronic commerce. This Directive should be implemented within a timescale similar to that for the implementation of the Directive on electronic commerce, since that Directive provides a harmonised framework of principles and provisions relevant *inter alia* to important parts of this Directive. This Directive is without prejudice to provisions relating to liability in that Directive.

(17) It is necessary, especially in the light of the requirements arising out of the digital environment, to ensure that collecting societies achieve a higher level of rationalisation and transparency with regard to compliance with competition rules.

(18) This Directive is without prejudice to the arrangements in the Member States concerning the management of rights such as extended collective licences.

(19) The moral rights of rightholders should be exercised according to the legislation of the Member States and the provisions of the Berne Convention for the Protection of Literary and Artistic Works, of the WIPO Copyright Treaty and of the WIPO Performances and Phonograms Treaty. Such moral rights remain outside the scope of this Directive.

(20) This Directive is based on principles and rules already laid down in the Directives currently in force in this area, in particular Directives 91/250/EEC(5), 92/100/EEC(6), 93/83/EEC(7), 93/98/EEC(8) and 96/9/EC(9), and it develops those principles and rules and places them in the context of the information society. The provisions of this Directive should be without prejudice to the provisions of those Directives, unless otherwise provided in this Directive.

(21) This Directive should define the scope of the acts covered by the reproduction right with regard to the different beneficiaries. This should be done in conformity with the *acquis communautaire*. A broad definition of these acts is needed to ensure legal certainty within the internal market.

(22) The objective of proper support for the dissemination of culture must not be achieved by sacrificing strict protection of rights or by tolerating illegal forms of distribution of counterfeited or pirated works.

(23) This Directive should harmonise further the author's right of communication to the public. This right should be understood in a broad sense covering all communication to the public not present at the place where the communication originates. This right should cover any such transmission or retransmission of a work to the public by wire or wireless means, including broadcasting. This right should not cover any other acts.

(24) The right to make available to the public subject-matter referred to in Article 3(2) should be understood as covering all acts of making available such subject-matter to members of the public not present at the place where the act of making available originates, and as not covering any other acts.

(25) The legal uncertainty regarding the nature and the level of protection of acts of on-demand transmission of copyright works and subject-matter protected by related rights over networks should be overcome by providing for harmonised protection at Community level. It should be made clear that all rightholders recognised by this Directive should have an exclusive right to make available to the public copyright works or any other subject-matter by way of interactive on-demand transmissions. Such interactive on-demand transmissions are characterised by the fact that members of the public may access them from a place and at a time individually chosen by them.

(26) With regard to the making available in on-demand services by broadcasters of their radio or television productions incorporating music from commercial phonograms as an integral part thereof, collective licensing arrangements are to be encouraged in order to facilitate the clearance of the rights concerned.

(27) The mere provision of physical facilities for enabling or making a communication does not in itself amount to communication within the meaning of this Directive.

(28) Copyright protection under this Directive includes the exclusive right to control distribution of the work incorporated in a tangible article. The first sale in the Community of the original of a work or copies thereof by the rightholder or with his consent exhausts the right to control resale of that object in the Community. This right should not be exhausted in respect of the original or of copies thereof sold by the rightholder or with his consent outside the Community. Rental and lending rights for authors have been established in Directive 92/100/EEC. The distribution right provided for in this Directive is without prejudice to the provisions relating to the rental and lending rights contained in Chapter 1 of that Directive.

(29) The question of exhaustion does not arise in the case of services and online services in particular. This also applies with regard to a material copy of a work or other subject-matter made by a user of such a service with the consent of the rightholder. Therefore, the same applies to rental and lending of the original and copies of works or other subject-matter which are services by nature. Unlike CD-ROM or CD-I, where the intellectual property is incorporated in a material medium, namely an item of goods, every online service is in fact an act which should be subject to authorisation where the copyright or related right so provides.

(30) The rights referred to in this Directive may be transferred, assigned or subject to the granting of contractual licences, without prejudice to the relevant national legislation on copyright and related rights.

(31) A fair balance of rights and interests between the different categories of rightholders, as well as between the different categories of rightholders and users of protected subject-matter must be safeguarded. The existing exceptions and limitations to the rights as set out by the Member States have to be reassessed in the light of the new electronic environment. Existing differences in the exceptions and limitations to certain restricted acts have direct negative effects on the functioning of the internal market of copyright and related rights. Such differences could well become more pronounced in view of the further development of transborder exploitation of works and cross-border activities. In order to ensure the proper functioning of the internal market, such exceptions and limitations should be defined more harmoniously. The degree of their harmonisation should be based on their impact on the smooth functioning of the internal market.

(32) This Directive provides for an exhaustive enumeration of exceptions and limitations to the reproduction right and the right of communication to the public. Some exceptions or limitations only apply to the reproduction right, where appropriate. This list takes due account of the different legal traditions in Member States, while, at the same time, aiming to ensure a functioning internal market. Member States should arrive at a coherent application of these exceptions and limitations, which will be assessed when reviewing implementing legislation in the future.

(33) The exclusive right of reproduction should be subject to an exception to allow certain acts of temporary reproduction, which are transient or incidental reproductions, forming an integral and essential part of a technological process and carried out for the sole purpose of enabling either efficient transmission in a network between third parties by an intermediary or a lawful use of a work or other subject-matter to be made. The acts of reproduction concerned should have no separate economic value on their own. To the extent that they meet these conditions, this exception should include acts which enable browsing as well as acts of caching to take place, including those which enable transmission systems to function efficiently, provided that the intermediary does not modify the information and does not interfere with the lawful use of technology, widely recognised and used by industry, to obtain data on the use of the information. A use should be considered lawful where it is authorised by the rightholder or not restricted by law.

(34) Member States should be given the option of providing for certain exceptions or limitations for cases such as educational and scientific purposes, for the benefit of public institutions such as libraries and archives, for purposes of news reporting, for quotations, for use by people with disabilities, for public security uses and for uses in administrative and judicial proceedings.

(35) In certain cases of exceptions or limitations, rightholders should receive fair compensation to compensate them adequately for the use made of their protected works or other subject-matter. When determining the form, detailed arrangements and possible level of such fair compensation, account should be taken of the particular

circumstances of each case. When evaluating these circumstances, a valuable criterion would be the possible harm to the rightholders resulting from the act in question. In cases where rightholders have already received payment in some other form, for instance as part of a licence fee, no specific or separate payment may be due. The level of fair compensation should take full account of the degree of use of technological protection measures referred to in this Directive. In certain situations where the prejudice to the rightholder would be minimal, no obligation for payment may arise.

(36) The Member States may provide for fair compensation for rightholders also when applying the optional provisions on exceptions or limitations which do not require such compensation.

(37) Existing national schemes on reprography, where they exist, do not create major barriers to the internal market. Member States should be allowed to provide for an exception or limitation in respect of reprography.

(38) Member States should be allowed to provide for an exception or limitation to the reproduction right for certain types of reproduction of audio, visual and audiovisual material for private use, accompanied by fair compensation. This may include the introduction or continuation of remuneration schemes to compensate for the prejudice to rightholders. Although differences between those remuneration schemes affect the functioning of the internal market, those differences, with respect to analogue private reproduction, should not have a significant impact on the development of the information society. Digital private copying is likely to be more widespread and have a greater economic impact. Due account should therefore be taken of the differences between digital and analogue private copying and a distinction should be made in certain respects between them.

(39) When applying the exception or limitation on private copying, Member States should take due account of technological and economic developments, in particular with respect to digital private copying and remuneration schemes, when effective technological protection measures are available. Such exceptions or limitations should not inhibit the use of technological measures or their enforcement against circumvention.

(40) Member States may provide for an exception or limitation for the benefit of certain non-profit making establishments, such as publicly accessible libraries and equivalent institutions, as well as archives. However, this should be limited to certain special cases covered by the reproduction right. Such an exception or limitation should not cover uses made in the context of online delivery of protected works or other subject-matter. This Directive should be without prejudice to the Member States' option to derogate from the exclusive public lending right in accordance with Article 5 of Directive 92/100/EEC. Therefore, specific contracts or licences should be promoted which, without creating imbalances, favour such establishments and the disseminative purposes they serve.

(41) When applying the exception or limitation in respect of ephemeral recordings made by broadcasting organisations it is understood that a broadcaster's own facilities include those of a person acting on behalf of and under the responsibility of the broadcasting organisation.

(42) When applying the exception or limitation for non-commercial educational and scientific research purposes, including distance learning, the non-commercial nature of the activity in question should be determined by that activity as such. The organisational structure and the means of funding of the establishment concerned are not the decisive factors in this respect.

(43) It is in any case important for the Member States to adopt all necessary measures to facilitate access to works by persons suffering from a disability which constitutes an obstacle to the use of the works themselves, and to pay particular attention to accessible formats.

(44) When applying the exceptions and limitations provided for in this Directive, they should be exercised in accordance with international obligations. Such exceptions and limitations may not be applied in a way which prejudices the legitimate interests of the rightholder or which conflicts with the normal exploitation of his work or other subject-matter. The provision of such exceptions or limitations by Member States should, in particular, duly reflect the increased economic impact that such exceptions or limitations may have in the context of the new electronic environment. Therefore, the scope of certain exceptions or limitations may have to be even more limited when it comes to certain new uses of copyright works and other subject-matter.

(45) The exceptions and limitations referred to in Article 5(2), (3) and (4) should not, however, prevent the definition of contractual relations designed to ensure fair compensation for the rightholders insofar as permitted by national law.

(46) Recourse to mediation could help users and rightholders to settle disputes. The Commission, in cooperation with the Member States within the Contact Committee, should undertake a study to consider new legal ways of settling disputes concerning copyright and related rights.

(47) Technological development will allow rightholders to make use of technological measures designed to prevent or restrict acts not authorised by the rightholders of any copyright, rights related to copyright or the sui generis right in databases. The danger, however, exists that illegal activities might be carried out in order to enable or facilitate the circumvention of the technical protection provided by these measures. In order to avoid fragmented legal approaches that could potentially hinder the functioning of the internal market, there is a need to provide for harmonised legal protection against circumvention of effective technological measures and against the provision of devices and products or services to this effect.

(48) Such legal protection should be provided in respect of technological measures that effectively restrict acts not authorised by the rightholders of any copyright, rights related to copyright or the sui generis right in databases without, however, preventing the normal operation of electronic equipment and its technological development. Such legal protection implies no obligation to design devices, products, components or services to correspond to technological measures, so long as such device, product, component or service does not otherwise fall under the prohibition of Article 6. Such legal protection should respect proportionality and should not prohibit those devices or activities which have a commercially significant purpose or use other than to circumvent the technical protection. In particular, this protection should not hinder research into cryptography.

(49) The legal protection of technological measures is without prejudice to the application of any national provisions which may prohibit the private possession of devices, products or components for the circumvention of technological measures.

(50) Such a harmonised legal protection does not affect the specific provisions on protection provided for by Directive 91/250/EEC. In particular, it should not apply to the protection of technological measures used in connection with computer programs, which is exclusively addressed in that Directive. It should neither inhibit nor prevent the development or use of any means of circumventing a technological measure that is necessary to enable acts to be undertaken in accordance with the terms of Article 5(3) or Article 6 of Directive 91/250/EEC. Articles 5 and 6 of that Directive exclusively determine exceptions to the exclusive rights applicable to computer programs.

(51) The legal protection of technological measures applies without prejudice to public policy, as reflected in Article 5, or public security. Member States should promote voluntary measures taken by rightholders, including the conclusion and implementation of agreements between rightholders and other parties concerned, to accommodate achieving the objectives of certain exceptions or limitations provided for in national law in accordance with this Directive. In the absence of such voluntary measures or agreements within a reasonable period of time, Member States should take appropriate measures to ensure that rightholders provide beneficiaries of such exceptions or limitations with appropriate means of benefiting from them, by modifying an implemented technological measure or by other means. However, in order to prevent abuse of such measures taken by rightholders, including within the framework of agreements, or taken by a Member State, any technological measures applied in implementation of such measures should enjoy legal protection.

(52) When implementing an exception or limitation for private copying in accordance with Article 5(2)(b), Member States should likewise promote the use of voluntary measures to accommodate achieving the objectives of such exception or limitation. If, within a reasonable period of time, no such voluntary measures to make reproduction for private use possible have been taken, Member States may take measures to enable beneficiaries of the exception or limitation concerned to benefit from it. Voluntary

measures taken by rightholders, including agreements between rightholders and other parties concerned, as well as measures taken by Member States, do not prevent rightholders from using technological measures which are consistent with the exceptions or limitations on private copying in national law in accordance with Article 5(2)(b), taking account of the condition of fair compensation under that provision and the possible differentiation between various conditions of use in accordance with Article 5(5), such as controlling the number of reproductions. In order to prevent abuse of such measures, any technological measures applied in their implementation should enjoy legal protection.

(53) The protection of technological measures should ensure a secure environment for the provision of interactive on-demand services, in such a way that members of the public may access works or other subject-matter from a place and at a time individually chosen by them. Where such services are governed by contractual arrangements, the first and second subparagraphs of Article 6(4) should not apply. Non-interactive forms of online use should remain subject to those provisions.

(54) Important progress has been made in the international standardisation of technical systems of identification of works and protected subject-matter in digital format. In an increasingly networked environment, differences between technological measures could lead to an incompatibility of systems within the Community. Compatibility and interoperability of the different systems should be encouraged. It would be highly desirable to encourage the development of global systems.

(55) Technological development will facilitate the distribution of works, notably on networks, and this will entail the need for rightholders to identify better the work or other subject-matter, the author or any other rightholder, and to provide information about the terms and conditions of use of the work or other subject-matter in order to render easier the management of rights attached to them. Rightholders should be encouraged to use markings indicating, in addition to the information referred to above, *inter alia* their authorisation when putting works or other subject-matter on networks.

(56) There is, however, the danger that illegal activities might be carried out in order to remove or alter the electronic copyright-management information attached to it, or otherwise to distribute, import for distribution, broadcast, communicate to the public or make available to the public works or other protected subject-matter from which such information has been removed without authority. In order to avoid fragmented legal approaches that could potentially hinder the functioning of the internal market, there is a need to provide for harmonised legal protection against any of these activities.

(57) Any such rights-management information systems referred to above may, depending on their design, at the same time process personal data about the consumption patterns of protected subject-matter by individuals and allow for the tracing of online behaviour. These technical means, in their technical functions, should incorporate

privacy safeguards in accordance with Directive 95/46/EC of the European Parliament and of the Council of 24 October 1995 on the protection of individuals with regard to the processing of personal data and the free movement of such data(10).

(58) Member States should provide for effective sanctions and remedies for infringements of rights and obligations as set out in this Directive. They should take all the measures necessary to ensure that those sanctions and remedies are applied. The sanctions thus provided for should be effective, proportionate and dissuasive and should include the possibility of seeking damages and/or injunctive relief and, where appropriate, of applying for seizure of infringing material.

(59) In the digital environment, in particular, the services of intermediaries may increasingly be used by third parties for infringing activities. In many cases such intermediaries are best placed to bring such infringing activities to an end. Therefore, without prejudice to any other sanctions and remedies available, rightholders should have the possibility of applying for an injunction against an intermediary who carries a third party's infringement of a protected work or other subject-matter in a network. This possibility should be available even where the acts carried out by the intermediary are exempted under Article 5. The conditions and modalities relating to such injunctions should be left to the national law of the Member States.

(60) The protection provided under this Directive should be without prejudice to national or Community legal provisions in other areas, such as industrial property, data protection, conditional access, access to public documents, and the rule of media exploitation chronology, which may affect the protection of copyright or related rights.

(61) In order to comply with the WIPO Performances and Phonograms Treaty, Directives 92/100/EEC and 93/98/EEC should be amended,

HAVE ADOPTED THIS DIRECTIVE:

CHAPTER I

OBJECTIVE AND SCOPE

Article 1

Scope

1. This Directive concerns the legal protection of copyright and related rights in the framework of the internal market, with particular emphasis on the information society.

2. Except in the cases referred to in Article 11, this Directive shall leave intact and shall in no way affect existing Community provisions relating to:

(a) the legal protection of computer programs;

(b) rental right, lending right and certain rights related to copyright in the field of intellectual property;
(c) copyright and related rights applicable to broadcasting of programmes by satellite and cable retransmission;
(d) the term of protection of copyright and certain related rights;
(e) the legal protection of databases.

CHAPTER II

RIGHTS AND EXCEPTIONS

Article 2

Reproduction right

Member States shall provide for the exclusive right to authorise or prohibit direct or indirect, temporary or permanent reproduction by any means and in any form, in whole or in part:

(a) for authors, of their works;
(b) for performers, of fixations of their performances;
(c) for phonogram producers, of their phonograms;
(d) for the producers of the first fixations of films, in respect of the original and copies of their films;
(e) for broadcasting organisations, of fixations of their broadcasts, whether those broadcasts are transmitted by wire or over the air, including by cable or satellite.

Article 3

Right of communication to the public of works and right of making available to the public other subject-matter

1. Member States shall provide authors with the exclusive right to authorise or prohibit any communication to the public of their works, by wire or wireless means, including the making available to the public of their works in such a way that members of the public may access them from a place and at a time individually chosen by them.

2. Member States shall provide for the exclusive right to authorise or prohibit the making available to the public, by wire or wireless means, in such a way that members of the public may access them from a place and at a time individually chosen by them:

(a) for performers, of fixations of their performances;
(b) for phonogram producers, of their phonograms;
(c) for the producers of the first fixations of films, of the original and copies of their films;

(d) for broadcasting organisations, of fixations of their broadcasts, whether these broadcasts are transmitted by wire or over the air, including by cable or satellite.

3. The rights referred to in paragraphs 1 and 2 shall not be exhausted by any act of communication to the public or making available to the public as set out in this Article.

Article 4

Distribution right

1. Member States shall provide for authors, in respect of the original of their works or of copies thereof, the exclusive right to authorise or prohibit any form of distribution to the public by sale or otherwise.

2. The distribution right shall not be exhausted within the Community in respect of the original or copies of the work, except where the first sale or other transfer of ownership in the Community of that object is made by the rightholder or with his consent.

Article 5

Exceptions and limitations

1. Temporary acts of reproduction referred to in Article 2, which are transient or incidental, which are an integral and essential part of a technological process and whose sole purpose is to enable:

(a) a transmission in a network between third parties by an intermediary, or
(b) a lawful use of a work or other subject-matter to be made, and which have no independent economic significance, shall be exempted from the reproduction right provided for in Article 2.

2. Member States may provide for exceptions or limitations to the reproduction right provided for in Article 2 in the following cases:

(a) in respect of reproductions on paper or any similar medium, effected by the use of any kind of photographic technique or by some other process having similar effects, with the exception of sheet music, provided that the rightholders receive fair compensation;
(b) in respect of reproductions on any medium made by a natural person for private use and for ends that are neither directly nor indirectly commercial, on condition that the rightholders receive fair compensation which takes account of the application or non-application of technological measures referred to in Article 6 to the work or subject-matter concerned;
(c) in respect of specific acts of reproduction made by publicly accessible libraries, educational establishments or museums, or by archives, which are not for direct or indirect economic or commercial advantage;

(d) in respect of ephemeral recordings of works made by broadcasting organisations by means of their own facilities and for their own broadcasts; the preservation of these recordings in official archives may, on the grounds of their exceptional documentary character, be permitted;
(e) in respect of reproductions of broadcasts made by social institutions pursuing non-commercial purposes, such as hospitals or prisons, on condition that the rightholders receive fair compensation.

3. Member States may provide for exceptions or limitations to the rights provided for in Articles 2 and 3 in the following cases:

(a) use for the sole purpose of illustration for teaching or scientific research, as long as the source, including the author's name, is indicated, unless this turns out to be impossible and to the extent justified by the non-commercial purpose to be achieved;
(b) uses, for the benefit of people with a disability, which are directly related to the disability and of a non-commercial nature, to the extent required by the specific disability;
(c) reproduction by the press, communication to the public or making available of published articles on current economic, political or religious topics or of broadcast works or other subject-matter of the same character, in cases where such use is not expressly reserved, and as long as the source, including the author's name, is indicated, or use of works or other subject-matter in connection with the reporting of current events, to the extent justified by the informatory purpose and as long as the source, including the author's name, is indicated, unless this turns out to be impossible;
(d) quotations for purposes such as criticism or review, provided that they relate to a work or other subject-matter which has already been lawfully made available to the public, that, unless this turns out to be impossible, the source, including the author's name, is indicated, and that their use is in accordance with fair practice, and to the extent required by the specific purpose;
(e) use for the purposes of public security or to ensure the proper performance or reporting of administrative, parliamentary or judicial proceedings;
(f) use of political speeches as well as extracts of public lectures or similar works or subject-matter to the extent justified by the informatory purpose and provided that the source, including the author's name, is indicated, except where this turns out to be impossible;
(g) use during religious celebrations or official celebrations organised by a public authority;
(h) use of works, such as works of architecture or sculpture, made to be located permanently in public places;
(i) incidental inclusion of a work or other subject-matter in other material;
(j) use for the purpose of advertising the public exhibition or sale of artistic works, to the extent necessary to promote the event, excluding any other commercial use;

(k) use for the purpose of caricature, parody or pastiche;
(l) use in connection with the demonstration or repair of equipment;
(m) use of an artistic work in the form of a building or a drawing or plan of a building for the purposes of reconstructing the building;
(n) use by communication or making available, for the purpose of research or private study, to individual members of the public by dedicated terminals on the premises of establishments referred to in paragraph 2(c) of works and other subject-matter not subject to purchase or licensing terms which are contained in their collections;
(o) use in certain other cases of minor importance where exceptions or limitations already exist under national law, provided that they only concern analogue uses and do not affect the free circulation of goods and services within the Community, without prejudice to the other exceptions and limitations contained in this Article.

4. Where the Member States may provide for an exception or limitation to the right of reproduction pursuant to paragraphs 2 and 3, they may provide similarly for an exception or limitation to the right of distribution as referred to in Article 4 to the extent justified by the purpose of the authorised act of reproduction.

5. The exceptions and limitations provided for in paragraphs 1, 2, 3 and 4 shall only be applied in certain special cases which do not conflict with a normal exploitation of the work or other subject-matter and do not unreasonably prejudice the legitimate interests of the rightholder.

CHAPTER III

PROTECTION OF TECHNOLOGICAL MEASURES AND RIGHTS-MANAGEMENT INFORMATION

Article 6

Obligations as to technological measures

1. Member States shall provide adequate legal protection against the circumvention of any effective technological measures, which the person concerned carries out in the knowledge, or with reasonable grounds to know, that he or she is pursuing that objective.

2. Member States shall provide adequate legal protection against the manufacture, import, distribution, sale, rental, advertisement for sale or rental, or possession for commercial purposes of devices, products or components or the provision of services which:

(a) are promoted, advertised or marketed for the purpose of circumvention of, or

(b) have only a limited commercially significant purpose or use other than to circumvent, or
(c) are primarily designed, produced, adapted or performed for the purpose of enabling or facilitating the circumvention of, any effective technological measures.

3. For the purposes of this Directive, the expression 'technological measures' means any technology, device or component that, in the normal course of its operation, is designed to prevent or restrict acts, in respect of works or other subject-matter, which are not authorised by the rightholder of any copyright or any right related to copyright as provided for by law or the sui generis right provided for in Chapter III of Directive 96/9/EC. Technological measures shall be deemed 'effective' where the use of a protected work or other subject-matter is controlled by the rightholders through application of an access control or protection process, such as encryption, scrambling or other transformation of the work or other subject-matter or a copy control mechanism, which achieves the protection objective.

4. Notwithstanding the legal protection provided for in paragraph 1, in the absence of voluntary measures taken by rightholders, including agreements between rightholders and other parties concerned, Member States shall take appropriate measures to ensure that rightholders make available to the beneficiary of an exception or limitation provided for in national law in accordance with Article 5(2)(a), (2)(c), (2)(d), (2)(e), (3)(a), (3)(b) or (3)(e) the means of benefiting from that exception or limitation, to the extent necessary to benefit from that exception or limitation and where that beneficiary has legal access to the protected work or subject-matter concerned.

A Member State may also take such measures in respect of a beneficiary of an exception or limitation provided for in accordance with Article 5(2)(b), unless reproduction for private use has already been made possible by rightholders to the extent necessary to benefit from the exception or limitation concerned and in accordance with the provisions of Article 5(2)(b) and (5), without preventing rightholders from adopting adequate measures regarding the number of reproductions in accordance with these provisions.

The technological measures applied voluntarily by rightholders, including those applied in implementation of voluntary agreements, and technological measures applied in implementation of the measures taken by Member States, shall enjoy the legal protection provided for in paragraph 1.

The provisions of the first and second subparagraphs shall not apply to works or other subject-matter made available to the public on agreed contractual terms in such a way that members of the public may access them from a place and at a time individually chosen by them.

When this Article is applied in the context of Directives 92/100/EEC and 96/9/EC, this paragraph shall apply mutatis mutandis.

Article 7

Obligations concerning rights-management information

1. Member States shall provide for adequate legal protection against any person knowingly performing without authority any of the following acts:

(a) the removal or alteration of any electronic rights-management information;
(b) the distribution, importation for distribution, broadcasting, communication or making available to the public of works or other subject-matter protected under this Directive or under Chapter III of Directive 96/9/EC from which electronic rights-management information has been removed or altered without authority, if such person knows, or has reasonable grounds to know, that by so doing he is inducing, enabling, facilitating or concealing an infringement of any copyright or any rights related to copyright as provided by law, or of the sui generis right provided for in Chapter III of Directive 96/9/EC.

2. For the purposes of this Directive, the expression 'rights-management information' means any information provided by rightholders which identifies the work or other subject-matter referred to in this Directive or covered by the sui generis right provided for in Chapter III of Directive 96/9/EC, the author or any other rightholder, or information about the terms and conditions of use of the work or other subject-matter, and any numbers or codes that represent such information.

The first subparagraph shall apply when any of these items of information is associated with a copy of, or appears in connection with the communication to the public of, a work or other subject-matter referred to in this Directive or covered by the sui generis right provided for in Chapter III of Directive 96/9/EC.

CHAPTER IV

COMMON PROVISIONS

Article 8

Sanctions and remedies

1. Member States shall provide appropriate sanctions and remedies in respect of infringements of the rights and obligations set out in this Directive and shall take all the measures necessary to ensure that those sanctions and remedies are applied. The sanctions thus provided for shall be effective, proportionate and dissuasive.

2. Each Member State shall take the measures necessary to ensure that rightholders whose interests are affected by an infringing activity carried out on its territory can bring an action for damages and/or apply for an injunction and, where appropriate, for the seizure of infringing material as well as of devices, products or components referred to in Article 6(2).
3. Member States shall ensure that rightholders are in a position to apply for an injunction against intermediaries whose services are used by a third party to infringe a copyright or related right.

Article 9

Continued application of other legal provisions

This Directive shall be without prejudice to provisions concerning in particular patent rights, trade marks, design rights, utility models, topographies of semiconductor products, type faces, conditional access, access to cable of broadcasting services, protection of national treasures, legal deposit requirements, laws on restrictive practices and unfair competition, trade secrets, security, confidentiality, data protection and privacy, access to public documents, the law of contract.

Article 10

Application over time

1. The provisions of this Directive shall apply in respect of all works and other subject-matter referred to in this Directive which are, on 22 December 2002, protected by the Member States' legislation in the field of copyright and related rights, or which meet the criteria for protection under the provisions of this Directive or the provisions referred to in Article 1(2).

2. This Directive shall apply without prejudice to any acts concluded and rights acquired before 22 December 2002.

Article 11

Technical adaptations

1. Directive 92/100/EEC is hereby amended as follows:

(a) Article 7 shall be deleted;
(b) Article 10(3) shall be replaced by the following: '3. The limitations shall only be applied in certain special cases which do not conflict with a normal exploitation of the subject-matter and do not unreasonably prejudice the legitimate interests of the rightholder.'

2. Article 3(2) of Directive 93/98/EEC shall be replaced by the following: '2. The rights of producers of phonograms shall expire fifty years after the fixation is made. However,

if the phonogram has been lawfully published within this period, the said rights shall expire fifty years from the date of the first lawful publication. If no lawful publication has taken place within the period mentioned in the first sentence, and if the phonogram has been lawfully communicated to the public within this period, the said rights shall expire fifty years from the date of the first lawful communication to the public.

However, where through the expiry of the term of protection granted pursuant to this paragraph in its version before amendment by Directive 2001/29/EC of the European Parliament and of the Council of 22 May 2001 on the harmonisation of certain aspects of copyright and related rights in the information society(11) the rights of producers of phonograms are no longer protected on 22 December 2002, this paragraph shall not have the effect of protecting those rights anew.'

Article 12

Final provisions

1. Not later than 22 December 2004 and every three years thereafter, the Commission shall submit to the European Parliament, the Council and the Economic and Social Committee a report on the application of this Directive, in which, *inter alia*, on the basis of specific information supplied by the Member States, it shall examine in particular the application of Articles 5, 6 and 8 in the light of the development of the digital market. In the case of Article 6, it shall examine in particular whether that Article confers a sufficient level of protection and whether acts which are permitted by law are being adversely affected by the use of effective technological measures. Where necessary, in particular to ensure the functioning of the internal market pursuant to Article 14 of the Treaty, it shall submit proposals for amendments to this Directive.

2. Protection of rights related to copyright under this Directive shall leave intact and shall in no way affect the protection of copyright.

3. A contact committee is hereby established. It shall be composed of representatives of the competent authorities of the Member States. It shall be chaired by a representative of the Commission and shall meet either on the initiative of the chairman or at the request of the delegation of a Member State.

4. The tasks of the committee shall be as follows:

(a) to examine the impact of this Directive on the functioning of the internal market, and to highlight any difficulties;
(b) to organise consultations on all questions deriving from the application of this Directive;
(c) to facilitate the exchange of information on relevant developments in legislation and case law, as well as relevant economic, social, cultural and technological developments;

(d) to act as a forum for the assessment of the digital market in works and other items, including private copying and the use of technological measures.

Article 13

Implementation

1. Member States shall bring into force the laws, regulations and administrative provisions necessary to comply with this Directive before 22 December 2002. They shall forthwith inform the Commission thereof.

When Member States adopt these measures, they shall contain a reference to this Directive or shall be accompanied by such reference on the occasion of their official publication. The methods of making such reference shall be laid down by Member States.

2. Member States shall communicate to the Commission the text of the provisions of domestic law which they adopt in the field governed by this Directive.

Article 14

Entry into force

This Directive shall enter into force on the day of its publication in the Official Journal of the European Communities.

Article 15

Addressees

This Directive is addressed to the Member States.

Done at Brussels, 22 May 2001.

For the European Parliament

The President

N. Fontaine

For the Council

The President

M. Winberg

(1) OJ C 108, 7.4.1998, p. 6 and

OJ C 180, 25.6.1999, p. 6.

(2) OJ C 407, 28.12.1998, p. 30.

(3) Opinion of the European Parliament of 10 February 1999 (OJ C 150, 28.5.1999, p. 171), Council Common Position of 28 September 2000 (OJ C 344, 1.12.2000, p. 1) and Decision of the European Parliament of 14 February 2001 (not yet published in the Official Journal). Council Decision of 9 April 2001.

(4) OJ L 178, 17.7.2000, p. 1.

(5) Council Directive 91/250/EEC of 14 May 1991 on the legal protection of computer programs (OJ L 122, 17.5.1991, p. 42). Directive as amended by Directive 93/98/EEC.

(6) Council Directive 92/100/EEC of 19 November 1992 on rental right and lending right and on certain rights related to copyright in the field of intellectual property (OJ L 346, 27.11.1992, p. 61). Directive as amended by Directive 93/98/EEC.

(7) Council Directive 93/83/EEC of 27 September 1993 on the coordination of certain rules concerning copyright and rights related to copyright applicable to satellite broadcasting and cable retransmission (OJ L 248, 6.10.1993, p. 15).

(8) Council Directive 93/98/EEC of 29 October 1993 harmonising the term of protection of copyright and certain related rights (OJ L 290, 24.11.1993, p. 9).

(9) Directive 96/9/EC of the European Parliament and of the Council of 11 March 1996 on the legal protection of databases (OJ L 77, 27.3.1996, p. 20).

(10) OJ L 281, 23.11.1995, p. 31.

(11) OJ L 167, 22.6.2001, p. 10.

APPENDIX II

The Streaming Regulation

Regulation (EU) 2017/1128 of the European Parliament and of the Council of 14 June 2017 on cross-border portability of online content services in the internal market

(Text with EEA relevance)

THE EUROPEAN PARLIAMENT AND THE COUNCIL OF THE EUROPEAN UNION,

Having regard to the Treaty on the Functioning of the European Union, and in particular Article 114 thereof,

Having regard to the proposal from the European Commission,

After transmission of the draft legislative act to the national parliaments,

Having regard to the opinion of the European Economic and Social Committee (1),

Having regard to the opinion of the Committee of the Regions (2),

Acting in accordance with the ordinary legislative procedure (3),

Whereas:

(1) Seamless access throughout the Union to online content services that are lawfully provided to consumers in their Member State of residence is important for the smooth functioning of the internal market and for the effective application of the principles of free movement of persons and services. Since the internal market comprises an area without internal borders relying, *inter alia*, on the free movement of persons and services, it is necessary to ensure that consumers can use portable online content services which offer access to content such as music, games, films, entertainment programmes or sports events, not only in their Member State of residence but also

when they are temporarily present in another Member State for purposes such as leisure, travel, business trips or learning mobility. Therefore, barriers that hamper access to and use of such online content services in such cases should be eliminated.

(2) The technological developments that have led to a proliferation of portable devices such as laptops, tablets and smartphones are increasingly facilitating the use of online content services by providing access to them regardless of the location of consumers. There is a rapidly growing demand on the part of consumers for access to content and innovative online services not only in their Member State of residence but also when they are temporarily present in another Member State.

(3) Consumers increasingly enter into contractual arrangements with service providers for the provision of online content services. However, consumers that are temporarily present in a Member State other than their Member State of residence often cannot continue to access and use the online content services that they have lawfully acquired the right to access and use in their Member State of residence.

(4) There are a number of barriers which hinder the provision of online content services to consumers temporarily present in a Member State other than their Member State of residence. Certain online services include content such as music, games, films or entertainment programmes which are protected by copyright or related rights under Union law. At present, the barriers to cross-border portability of online content services differ from one sector to another. The barriers stem from the fact that the rights for the transmission of content protected by copyright or related rights, such as audiovisual works, are often licensed on a territorial basis, as well as from the fact that providers of online content services might choose to serve specific markets only.

(5) The same applies to content, such as sports events, which is not protected by copyright or related rights under Union law but which could be protected by copyright or related rights under national law or by virtue of other specific national legislation and which is often also licensed by the organisers of such events or offered by providers of online content services on a territorial basis. Transmissions of such content by broadcasting organisations are protected by related rights which have been harmonised at Union level. Moreover, transmissions of such content often include copyright-protected elements such as music, opening or closing video sequences or graphics. Also, certain aspects of transmissions of such content, specifically those relating to broadcasting events of major importance for society as well as to short news reports on events of high interest to the public, have been harmonised by Directive 2010/13/EU of the European Parliament and of the Council (4). Finally, audiovisual media services within the meaning of Directive 2010/13/EU include services which provide access to content such as sports events, news or current affairs.

(6) Increasingly, online content services are marketed in a package in which content which is not protected by copyright or related rights is not separable from content which is protected by copyright or related rights without substantially lessening the

value of the service provided to consumers. This is especially the case with premium content such as sports events or other events of significant interest to consumers. In order to enable providers of online content services to provide to consumers full access to their online content services when consumers are temporarily present in a Member State other than their Member State of residence, it is indispensable that this Regulation also covers such content used by online content services and therefore that it applies to audiovisual media services within the meaning of Directive 2010/13/EU as well as to transmissions of broadcasting organisations in their entirety.

(7) The rights in works protected by copyright and in subject-matter protected by related rights ('works and other protected subject-matter') are harmonised, *inter alia*, in Directives 96/9/EC (5), 2001/29/EC (6), 2006/115/EC (7) and 2009/24/EC (8) of the European Parliament and of the Council. The provisions of international agreements in the area of copyright and related rights concluded by the Union in particular the Agreement on Trade-Related Aspects of Intellectual Property Rights annexed as Annex 1C to the Agreement establishing the World Trade Organization of 15 April 1994, the WIPO Copyright Treaty of 20 December 1996, and the WIPO Performances and Phonograms Treaty of 20 December 1996, as amended, form an integral part of the Union legal order. Union law should, insofar as is possible, be interpreted in a manner that is consistent with international law.

(8) It is essential that providers of online content services that make use of works or other protected subject-matter, such as books, audiovisual works, recorded music or broadcasts have the right to use such content for the relevant territories.

(9) The transmission by providers of online content services of content that is protected by copyright or related rights requires the authorisation of the relevant rightholders, such as authors, performers, producers or broadcasting organisations, regarding the content included in the transmission. This is equally true when such transmission takes place for the purpose of allowing a consumer to carry out a download in order to use an online content service.

(10) The acquisition of a licence for relevant rights is not always possible, in particular when rights in content are licensed on an exclusive basis. In order to ensure that territorial exclusivity is effectively complied with, providers of online content services often undertake, in their licence contracts with rightholders, including broadcasting organisations or events organisers, to prevent their subscribers from accessing and using their services outside the territory for which the providers hold the licence. Such contractual restrictions imposed on providers require them to take measures such as disallowing access to their services from Internet Protocol (IP) addresses located outside the territory concerned. Therefore, one of the obstacles to the cross-border portability of online content services is to be found in the contracts concluded between the providers of online content services and their subscribers, which reflect the territorial restriction clauses included in contracts concluded between those providers and the rightholders.

(11) The case law of the Court of Justice of the European Union should be taken into account when balancing the objective of protecting intellectual property rights with the fundamental freedoms guaranteed by the Treaty on the Functioning of the European Union (TFEU).

(12) Therefore, the objective of this Regulation is to adapt the harmonised legal framework on copyright and related rights and to provide a common approach to the provision of online content services to subscribers temporarily present in a Member State other than their Member State of residence by removing barriers to cross-border portability of online content services which are lawfully provided. This Regulation should ensure cross-border portability of online content services in all sectors concerned and hence provide consumers with an additional means of accessing online content lawfully, without affecting the high level of protection guaranteed by copyright and related rights in the Union, without changing the existing licensing models, such as territorial licensing, and without affecting the existing financing mechanisms. The concept of cross-border portability of online content services should be distinguished from that of cross-border access by consumers to online content services provided in a Member State other than their Member State of residence, which is not covered by this Regulation.

(13) Given the Union instruments that exist in the field of taxation, it is necessary to exclude the field of taxation from the scope of this Regulation. Therefore, this Regulation should not affect the application of any provision related to taxation.

(14) This Regulation defines several concepts necessary for its application, including the Member State of residence. The Member State of residence should be determined taking into account the objectives of this Regulation and the necessity to ensure its uniform application in the Union. The definition of the Member State of residence implies that the subscriber has his or her actual and stable residence in that Member State. A provider of an online content service who has verified the Member State of residence in accordance with this Regulation should be allowed to assume, for the purposes of this Regulation, that the Member State of residence as verified is the only Member State of residence of the subscriber. Providers should not be obliged to verify whether their subscribers are also subscribers to an online content service in another Member State.

(15) This Regulation should apply to online content services that providers, after having obtained the relevant rights from rightholders in a given territory, provide to their subscribers on the basis of a contract, by any means including streaming, downloading, through applications or any other technique which allows use of that content. For the purposes of this Regulation, the term contract should be regarded as covering any agreement between a provider and a subscriber, including any arrangement by which the subscriber accepts the provider's terms and conditions for the provision of online content services, whether against payment of money or without such payment. A registration to receive content alerts or a mere acceptance of HTML

cookies should not be regarded as a contract for the provision of online content services for the purposes of this Regulation.

(16) An online service which is not an audiovisual media service within the meaning of Directive 2010/13/EU and which uses works, other protected subject-matter or transmissions of broadcasting organisations in a merely ancillary manner should not be covered by this Regulation. Such services include websites that use works or other protected subject-matter only in an ancillary manner such as graphical elements or music used as background, where the main purpose of such websites is, for example, the sale of goods.

(17) This Regulation should apply only to online content services which subscribers can effectively access and use in their Member State of residence without being limited to a specific location, as it is not appropriate to require providers of online content services that do not offer portable online content services in the Member State of residence of a subscriber to do so across borders.

(18) This Regulation should apply to online content services which are provided against payment of money. Providers of such services are in a position to verify the Member State of residence of their subscribers. The right to use an online content service should be regarded as acquired against payment of money, whether such payment is made directly to the provider of the online content service, or to another party such as a provider offering a package combining an electronic communications service and an online content service operated by another provider. For the purposes of this Regulation, the payment of a mandatory fee for public broadcasting services should not be regarded as a payment of money for an online content service.

(19) Providers of online content services should not subject their subscribers to any additional charges for the provision of cross-border portability of online content services in accordance with this Regulation. It is possible however that subscribers, in order to access and use online content services in Member States other than their Member State of residence, could be subject to fees payable to operators of electronic communications networks used to access such services.

(20) Providers of online content services which are provided without payment of money generally do not verify the Member State of residence of their subscribers. The inclusion of such online content services in the scope of this Regulation would involve a major change to the way those services are delivered and involve disproportionate costs. However, the exclusion of those services from the scope of this Regulation would mean that providers of those services would not be able to take advantage of the legal mechanism which is provided for in this Regulation and which enables providers of online content services to offer cross-border portability of such services, even when they decide to invest in means that allow them to verify their subscribers' Member State of residence. Accordingly, providers of online content services which are provided without payment of money should be able to opt to be included in the scope of this

Regulation provided that they comply with the requirements on the verification of the Member State of residence of their subscribers. If such providers exercise that option, they should comply with the same obligations as imposed under this Regulation upon the providers of online content services which are provided against payment of money. Furthermore, they should inform the subscribers, the relevant holders of copyright and related rights and the relevant holders of any other rights in the content of the online content service of their decision to exercise that option in a timely manner. Such information could be provided on the provider's website.

(21) In order to ensure the cross-border portability of online content services, it is necessary to require providers of online content services covered by this Regulation to enable subscribers to use such services in the Member State in which they are temporarily present in the same manner as in their Member State of residence. Subscribers should have access to online content services offering the same content on the same range and number of devices, for the same number of users and with the same range of functionalities as those offered in their Member State of residence. It is essential that the obligation to provide cross-border portability of online content services be mandatory and therefore the parties should not be able to exclude it, derogate from it or vary its effect. Any action by a provider which would prevent subscribers from accessing or using the service while temporarily present in a Member State other than their Member State of residence, for example, restrictions to the functionalities of the service or to the quality of its delivery should be considered to be a circumvention of the obligation to provide cross-border portability of online content services and therefore contrary to this Regulation.

(22) Requiring that the delivery of online content services to subscribers temporarily present in a Member State other than their Member State of residence be of the same quality as in the Member State of residence could result in high costs for providers of online content services and thus ultimately for subscribers. Therefore, it is not appropriate for this Regulation to require that providers ensure a quality of delivery of such services that would be beyond the quality available via the local online access chosen by a subscriber while temporarily present in another Member State. In such cases the provider should not be liable if the quality of delivery of the service is lower. Nevertheless, if the provider expressly guarantees a certain quality of delivery to subscribers while temporarily present in another Member State, it should be bound by that guarantee. The provider, on the basis of the information in its possession, should provide its subscribers in advance with information concerning the quality of delivery of an online content service in Member States other than their Member State of residence, in particular the fact that the quality of delivery could differ from that applicable in their Member State of residence. The provider should not be under an obligation to actively seek information on the quality of delivery of a service in Member States other than the subscriber's Member State of residence. The relevant information could be provided on the provider's website.

(23) In order to ensure that providers of online content services covered by this Regulation comply with the obligation to provide cross-border portability of their services, without acquiring the relevant rights in another Member State, it is necessary to stipulate that those providers should always be entitled to provide such services to subscribers when they are temporarily present in a Member State other than their Member State of residence. This should be achieved by establishing that the provision of, access to and use of such online content services should be deemed to occur in the subscriber's Member State of residence. This legal mechanism should apply for the sole purpose of ensuring the cross-border portability of online content services. An online content service should be considered to be provided lawfully if both the service and the content are provided in a lawful manner in the Member State of residence. This Regulation, and in particular the legal mechanism by which the provision of, access to and use of an online content service are deemed to occur in the subscriber's Member State of residence, does not prevent a provider from enabling the subscriber to additionally access and use the content lawfully offered by the provider in the Member State where the subscriber is temporarily present.

(24) For the licensing of copyright or related rights, the legal mechanism laid down in this Regulation means that relevant acts of reproduction, communication to the public and making available of works and other protected subject-matter, as well as the acts of extraction or re-utilization in relation to databases protected by sui generis rights, which occur when the service is provided to subscribers when they are temporarily present in a Member State other than their Member State of residence, should be deemed to occur in the subscribers' Member State of residence. Providers of online content services covered by this Regulation, therefore, should be deemed to carry out such acts on the basis of the respective authorisations from the rightholders concerned for the Member State of residence of their subscribers. Whenever providers have the right to carry out acts of communication to the public or reproduction in their subscribers' Member State of residence on the basis of an authorisation from the rightholders concerned, subscribers who are temporarily present in a Member State other than their Member State of residence should be able to access and use the service and where necessary carry out any relevant acts of reproduction, such as downloading, which they would be entitled to do in their Member State of residence. The provision of an online content service by providers to subscribers temporarily present in a Member State other than their Member State of residence and the access to and use of the service by such subscribers in accordance with this Regulation should not constitute a breach of copyright or related rights or any other rights relevant for the provision of, access to and use of the online content service.

(25) Providers of online content services covered by this Regulation should not be liable for the breach of any contractual provisions that are contrary to the obligation to enable their subscribers to use such services in the Member State in which they are temporarily present. Therefore, clauses in contracts designed to prohibit or limit the cross-border portability of such online content services should be unenforceable. The providers and holders of rights relevant for the provision of online content services

should not be allowed to circumvent the application of this Regulation by choosing the law of a third country as the law applicable to contracts between them. The same should apply to contracts concluded between providers and subscribers.

(26) This Regulation should enable subscribers to enjoy online content services to which they have subscribed in their Member State of residence when they are temporarily present in another Member State. Subscribers should be eligible for cross-border portability of online content services only if they reside in a Member State of the Union. Therefore, this Regulation should oblige providers of online content services to make use of reasonable, proportionate and effective means in order to verify the Member State of residence of their subscribers. To that end, providers should use the means of verification listed in this Regulation. This does not preclude agreement between providers and rightholders on those means of verification within the limits of this Regulation. The objective of the list is to provide legal certainty as to the means of verification to be used by providers as well as to limit interference with subscribers' privacy. In each case, account should be taken of the effectiveness and proportionality of a particular means of verification in a given Member State and for a given type of online content service. Unless the subscriber's Member State of residence can be verified with sufficient certainty on the basis of a single means of verification, providers should rely on two means of verification. In cases where the provider has reasonable doubts concerning the subscriber's Member State of residence, the provider should be able to repeat the verification of the subscriber's Member State of residence. The provider should implement the necessary technical and organisational measures required under applicable data protection rules for the processing of personal data collected for the purpose of verification of the subscriber's Member State of residence under this Regulation. Examples of such measures include providing transparent information to the individuals about the methods used for, and the purpose of, the verification, and appropriate security measures.

(27) In order to verify the subscriber's Member State of residence, the provider of an online content service should rely, if possible, on information which is in the provider's possession, such as billing information. As regards contracts concluded prior to the date of application of this Regulation and as regards the verification carried out upon renewal of a contract, the provider should be allowed to request the subscriber to provide the information necessary to verify the subscriber's Member State of residence only when it cannot be determined on the basis of information which is already in the provider's possession.

(28) IP address checks performed under this Regulation should be conducted in accordance with Directives 95/46/EC (9) and 2002/58/EC (10) of the European Parliament and of the Council. In addition, for the purpose of verification of the subscriber's Member State of residence what matters is not the precise location of the subscriber, but rather the Member State in which the subscriber is accessing the

service. Accordingly, data on the subscriber's precise location or any other personal data should neither be collected nor processed for that purpose. Where the provider has reasonable doubts concerning the subscriber's Member State of residence and carries out an IP address check to verify the Member State of residence, the sole purpose of such checks should be to establish whether the subscriber is accessing or using the online content service within or outside the Member State of residence. Therefore, in such cases, the data resulting from the checking of IP addresses should only be collected in binary format and in compliance with applicable data protection rules. The provider should not exceed that level of detail.

(29) A holder of copyright, related rights, or any other rights in the content of an online content service should remain able to exercise contractual freedom to authorise such content to be provided, accessed and used under this Regulation without verification of the Member State of residence. This can be particularly relevant in sectors such as music and e-books. Each rightholder should be able to take such decisions freely when entering into contracts with providers of online content services. Contracts between providers and rightholders should not restrict the possibility for rightholders to withdraw such authorisation subject to giving reasonable notice to the provider. The authorisation given by an individual rightholder does not as such release the provider from the obligation to verify the subscriber's Member State of residence. It is only in cases where all the holders of copyright, related rights or any other rights in the content used by the provider decide to authorise their content to be provided, accessed and used without verification of the subscriber's Member State of residence that the obligation to verify should not apply, and the contract between the provider and the subscriber for the provision of an online content service should be used to determine the latter's Member State of residence. All other aspects of this Regulation should remain applicable in such cases.

(30) This Regulation respects fundamental rights and observes the principles recognised in the Charter of Fundamental Rights of the European Union ('Charter'). Accordingly, this Regulation should be interpreted and applied in accordance with those rights and principles, in particular the right to respect for private and family life, the right to protection of personal data, the right to freedom of expression, the freedom to conduct a business and the right to property, including intellectual property. Any processing of personal data under this Regulation should respect fundamental rights, including the right to respect for private and family life and the right to protection of personal data under Articles 7 and 8 of the Charter, and it is essential that such processing be in compliance with Directives 95/46/EC and 2002/58/EC. In particular, providers of online content services should ensure that any processing of personal data under this Regulation is necessary, reasonable and proportionate in order to achieve the relevant purpose. Where authentication of a subscriber is sufficient in order to provide the service, identification of the subscriber should not be required. Data collected pursuant to this Regulation for the purposes of verification of the Member State of residence

should not be stored by the provider longer than necessary to complete such verification. Such data should be immediately and irreversibly destroyed after the verification is completed. However, this is without prejudice to the storage of data which was collected for another legitimate purpose, subject to applicable data protection rules, including rules concerning the storage of that data.

(31) Contracts under which content is licensed are usually concluded for a relatively long duration. Consequently, and in order to ensure that all consumers residing in the Union can enjoy cross-border portability of online content services on an equal basis in time and without any undue delay, this Regulation should also apply to contracts concluded and rights acquired before the date of its application if those contracts and rights are relevant for the cross-border portability of an online content service provided after that date. Such application of this Regulation is also necessary in order to ensure a level playing field for providers of online content services covered by this Regulation operating in the internal market, particularly for SMEs, by enabling providers that concluded contracts with rightholders for a long duration to offer cross-border portability to their subscribers, independently of the provider's ability to renegotiate such contracts. Moreover, such application of this Regulation should ensure that when providers make arrangements necessary for the cross-border portability of their services, they will be able to offer such portability with regard to the entirety of their online content. This should also apply to providers of online content services that offer packages combining electronic communications services and online content services. Finally, such application of this Regulation should also allow rightholders not to have to renegotiate their existing licensing contracts in order to enable providers to offer cross-border portability of their services.

(32) Accordingly, since this Regulation will apply to some contracts concluded and rights acquired before the date of its application, it is also appropriate to provide for a reasonable period between the date of entry into force of this Regulation and the date of its application, so as to allow rightholders and providers of online content services covered by this Regulation to make the arrangements necessary to adapt to the new situation, as well as to allow providers to amend the terms of use of their services. Changes to the terms of use of online content services offered in packages combining an electronic communications service and an online content service that are made strictly in order to comply with the requirements of this Regulation should not trigger for subscribers any right under national laws transposing the regulatory framework for electronic communications networks and services to withdraw from contracts for the provision of such electronic communications services.

(33) This Regulation is aimed at improving competitiveness by fostering innovation in online content services and attracting more consumers. This Regulation should not affect the application of the rules of competition, and in particular Articles 101 and 102 TFEU. The rules provided for in this Regulation should not be used to restrict competition in a manner contrary to the TFEU.

(34) This Regulation should not affect the application of Directive 2014/26/EU of the European Parliament and of the Council (11) and in particular Title III thereof. This Regulation is consistent with the objective of facilitating the lawful access to content, which is protected by copyright or related rights, as well as services linked thereto.

(35) In order to achieve the objective of ensuring cross-border portability of online content services in the Union, it is appropriate to adopt a regulation, which is directly applicable in Member States. This is necessary in order to guarantee a uniform application of the cross-border portability rules across Member States and their entry into force at the same time with regard to all online content services. Only a regulation ensures the degree of legal certainty which is necessary in order to enable consumers to fully benefit from cross-border portability across the Union.

(36) Since the objective of this Regulation, namely the adaptation of the legal framework so that cross-border portability of online content services is provided in the Union, cannot be sufficiently achieved by the Member States but can rather, by reason of its scale and effects, be better achieved at Union level, the Union may adopt measures in accordance with the principle of subsidiarity as set out in Article 5 of the Treaty on European Union. In accordance with the principle of proportionality as set out in that Article, this Regulation does not go beyond what is necessary in order to achieve that objective. In particular, this Regulation does not substantially affect the way the rights are licensed and does not oblige rightholders and providers to renegotiate contracts. Moreover, this Regulation does not require that providers take measures to ensure the quality of delivery of online content services outside the Member State of residence of the subscribers. Finally, this Regulation does not apply to providers that offer online content services without payment of money and who do not exercise the option to enable the cross-border portability of their services. Therefore, it does not impose any disproportionate costs,

HAVE ADOPTED THIS REGULATION:

Article 1

Subject-matter and scope

1. This Regulation introduces a common approach in the Union to the cross-border portability of online content services, by ensuring that subscribers to portable online content services which are lawfully provided in their Member State of residence can access and use those services when temporarily present in a Member State other than their Member State of residence.

2. This Regulation shall not apply to the field of taxation.

Article 2

Definitions

For the purposes of this Regulation, the following definitions apply:

(1) 'subscriber' means any consumer who, on the basis of a contract for the provision of an online content service with a provider whether against payment of money or without such payment, is entitled to access and use such service in the Member State of residence;
(2) 'consumer' means any natural person who, in contracts covered by this Regulation, is acting for purposes which are outside that person's trade, business, craft or profession;
(3) 'Member State of residence' means the Member State, determined on the basis of Article 5, where the subscriber has his or her actual and stable residence;
(4) 'temporarily present in a Member State' means being present in a Member State other than the Member State of residence for a limited period of time;
(5) 'online content service' means a service as defined in Articles 56 and 57 TFEU that a provider lawfully provides to subscribers in their Member State of residence on agreed terms and online, which is portable and which is:
   (i) an audiovisual media service as defined in point (a) of Article 1 of Directive 2010/13/EU, or
   (ii) a service the main feature of which is the provision of access to, and the use of, works, other protected subject-matter or transmissions of broadcasting organisations, whether in a linear or an on-demand manner;
(6) 'portable' means a feature of an online content service whereby subscribers can effectively access and use the online content service in their Member State of residence without being limited to a specific location.

Article 3

Obligation to enable cross-border portability of online content services

1. The provider of an online content service provided against payment of money shall enable a subscriber who is temporarily present in a Member State to access and use the online content service in the same manner as in the Member State of residence, including by providing access to the same content, on the same range and number of devices, for the same number of users and with the same range of functionalities.

2. The provider shall not impose any additional charges on the subscriber for the access to and the use of the online content service pursuant to paragraph 1.

3. The obligation set out in paragraph 1 shall not extend to any quality requirements applicable to the delivery of an online content service that the provider is subject to

when providing that service in the Member State of residence, unless otherwise expressly agreed between the provider and the subscriber.

The provider shall not take any action to reduce the quality of delivery of the online content service when providing the online content service in accordance with paragraph 1.

4. The provider shall, on the basis of the information in its possession, provide the subscriber with information concerning the quality of delivery of the online content service provided in accordance with paragraph 1. The information shall be provided to the subscriber prior to providing the online content service in accordance with paragraph 1 and by means which are adequate and proportionate.

Article 4

Localisation of the provision of, access to and use of online content services

The provision of an online content service under this Regulation to a subscriber who is temporarily present in a Member State, as well as the access to and the use of that service by the subscriber, shall be deemed to occur solely in the subscriber's Member State of residence.

Article 5

Verification of the Member State of residence

1. At the conclusion and upon the renewal of a contract for the provision of an online content service provided against payment of money, the provider shall verify the Member State of residence of the subscriber by using not more than two of the following means of verification and shall ensure that the means used are reasonable, proportionate and effective:

(a) an identity card, electronic means of identification, in particular those falling under the electronic identification schemes notified in accordance with Regulation (EU) No 910/2014 of the European Parliament and of the Council (12), or any other valid identity document confirming the subscriber's Member State of residence;
(b) payment details such as the bank account or credit or debit card number of the subscriber;
(c) the place of installation of a set top box, a decoder or a similar device used for supply of services to the subscriber;
(d) the payment by the subscriber of a licence fee for other services provided in the Member State, such as public service broadcasting;
(e) an Internet or telephone service supply contract or any similar type of contract linking the subscriber to the Member State;
(f) registration on local electoral rolls, if the information concerned is publicly available;

(g) payment of local taxes, if the information concerned is publicly available;
(h) a utility bill of the subscriber linking the subscriber to the Member State;
(i) the billing address or the postal address of the subscriber;
(j) a declaration by the subscriber confirming the subscriber's address in the Member State;
(k) an Internet Protocol (IP) address check, to identify the Member State where the subscriber accesses the online content service.

The means of verification under points (i) to (k) shall only be used in combination with one of the means of verification under points (a) to (h), unless the postal address under point (i) is included in a publicly available official register.

2. If the provider has reasonable doubts about the subscriber's Member State of residence in the course of the duration of the contract for the provision of an online content service, the provider may repeat the verification of the Member State of residence of the subscriber, in accordance with paragraph 1. In such a case, however, the means of verification under point (k) may be used as a sole means. Data resulting from the use of the means of verification under point (k) shall be collected in binary format only.

3. The provider shall be entitled to request the subscriber to provide the information necessary to determine the subscriber's Member State of residence in accordance with paragraphs 1 and 2. If the subscriber fails to provide that information, and as a result the provider is unable to verify the subscriber's Member State of residence, the provider shall not, on the basis of this Regulation, enable the subscriber to access or use the online content service when the subscriber is temporarily present in a Member State.

4. The holders of copyright or related rights or those holding any other rights in the content of an online content service may authorise the provision of, access to and use of their content under this Regulation without verification of the Member State of residence. In such cases, the contract between the provider and the subscriber for the provision of an online content service shall be sufficient to determine the subscriber's Member State of residence.

The holders of copyright or related rights or those holding any other rights in the content of an online content service shall be entitled to withdraw the authorisation given pursuant to the first subparagraph subject to giving reasonable notice to the provider.

5. The contract between the provider and the holders of copyright or related rights or those holding any other rights in the content of an online content service shall not restrict the possibility for such holders of rights to withdraw the authorisation referred to in paragraph 4.

Article 6

Cross-border portability of online content services provided without payment of money

1. The provider of an online content service provided without payment of money may decide to enable its subscribers who are temporarily present in a Member State to access and use the online content service on condition that the provider verifies the subscriber's Member State of residence in accordance with this Regulation.

2. The provider shall inform its subscribers, the relevant holders of copyright and related rights and the relevant holders of any other rights in the content of the online content service of its decision to provide the online content service in accordance with paragraph 1, prior to providing that service. The information shall be provided by means which are adequate and proportionate.

3. This Regulation shall apply to providers that provide an online content service in accordance with paragraph 1.

Article 7

Contractual provisions

1. Any contractual provisions, including those between providers of online content services and holders of copyright or related rights or those holding any other rights in the content of online content services, as well as those between such providers and their subscribers, which are contrary to this Regulation, including those which prohibit cross-border portability of online content services or limit such portability to a specific time period, shall be unenforceable.

2. This Regulation shall apply irrespective of the law applicable to contracts concluded between providers of online content services and holders of copyright or related rights or those holding any other rights in the content of online content services, or to contracts concluded between such providers and their subscribers.

Article 8

Protection of personal data

1. The processing of personal data carried out within the framework of this Regulation including, in particular, for the purposes of verification of the subscriber's Member State of residence under Article 5, shall be carried out in compliance with Directives 95/46/EC and 2002/58/EC. In particular, the use of the means of verification in accordance with Article 5 and any processing of personal data under this Regulation, shall be limited to what is necessary and proportionate in order to achieve its purpose.

2. Data collected pursuant to Article 5 shall be used solely for the purpose of verifying the subscriber's Member State of residence. They shall not be communicated, transferred, shared, licensed or otherwise transmitted or disclosed to holders of copyright or

related rights or to those holding any other rights in the content of online content services, or to any other third parties.

3. Data collected pursuant to Article 5 shall not be stored by the provider of an online content service longer than necessary to complete a verification of a subscriber's Member State of residence pursuant to Article 5(1) or (2). On completion of each verification, the data shall be immediately and irreversibly destroyed.

Article 9

Application to existing contracts and rights acquired

1. This Regulation shall apply also to contracts concluded and rights acquired before the date of its application if they are relevant for the provision of, access to and use of an online content service, in accordance with Articles 3 and 6, after that date.

2. By 2 June 2018, the provider of an online content service provided against payment of money shall verify, in accordance with this Regulation, the Member State of residence of those subscribers who concluded contracts for the provision of the online content service before that date.

Within two months of the date upon which the provider of an online content service provided without payment of money first provides the service in accordance with Article 6, the provider shall verify, in accordance with this Regulation, the Member State of residence of those subscribers who concluded contracts for the provision of the online content service before that date.

Article 10

Review

By 2 April 2021, and as required thereafter, the Commission shall assess the application of this Regulation in the light of legal, technological and economic developments, and submit to the European Parliament and to the Council a report thereon.

The report referred to in the first paragraph shall include, *inter alia*, an assessment of the application of the verification means of the Member State of residence referred to in Article 5, taking into account newly developed technologies, industry standards and practices, and, if necessary, consider the need for a review. The report shall pay special attention to the impact of this Regulation on SMEs and the protection of personal data. The Commission's report shall be accompanied, if appropriate, by a legislative proposal.

Article 11

Final provisions

1. This Regulation shall enter into force on the twentieth day following that of its publication in the Official Journal of the European Union.

2. It shall apply from 1 April 2018.

This Regulation shall be binding in its entirety and directly applicable in all Member States.

Done at Strasbourg, 14 June 2017.

For the European Parliament

The President

A. TAJANI

For the Council

The President

H. DALLI

(1) OJ C 264, 20.7.2016, p. 86.

(2) OJ C 240, 1.7.2016, p. 72.

(3) Position of the European Parliament of 18 May 2017 (not yet published in the Official Journal) and decision of the Council of 8 June 2017.

(4) Directive 2010/13/EU of the European Parliament and of the Council of 10 March 2010 on the coordination of certain provisions laid down by law, regulation or administrative action in Member States concerning the provision of audiovisual media services (Audiovisual Media Services Directive) (OJ L 95, 15.4.2010, p. 1).

(5) Directive 96/9/EC of the European Parliament and of the Council of 11 March 1996 on the legal protection of databases (OJ L 77, 27.3.1996, p. 20).

(6) Directive 2001/29/EC of the European Parliament and of the Council of 22 May 2001 on the harmonisation of certain aspects of copyright and related rights in the information society (OJ L 167, 22.6.2001, p. 10).

(7) Directive 2006/115/EC of the European Parliament and of the Council of 12 December 2006 on rental right and lending right and on certain rights related to copyright in the field of intellectual property (OJ L 376, 27.12.2006, p. 28).

(8) Directive 2009/24/EC of the European Parliament and of the Council of 23 April 2009 on the legal protection of computer programs (OJ L 111, 5.5.2009, p. 16).

(9) Directive 95/46/EC of the European Parliament and of the Council of 24 October 1995 on the protection of individuals with regard to the processing of personal data and on the free movement of such data (OJ L 281, 23.11.1995, p. 31). Directive 95/46/EC is repealed and replaced, with effect from 25 May 2018, by Regulation (EU) 2016/679 of the European Parliament and of the Council of 27 April 2016 on the protection of natural persons with regard to the processing of personal data and on the free movement of such data, and repealing Directive 95/46/EC (General Data Protection Regulation) (OJ L 119, 4.5.2016, p. 1).

(10) Directive 2002/58/EC of the European Parliament and of the Council of 12 July 2002 concerning the processing of personal data and the protection of privacy in the electronic communications sector (Directive on privacy and electronic communications) (OJ L 201, 31.7.2002, p. 37).

(11) Directive 2014/26/EU of the European Parliament and of the Council of 26 February 2014 on collective management of copyright and related rights and multi-territorial licensing of rights in musical works for online use in the internal market (OJ L 84, 20.3.2014, p. 72).

(12) Regulation (EU) No 910/2014 of the European Parliament and of the Council of 23 July 2014 on electronic identification and trust services for electronic transactions in the internal market and repealing Directive 1999/93/EC (OJ L 257, 28.8.2014, p. 73).

Bibliography

BOOKS

Bently, L., Sherman, B., Gangjee, D., Johnson, P., Intellectual Property Law, Fifth Edition (Oxford University Press, 2018).

Czarnota, B., Hart, R., Legal Protection of Computer Programs in Europe, A Guide to the EC Directive, (Butterworths, 1991, reprinted 1993).

Derclaye, E. (ed.), Research Handbook on the Future of EU Copyright, (Edward Elgar, 2009).

Depreeuw, S., 'The Variable Scope of the Exclusive Rights in Copyright', (Kluwer Law International, 2014).

Dreier, T., Hugenholtz, B.P. (eds), Concise European Copyright Law, Second edition (Kluwer Law International, 2016).

Dreier, T., Kur, A., European Intellectual Property Law, (Edward Elgar Publishing, 2013).

Okediji, R. (ed.), Copyright Law in an Age of Limitations and Exceptions, (Cambridge University Press, 2017).

Justine Pila, J., Torremans, P., European Intellectual Property Law, (Oxford University Press, 2016).

Mezei, P., Copyright Exhaustion. Law and Policy in the United States and the European Union, (Cambridge University Press, 2018).

Lundstedt, L., Territoriality in Intellectual Property Law, (Stockholm University Department of Law, 2016).

Torresman, P., Holyoak and Torremans Intellectual Property Law, Eighth edition (Oxford University Press, 2016).

Walter, M. and von Lewinski, S. (eds), European Copyright Law, A Commentary, (Oxford University Press, 2018).

Weinstock Netanel, L., Copyright, What Everyone Needs to Know, (Oxford University Press, 2018).

Wolk, S. Szkalej, K. (eds), Employees' Intellectual Property Rights, Second edition (Kluwer Law International, 2018).

Quintas, J.P., Copyright in the Age of Online Access, Alternative Compensation Systems in EU Law, (Kluwer Law International, 2017).

ACADEMIC ARTICLES AND BOOK CHAPTERS

Dussolier, S., The Protection of Technological Measures: Much Ado about Nothing or Silent Remodelling of Copyright?, in Dreyfuss, R.C., Ginsburg, J.C. (eds), *Intellectual Property at the Edge: The Contested Contours of IP* (Cambridge University Press, 2014).

Favale, M., Kretschmer, M., Torremans, P., Is There a EU Copyright Jurisprudence? An Empirical Analysis of the Workings of the European Court of Justice, 79(1) Modern L.R. 31 (2016).

Favale, M., Approximation and DRM: Can Digital Locks Respect Copyright Exceptions?, 19 Int'l J.L. & Info. Tech. 306 (2011).

Geiger, C., Griffiths, J., Senftleben, M., Bently, L., Xalabarder, R., Limitations and Exceptions as Key Elements of the Legal Framework for Copyright in the European Union – Opinion of the European Copyright Society on the Judgment of the CJEU in Case C-201/13 Deckmyn, 46(1) IIC 93 (2011).

Geiger, C., Gervais, D., Senftleben, M., The Three-Step Test Revisited: How to Use the Test's Flexibility in National Copyright Law, 29(3) Am. U. Int'l L. Rev. 582 (2014).

Hugenholtz, B., Senftleben, M., Fair Use in Europe. In Search of Flexibilities, Institute for Information Law Research Paper No. 2012-33 (2012).

Husovec, M., Intellectual Property Rights and Integration by Conflict: The Past, Present and Future, 18 C.Y.E.L.S. 239 (2016).

Kur, A., Of Oceans, Islands, and Inland Water – How Much Room for Exceptions and Limitations under the Three Step-Test?, MPI for IP, Competition & Tax Law Research Paper Series No. 08-04 (2008).

Liu, J. P., Paracopyright – A Peculiar Right to Control Access, in Dreyfuss, R.C., Ginsburg, J.C. (eds), *Intellectual Property at the Edge: The Contested Contours of IP* (Cambridge University Press, 2014).

Quintais, J.P., Untangling the Hyperlinking Web: In Search of the Online Right of Communication to the Public, JWIP (2018) (forthcoming in print) https://doi.org/10.1111/jwip.12107.

Quintais, J.P., Rendas, T., EU Copyright Law and the Cloud: VCAST and the Intersection of Private Copying and Communication to the Public, 13(9) JIPLP 711 (2018).

Rendas, T., Copyright, Technology and the CJEU: An Empirical Study, 49(2) IIC 153 (2018).

Rognstad, O., Legally Flawed but Politically Sound? Digital Exhaustion of Copyright in Europe after UsedSoft, 1 Oslo L.R. 1 (2014).

Rosati, E., Online Copyright Exhaustion in a Post-Allposters World, 10(9) JIPLP 673 (2015).

Rosati, E., Originality in EU Copyright. Full Harmonization Through Case Law, Cheltenham (2013).

Wolk, S., The Software Business in Transit – Will Exhaustion and Defining Sale or Licence Soon Be Irrelevant?, IMC Paper 2014/1 (2014).

OPINIONS AND INTERNET BLOG POSTS

European Copyright Society, General Opinion on the EU Copyright Reform Package, 24 January 2017, available at https://europeancopyrightsocietydotorg.files.wordpress.com/2015/12/ecs-opinion-on-eu-copyright-reform-def.pdf (last visited 5 September 2018).

Ricolfi, M., Xalabarder, R., van Eechoud, M., A Statement from EU Academics on Proposed Press Publishers' Right, 24 April 2018, available at: https://www.ivir.nl/academics-against-press-publishers-right/ (last visited 5 September 2018).

Samuelson, P., The EU's Controversial Digital Single Market Directive – Part I: Why the Proposed Internet Content Filtering Mandate Was So Controversial, Kluwer Copyright Blog, 10 July 2018, available at http://copyrightblog.kluweriplaw.com/2018/07/10/eus-controversial-digital-single-market-directive-part-proposed-internet-content-filtering-mandate-controversial/ (last visited 5 September 2018).

Samuelson, P., The EU's Controversial Digital Single Market Directive – Part II: Why the Proposed Mandatory Text – and Data-Mining Exception is Too Restrictive, Kluwer Copyright Blog, 12 July 2018, available at http://copyrightblog.kluweriplaw.com/2018/07/12/eus-controversial-digital-single-market-directive-part-ii-proposed-mandatory-text-data-mining-exception-restrictive/ (last visited 5 September 2018).

Szkalej, K., Wolk, S., Blocking Injunctions Against ISPs in Sweden – The Swedish Court Doesn't Wait for the CJEU, Kluwer Copyright Blog, 1 March 2017, available at http://copyrightblog.kluweriplaw.com/2017/03/01/blocking-injunctions-against-isps-in-sweden-the-swedish-court-doesnt-wait-for-the-cjeu/ (last visited 5 September 2018).

von Lewinski, S., Comments on Article 13 and Related Provisions in the JURI Committee Report for a Directive on Copyright in the Digital Single Market, Kluwer Copyright Blog, 3 September 2018, available at http://copyrightblog.kluweriplaw.com/2018/09/03/comments-article-13-related-provisions-juri-committee-report-directive-copyright-digital-single-market/ (last visited 5 September 2018).

Wolk, S., EU Court Rules That Back-up Copies Cannot Be Resold, Kluwer Copyright Blog, 20 October 2016, available at http://copyrightblog.kluweriplaw.com/2016/10/20/eu-court-rules-that-back-up-copies-cannot-be-resold/ (last visited 5 September 2018).

Wolk, S., Provider of Free Wi-Fi Is Not Liable for Copyright Infringement, Kluwer Copyright Blog, 22 September 2016, available at http://copyrightblog.kluweriplaw.com/2016/09/22/provider-of-free-wi-fi-is-not-liable-for-copyright-infringement/ (last visited 5 September 2018).

Table of Cases

European Court of Human Rights (ECtHR)

Court of Justice of the European Union (CJEU)

Table of Legislation

International Treaties and Conventions

International: Secondary Sources

European Union: Treaties and Charter

European Union: Regulations

European Union: Directives

are blind, visually impaired or otherwise print-disabled and amending Directive 2001/29/EC on the harmonisation of certain aspects of copyright and related rights in the information society [2017] OJ L 242/6, **8**, **82**

European Union: Decisions and Notices

Council Decision of 22 December 1994 concerning the conclusion on behalf of the European Community, as regards matters within its competence, of the agreements reached in the Uruguay Round multilateral negotiations (1986–1994) [1994] OJ L 336/1, **3**

Council Decision of 16 March 2000 on the approval, on behalf of the European Community, of the WIPO Copyright Treaty and the WIPO Performances and Phonograms Treaty [2000] OJ L89/6, **3**

Council Decision (EU) 2018/254 of 15 February 2018 on the conclusion on behalf of the European Union of the Marrakesh Treaty to Facilitate Access to Published Works for Persons who are Blind, Visually Impaired, or otherwise Print Disabled [2018] OJ L48/1, **3**

Council Notice on the Agreement on a Unified Patent Court [2013] OJ C 175/1, 20 June 2013, **139**

European Union: Preparatory documents, Reports, Opinions, Memoranda, Staff Working Documents

Article 29 Working Party, 'Opinion 4/2007 on the concept of personal data' WP 136, adopted 20 June 2007, **94**

Commission, 'Green Paper on copyright and the challenge of technology – copyright issues requiring immediate action' COM(88) 172 final, 7 June 1988, **5**, **33**, **45**, **68**, **110**

Commission, 'Proposal for a Council Directive on the legal protection of computer programs' (Explanatory Memorandum) COM(88) 816 final – SYN 183, 5 January 1989, **33**, **36**, **38**, **45**, **111**

Commission, 'Amended Proposal for a Council Directive on the legal protection of computer programs' COM(90) 509 final – SYN 183, 18 October 1990, **68**

Commission, 'Follow-up to the Green Paper – Working programme of the Commission in the field of copyright and neighbouring rights, COM(90) 584 final, 17 January 1991, **5**

Commission, 'Copyright and related rights in the information society' (Green Paper) COM(95) 382 final, 19 July 1995, **68**

Commission, 'Follow-up to the Green Paper on copyright and related rights in the information society' (Communication) COM(96) 586 final, 20 November 1996, **68**

Commission, 'Proposal for a European Parliament and Council Directive on the harmonization of certain aspects of copyright and related rights in the Information Society' COM(97) 628 final, 10 December 1997, **115**, **126**

Commission, 'Report on the implementation and effects of Directive 91/250/EEC on the legal protection of computer programs' COM(2000) 199 final, 10 April 2000, **33**, **45**, **46**, **111**

Commission, 'Application of the Charter of Fundamental Rights of the European Union' (Memorandum) SEC(2001) 380/3, 13 March 2001, **11**

Commission, 'Staff working paper on the review of the EC legal framework in the field of copyright and related rights' SEC(2004) 995, 19 July 2004, **33**, **45**

Commission, 'Compliance with the Charter of Fundamental Rights in Commission Legislative Proposals. Methodology for systematic and rigorous monitoring' (Communication) COM(2005) 172 final, 24 April 2005, **11**

Commission, 'Report to the Council, the European Parliament and the Economic and Social Committee on the application of Directive 2001/29/EC on the harmonisation of certain aspects of copyright and related rights in the information society' (Staff Working Document) SEC(2007) 1556, 30 November 2011, **128**

Commission, 'Report on the responses to the Public Consultation on the Review of the EU Copyright Rules', DG Internal Market and Services, July 2014, **84**

Commission, 'A Digital Single Market Strategy for Europe' (Communication) COM(2015) 192 final, 6 May 2015, **9**, **83**

Commission, 'Proposal for a Directive on certain aspects concerning contracts for the supply of digital content' COM(2015) 634 final, 9 December 2015, **9**, **83**, **101**

Commission, 'Proposal for a Regulation on ensuring the cross-border portability of online content services in the internal market' COM(2015) 627 final, 9 December 2015, **83**, **106**

Commission, 'Impact Assessment accompanying the document Proposal for a Regulation of the European Parliament and of the Council to ensure the cross-border portability of online content services in the internal market' (Staff Working Document) SWD(2015) 270 final, 9 December 2015, **88**

Commission, 'Proposal for a Directive amending Directive 2010/13/EU on the coordination of certain provisions laid down by law, regulation or administrative action in Member States concerning the provision of audiovisual media services in view of changing market realities' COM/2016/0287 final, 25 May 2016, **8**, **82**

Commission, 'Promoting a fair, efficient and competitive European copyright-based economy in the Digital Single Market' (Communication) COM(2016) 592 final, 14 September 2016, **9**

Commission, 'Proposal for a Directive on copyright in the Digital Single Market' COM(2016) 593 final, 14 September 2016, **9**

Commission, 'Proposal for a Regulation laying down rules on the exercise of copyright and related rights applicable to certain online transmissions of broadcasting organisations and retransmissions of television and radio programmes' COM(2016) 594 final, 14 September 2016, **9**

European Committee of the Regions, 'Modernisation of the EU Copyright Rules' (Opinion) SEDEC-VI-009, 8 April 2016, **92**

European Economic and Social Committee, 'Opinion on the Proposal for a Regulation of the European Parliament and of the Council on ensuring the cross-border portability of online content services in the internal market' INT/781 27 April 2016, **92**

European Parliament, 'Position of the European Parliament with a view to the adoption of Regulation (EU) 2017/ … of the European Parliament and of the Council on cross-border potability of online content services in the internal market' EP-PE_TC1-COD(2015)0284 adopted at first reading on 18 May 2017, **92**

European Parliament, 'Report on the proposal for a regulation of the European Parliament and of the Council on ensuring the cross-border potability of online content services in the internal market' Committee on Legal Affairs, A8-0378/2016, 9 December 2016, **93**

National legislation

Belgium: *Loi du 30 juin 1994 relative au droit d'auteur et aux droits voisins* (Law of 30 June 1994 on copyright and related rights), **145**

The Netherlands: *Wet van 23 september 1912, houdende nieuwe regeling van het auteursrecht* (Law of 23 September 1912, containing a new regulation on copyright), **104**

Sweden: *Lag (1960:729) om upphovsrätt till litterära och konstärliga verk* (Law (1960:729) on copyright to literary and artistic works), **131**, **137**

United Kingdom: Copyright, Designs and Patents Act 1988 (c.48), **31**, **41**, **68**, **131**

www.ingramcontent.com/pod-product-compliance
Ingram Content Group UK Ltd.
Pitfield, Milton Keynes, MK11 3LW, UK
UKHW020815290926
15470UKWH00003B/1170

9 789041 183699